Contents

Introduction

The *Grammar Rules!* Series

Grammar Rules! is an award-winning series of six student books and two Teacher Resource Books, which have been reproduced in a second edition. This second edition includes a disc in the Teacher Resource Books, Scope and Sequence charts updated for the Australian Curriculum and reflection activities in student books 1–4 to allow students to assess their own progress.

The *Grammar Rules!* series provides a context-based approach to grammar teaching and learning to ensure that students understand how to use their knowledge of grammar when constructing their own texts and responding to the texts of others. The series supports teaching and learning in English as described in the Language, Literature and Literacy Strands of the Australian Curriculum, English.

The sample texts and associated activities in the Student Books, as well as the supplementary activities suggested in the Teacher Resource Books, provide opportunities for students to develop the general capabilities of critical and creative thinking, personal and social capability, ethical understanding and intercultural understanding, as defined and described in the Australian Curriculum, English. Where possible, suggested activities also address ICT capabilities and cross-curriculum priorities.

Grammar Rules! shows students how grammatical structures and features function in texts to achieve meaning, from the contextual level of the whole text down to sentence and clause level and to the level of word groups, individual words and word parts. The series deals with the appropriate grammatical structures for particular types of texts, purposes for using language, and audiences.

The student books and Teacher Resource Books include **Scope and Sequence** charts. These charts give an overview of the whole program. They are also a useful index to the lessons and topics in each unit. Teachers can use the Grammar Program Checklists on **Reproducible 1** (page 109) and **Reproducible 2** (page 110) in their programs to keep track of the grammar concepts covered in class. The checklists are based on the Scope and Sequence charts in the *Grammar Rules!* student books. Teachers can use the Comment column to write their evaluation of any grammar activities undertaken with students and to note any follow-up activities required, or further comments.

The student books include 35 **units** of work for students to complete, including 6 Revision Units, which can be used for assessment purposes. Each Unit focuses on one or more aspects of grammar, but the units also lend themselves to extension or enrichment with further aspects of grammar able to be explored if the teacher chooses or if students are ready, interested or in need of extension. Each unit builds upon knowledge gained in previous units.

The units cover a range of informative, imaginative and persuasive texts. Each individual unit in the student books is based on a **model text** that establishes the context for both the grammar focus of the unit and the grammar activities included in the unit. Teachers and students can explore the structure and meaning of each text before exploring the grammar in that context.

Each unit concludes with a **Try it yourself!** activity. This activity enables students to further extend their understanding of the type of text as well as demonstrate their knowledge of the grammar covered in the unit. The Try it yourself! refocuses students' attention on the influence of context and text on grammar choices.

Each *Grammar Rules!* student book includes a pull-out section with a **Student Writing Log**. The Writing Log provides a way for students to keep track of the types of texts and text forms they are writing, and the grammar they are attempting to use in the context of their writing. The Writing Logs support students' independence and encourage students to develop responsibility for their own writing tasks.

Footers at the end of each unit are cross-referenced with the Scope and Sequence charts. Along with the Scope and Sequence charts, they are a useful reference for teachers when programming or when looking for a particular grammatical concept.

TEACHER RESOURCE BOOK

3-6

GRAMMAR RULES!

Second edition

Tanya Gibb

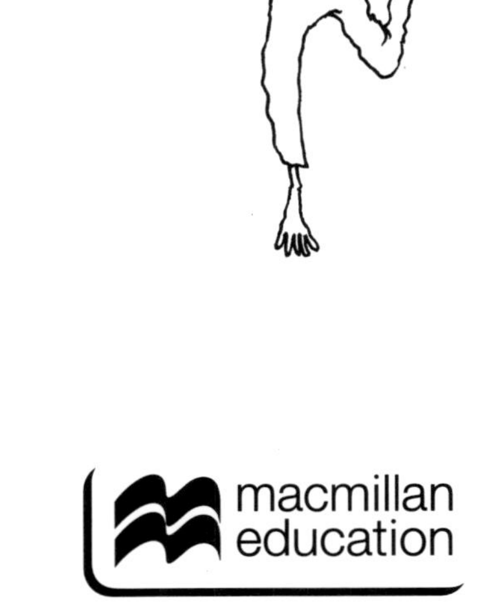

macmillan education

This edition published in 2016 by

macmillan education

MACMILLAN SCIENCE AND EDUCATION AUSTRALIA PTY LTD
15–19 Claremont Street, South Yarra 3141
Visit our website at www.macmillaneducation.com.au
Associated companies and representatives throughout the world.

First published in 2008.

Publisher: First edition Sharon Dalgleish
Designers: Trish Hayes and Stephen Michael King
Illustrator: Stephen Michael King

Printed in the UK by CLOC Ltd
MEA9_19_01

What is Grammar?

Grammar is a system for organising language. It is a tool for making meaning and it is a body of knowledge in its own right. Grammar is essential for communicating effectively. It enables speakers and writers to get their message across to readers and listeners. It enables readers and listeners to interpret and analyse the way information and opinions are constructed to shape their view of the world. An understanding of the way grammar works in texts is important for effective language use across learning areas.

How to Develop a Whole-School Grammar Policy

On pages 6 and 7 you'll find a sample policy to use as a starting point to develop your own whole-school grammar policy. A whole-school policy could contain the following sections:

Philosophical Statement and Rationale
These statements explain why the school has decided to implement a whole-school policy; what the school values or believes about the teaching and learning of grammar; and how grammar is relevant to the particular learning needs of students enrolled in the school.

Aim/s
This should clearly articulate the overall aim/s of a whole-school approach to grammar.

Objectives
These are broad statements of the values and attitudes, skills and knowledge that are promoted by the school's policy.

Student Assessment
This part of the school's policy should clearly articulate the ways of collecting, recording, storing and using assessment information in the school. Assessment information can be cross-referenced to the Australian Curriculum and each state's syllabus documents.

Teaching Implications
These should cover:
- how grammar will be taught in each year group
- how grammar will be taught to the range of learners in the school
- how and when students will be assessed and how the assessment information will be reported to families
- the purchasing of resources and support materials
- teacher professional development and the training requirements of volunteers.

Evaluation
How will the policy be evaluated, by whom and in what time frame? What will be done with the evaluation information? How, when and by whom will the policy be revised?

Grammaville State School

Whole-School Grammar Policy

Philosophy

The staff and families at Grammaville State School value the home languages and social dialects of students and families at the school and recognise that these provide effective means of communication in particular community situations. However, the staff and families at Grammaville State School believe that an understanding of the grammar of Standard Australian English will enable students to:

- create effective texts for a range of social purposes in the wider community
- analyse the texts constructed by others and understand the way language choices affect meaning
- learn more effectively across learning areas
- participate equitably in Australian society.

Rationale

A coherent, systematic teaching approach to grammar and different types of texts will ensure that students develop the knowledge and skills essential for effective communication in English and have fair and equitable access to opportunities beyond school, based on their ability to use Standard Australian English.

Aim

All students will be provided with systematic and sequential instruction in English grammar in the context of a range of informative, imaginative and persuasive texts, so that they:

- develop positive attitudes to learning in English
- experience success in creating a range of grammatically well-constructed texts to achieve social purposes (recount, inform, persuade, argue, explain, respond, describe, entertain, narrate, direct, instruct, discuss)
- use, appreciate, critically analyse and evaluate texts constructed by others.

Objectives

1. Students will value grammar and develop confidence in themselves as users of English.
2. Students will develop knowledge of language structures and features appropriate in different contexts for different purposes and audiences.
3. Students will use their knowledge of language structures and features in a range of texts in their own reading, writing, talking, listening and viewing.

Curriculum Links

See Australian Curriculum, English.

Refer to the Scope and Sequence charts from the *Grammar Rules!* Teacher Resource Books and student books.

Student Assessment

Information about student achievement in grammar will be collected spontaneously during class work and using a combination of students' writing samples and students' spoken texts.

Assessment information will also be collected on a regular and systematic basis using the Revision units provided in the *Grammar Rules!* student books as well as through specific tasks set for students, such as those in the student books' **Try it yourself!** sections.

Students will engage in self-assessment using the pull-out pages in their *Grammar Rules!* student books to record their use of different types of texts and grammar. Students can reflect on their progress in grammar within the context of their own writing, and record issues discussed in writing conferences held with the teacher.

Information about students' language achievements will be recorded and this information will be provided to families informally, as the need arises, and formally, in response to requests from families or as determined by the teacher.

Families will be provided with half-yearly and yearly written reports that outline grammar progress and development.

Teaching Implications

The school will implement this policy commencing Term 1 of ______ (year) in all classes.

Grammar instruction will be integrated across all areas of learning. Grammar instruction will be supported by the classroom expectation that all students will engage in writing and speaking, daily, for a variety of purposes and audiences.

Grammar instruction will be planned for daily, as well as occur spontaneously during the course of any activity that provides a teaching opportunity for grammar.

Support Material/Resources

Grammar Rules! resources will be purchased for each student and class teacher.

Whole-staff training and professional development opportunities in grammar will be organised.

Evaluation

Evaluation of the policy and policy review will be ongoing. Year-group meetings will be held monthly.

Year groups will provide written feedback to the Grammar Committee about the impact of this policy on students and staff.

The Grammar Committee will compile a written report for the school community on the progress of policy implementation and make further recommendations to school management regarding teacher training, resources (personnel and equipment), and so on.

Key things to remember:

- Integrate grammar across the curriculum.
- Teach grammar in context as it arises in students' own written and spoken texts and the texts students are using.
- Teach grammar by creating contexts for learning grammar.
- Teach grammar at the point of need for individual students as well as to the whole class, as appropriate, or to groups of students with similar needs.
- Consider ways to teach special groups such as ESL students.

Glossary

absolute adjective
an adjective that does not have a comparative or superlative form *(dead)*

abstract noun
a noun for something that cannot be seen, heard or touched, such as an emotion or an idea *(love)*

active voice
when the **subject of the verb** is doing the action *(The Egyptians built pyramids.)*

adjectival clause
a **dependent clause** that does the job of an **adjective** by describing a **noun** or **pronoun** *(James is a boy who runs like the wind.)*

adjectival phrase
a phrase that does the job of an adjective by adding meaning to a **noun** or **pronoun**. It describes a noun and usually comes after the main noun in a noun group *(the cupcake with the chocolate sprinkles)*.

adjective
a word that tells more about a **noun** or **pronoun** (see also **classifying adjective, descriptive adjective, number adjective, possessive adjective**)

adverb
a word that adds meaning to a **verb** *(rolled slowly)*, an **adjective** *(very pretty)* or another **adverb** *(really well)*. Adverbs can tell how *(quickly)*; when *(soon, now, then)*; where *(here, there)*.

adverbial clause
a **dependent clause** that does the job of an **adverb**. An adverbial clause can tell how, when, where or why an action occurs. *(The branch snapped when the cat ran along it.)*

adverbial phrase
a phrase that does the job of an adverb by telling how, when, where or why *(The branch snapped along its length.)*

alliteration
when words begin with the same sound *(slippery slugs)*

antonym
a word that means the opposite of another word *(clean/dirty)*

auxiliary verb
a verb that helps another verb *(is called)*. Modal auxiliary verbs help to show **modality** *(should come)*.

being or having verb
see **relating verb**

classifying adjective
an adjective that classifies or tells the group that a **noun** belongs to *(tennis match)*

clause
a group of words that expresses an idea and contains a **verb** *(I caught the ball)*

collective noun
a name for a group of things *(herd, bunch, pod)*

collocation
the term used for words that are likely to be used together *(light bulb, light switch)*

command
a sentence that tells someone to do something *(Finish your work.)*

common noun
an everyday naming word

comparative and superlative adjectives
the forms of an adjective that show degrees of comparison *(pretty* – positive, *prettier* – comparative, *prettiest* – superlative*)*

complex sentence
a sentence that has a main clause (an **independent clause**) and one or more **dependent clauses** that add meaning to the main clause *(If the dog barks, the cat will run away.)*

complex verb
a **verb group** that contains more than one main verb. Each single verb contributes equally to the meaning of the verb group. *(remembered thinking, started running)*

compound noun
a noun made by combining two or more words (joining – *Sunday,* two words – *light switch,* hyphens – *father-in-law)*

compound sentence
a sentence containing more than one **clause**, where each clause is an **independent clause** that makes sense on its own *(I will walk and she will drive.)*

concrete noun
a noun for something that can be seen, heard or touched

conjunction
a joining word that links words, **phrases** or **clauses** in a **sentence**. Conjunctions are **connectives**.

connective
a word or words that connect ideas and events in a text by adding information, comparing things, showing one thing causes another, showing time sequence, or showing logical sequence

contraction
a shortened form of a word or words where letters are left out. An apostrophe shows that a letter or letters have been left out. *(I'm, what's)*

definite and indefinite articles
types of **determiners** in the **noun group** that indicate specific or definite things *(the cat)*, or general or indefinite things *(a cat, an orange)*

descriptive adjective
an adjective that describes aspects of a noun such as colour, shape, size and texture

determiner
a word in a **noun group** such as an article (*a, an, the*) or a word that points out *(that apple)*

doing verb
a word that represents an action *(jump, ate, is skipping)*

ellipsis
when words have been left out of a sentence. Meaning is implied but not stated in words.

emotive word
a word that appeals to the emotions. Emotive words are often used in the media, in exposition texts *(the slaughter of whales)* and in advertising *(Don't miss out!)*.

valuative language
language that represents the author's personal opinions and judgements about something *(delicious food, brave explorer)*

exclamation
a sentence that shows strong emotion, such as anger or surprise, or gives a warning or command. An **exclamation** ends in an exclamation mark. *(Wow! Look out! I love it!)*

helping verb
see **auxiliary verb**

homophone
a word that sounds the same as another word but is spelled differently and has a different meaning *(flour/flower)*

indefinite article
see **definite and indefinite articles**

independent clause
a clause that makes sense on its own (a main clause)

irregular verb
a verb that does not follow the regular pattern of adding *–d* or *–ed* to form past tense but forms past tense in other ways *(ate, ran)*

lexical chain
a chain of words that represents a particular content strand in a text

modality
the degree of certainty, usualness or obligation the speaker or writer has about something. **High modality** is certain; **low modality** is less certain. *(It will rain* – high*; It might rain* – low; *It won't rain* – high*)*

nominalisation
a form of abstraction where **verbs** are turned into **nouns** *(the rehabilitation and release of injured wildlife)*

noun
a word for a person, place, animal or thing

noun group
a group of words that contains a main **noun** and other words that tell more about the main noun

number adjective
an adjective in the **noun group** that tells the quantity or order of a **noun**

onomatopoeia
when words sound like the things they represent *(whiz, clunk)*

passive voice
when the **subject of the verb** has the action done to it *(Pyramids were built by Egyptians.)*

personal pronoun
a **pronoun** that replaces a **noun** for a person, place, animal or thing. Personal pronouns can be 1st person (*I, me, we, us*), 2nd person (*you*) or 3rd person (*her, him, she, he, them, they, it*).

phrase
a group of words that go together to make meaning. A phrase usually does not include a **verb**. *(during the week, to the beach)*

plural noun
the form of the **noun** used for more than one person, place, animal or thing

possessive adjective
a word in the noun group that shows possession *(his hat)*

possessive pronoun
a **pronoun** that shows ownership *(The red car is ours.)*

preposition
a word that shows the relationship between a **noun** or **pronoun** and another word *(in, under, with, by)*

prepositional phrase
a **preposition** linked to a **noun**, **pronoun** or **noun group**. A prepositional phrase can tell where *(by the road)*; when *(in the morning)*; how *(by a falling rock)*; or with whom *(with him)*.

pronoun
a word that can replace a **noun**, including a demonstrative pronoun *(Do you want this?)*

proper noun
a name for a particular person, place, animal or thing, beginning with a capital letter

question
a **sentence** that asks for information or an opinion. A question ends in a question mark.

quoted (direct) speech
the actual speech someone says

reference chain
a chain of **reference words** (usually **pronouns**) that refer to the same person, place, animal or thing throughout a text; used to avoid repeatedly using the same **noun**

reference word
a word used to refer to something mentioned elsewhere in a text *(The koala . . . it)*

regular verb
a verb that forms its past tense with the suffix *–d* or *–ed*

relating verb
a being or having word *(is, has, was)*

relative pronoun
a pronoun that relates to people, places, animals or things already mentioned in a text *(that, which, who, whom, whose)*

reported (indirect) speech
speech that is not quoted directly

saying verb
a verb that shows something is being said *(shout, talking, yelled)*

sentence
a group of words that makes sense on its own and includes at least one **verb**

simple sentence
a sentence that consists of a single **clause**

singular noun
the form of the noun used for a single person, place, animal or thing

speech marks
marks used to show words that are spoken in **quoted (direct) speech**, also called inverted commas or quotation marks

statement
a **sentence** that presents a fact or an opinion. A statement ends in a full stop.

subject of the verb
find the **subject** of the **verb** by asking who or what the verb is about

subordinate (dependent) clause
a clause that adds information to a main or **independent clause**. It does not make sense on its own. *(<u>When it's my birthday</u>, I'll have a fancy dress party.)*

superlative adjective
see **comparative and superlative adjectives**

synonym
a word that has a similar meaning to another word *(small/little)*

tenor
refers to the roles and relationships of the people involved in the language situation

tense
refers to the ways in which time is represented in the forms of the **verb**. Tense is described as past, present or future.

theme
theme is the starting point of the message in the clause. It is the first grammatical component of the clause.

thinking or feeling verb
a verb that represents a mental activity *(loving, hoping, believing)*

verb
a doing, being or having, thinking or feeling, or saying word

verb group
a group of words that does the job of a **verb**. It can contain a main verb and an **auxiliary verb** *(should try, is dancing)* or two verbs that contribute equally to the meaning *(remembered feeling* – this type is also know as a **complex verb**).

vocative
a name or title used to address a person and signal the nature of the relationship between the language users and their relative status *(Sir, Mum, Darling)*

Teaching and Learning Activities

Displays

To help students develop an understanding of grammar it is useful to begin with the relevant types of texts across learning areas and the way the grammar functions in those types of texts. Examples of useful texts across learning areas could include:

- factual books related to topics being undertaken in class
- newspapers
- picture books
- play scripts
- novels
- poetry
- magazines
- advertising leaflets
- business letters
- informal letters
- emails
- postcards
- diaries and journals
- travel brochures
- scientific explanations
- comic strips
- song lyrics

Organise classroom displays of models of the different types of texts with the structures clearly outlined for students. For example, models of procedural texts could include: rules for maths games, rules for classroom behaviour, rules for sports, instructions for classroom organisation, directions to get to various parts of the school from the classroom, instructions for cleaning the class fish tank or caring for class plants, recipes for modelling clay or favourite family treats, maps of the suburb or area, maps of the school grounds and so on.

Display grammar definition posters as well as posters to illustrate proverbs, metaphor, idiom and simile; word banks (lexical chains) for topic lists; word banks for thinking and feeling verbs; verbs to use for 'saying' other than *said*; time connectives; prepositions; <u>how</u> adverbs; maps with proper nouns for place names; homophones and so on. Add to word banks as students discover extra possibilities.

It is important to develop a common classroom language to discuss grammar. Students need to learn **grammar terminology** to be able to effectively discuss what's going on in texts. All subjects have terminology, including maths, visual arts, music and science. Without terminology students and teachers are limited in their capacity to talk about the language of a text. Making grammar terminology a regular part of classroom discussions will enable students to become more comfortable with it as it becomes more familiar to them.

Display examples of students' written texts that show writing for a variety of social purposes, topics and audiences.

Provide different audiences for students' spoken texts – peers, other classes, small groups, whole-school assemblies, family members, invited guests such as senior citizens, imaginary guests and so on.

Modelling and Demonstration

Demonstrate for students how to write different types of texts. Construct texts in front of the class or a particular group of students. Tell students what you are thinking as you write. For example, when demonstrating the construction of a recount, talk out loud about chronological sequence, time words and past tense. Articulate for students why you have included particular events, what is significant about them and therefore why they belong in the recount. Model how you think about your writing as you write. This shows students that writers change their minds, reorder things, cross out, consider different ways to write things, choose 'better' words and self-correct as they write.

Joint and Collaborative Writing

Write texts with students as a collaboration. For example, after a class excursion to a park, nature reserve or botanical gardens, jointly construct a description. Ask students to contribute noun groups with adjectives and adjectival phrases. Ask them for figurative language, such as simile, personification or metaphor. Ask them how you should connect the ideas in the text in a logical sequence, which verb groups would be appropriate and so on.

Have students engage in collaborative language tasks in pairs or small groups where they discuss the purpose, structure and grammar of their texts. Collaborative and group work consolidates learning for those students who have learned particular aspects of grammar, and supports and extends those students who are still developing in that area. Students who are more capable or who are gifted in verbal-linguistic intelligence deserve opportunities to work on language tasks together or with students in other classes, otherwise they might resent always being teamed with less verbal-linguistically able students. Working in ability groups enables gifted students to extend and challenge each other.

In any group work, encourage students to articulate for each other the grammar choices they are making when they collaboratively construct texts. Model this when you demonstrate how to create particular texts for particular purposes.

Use published texts as models for innovation:

Cinderella → 'Cinderfella'

Red Riding Hood → 'Robert Riding Hood'

Sleeping Beauty → 'Sleeping Bernie'

The Very Hungry Caterpillar → 'The Very Hungry Caterpillar Dog'

Where the Wild Things Are → 'When the Wild Things Came'

Activities to Support Grammar Learning

Anthology Drama

Students perform a series of drama pieces as a collection or anthology, linked by narration, music, signs or in some other way. This strategy is useful for exploring time frames, sequencing, cause and effect, connectives, and adverbial phrases that tell when in novels as well as point of view.

To create anthology drama for a novel divide the class into groups. Allocate a specific section of the novel to each group to dramatise. The sections could be identified based on time frames and significant events or based on particular characters and their points of view of events. The narrator could be a third person narrator or it could be a character narrating from a particular point of view. It is also possible to have two characters as narrators of the anthology giving different points of view of the same events. Students could use various forms of dramatisation for the segments including scripted drama, developed improvisations and **Readers' Theatre** (see page 18).

Anthology drama works well to help students establish time patterns in narratives because narratives can be written in chronological order; they can begin with a prologue and then proceed in a time sequence; they can use flashback and flash forward; or they can contain dual time frames.

Cloze

Cloze involves deleting words or word groups from a text and asking students to use their knowledge of the way texts are structured and the grammar of texts to work out the missing words. Cloze works particularly well to identify students' understanding of reference chains, articles, determiners, adjectives and verb tense. It is usually best to focus on one aspect of grammar only in a cloze activity.

Jigsaw cloze involves cutting a text into chunks (paragraphs, sentences) and asking students to reassemble the pieces in the correct order. Jigsaw cloze works well to identify students' knowledge of text structures, particularly procedures (directions, instructions and recipes), recounts, expositions and information reports. Oral cloze involves the teacher reading to students (particularly narratives), pausing during the reading and asking for predictions about what might happen next. Students need to identify aspects of the text that enabled them to make their predictions. Sentence cloze involves cutting a sentence into individual words or word groups (grammatical parts) and having students use their knowledge of grammar to reassemble them. This is more applicable to lower primary students or to students learning English as a second language.

Debates

Debates are particularly useful for teaching students about modality and asserting a point of view. Students need to present opinions and reasons in a logical sequence. They learn to use connectives to link arguments. They use emotive language to convince listeners to adopt a point of view. They manipulate modality to sound more convincing and persuasive. They make use of vocatives to engage the audience.

Parliamentary debates are formal debates. They involve two teams (the 'affirmative' and the 'negative' or the 'government' and the 'opposition'). Students take turns to present their arguments as first, second and third speakers for their teams. Their arguments are prepared and written in advance. The first speakers for each team outline their team's arguments. The second speakers present the substance of the arguments. The final speakers provide a summation or restatement of the team's position. The final speaker also responds to the points raised by the other team. This is called the 'right of rebuttal'.

Students learn to use cue cards. They also learn how to use their voice in presenting an argument to express high modality (tone, inflection, pitch, pace, pause, emphasis).

Polarised debates are less formal debates. Arguments are not written before the debate. Students make decisions about their point of view as the debate proceeds. Usually a topic statement is presented and then students who agree with the statement stand on one side of the room. Students who disagree stand on the opposite side of the room. Students who are undecided stand across the middle of the room to make a horseshoe shape. Students learn that it is acceptable to change your opinion as you listen to the convincing opinions of others. Students can cross the room as they change their minds. Usually the polarised debate finishes when every student has had an opportunity to present a point of view. Usually students realise that few issues are black and white and that in all arguments there are shades of grey or valid points on all sides of the issue. It is useful to have students write a discussion text after the debate. Their discussion should outline the main points raised by different sides of the issue and then end with a statement of their own position on the issue. Connectives such as *on the one hand, on the other hand, alternatively,* will be useful in a discussion.

Dictagloss

This strategy assists students in learning how to make notes from teacher talks, the teacher reading information, or film and television documentaries. Students need to note down the lexical chains (chains of content words). These will be noun groups, circumstances and verb groups. The term 'dictagloss' comes from the words 'dictation' and 'glossary'. The students create a glossary of content words. Students do not need to write every word. They need to write key words and phrases. Then they use their understanding of the way texts are structured to re-create the whole text, adding aspects of grammar that make the text cohesive, such as connectives. Students can work independently or in groups. Group discussion is often useful to reinforce understandings and to support students who initially are not as effective at listening, note making or reconstructing their content words into a cohesive text.

Dramatisation

Dramatise familiar children's rhymes and songs, such as *Miss Polly had a Dolly who was Sick, Sick, Sick,* to focus on saying verbs, adjectives, quoted (direct) speech, dialogue, commands and stereotyping. Allocate characters to students. Have one student act as Director with a cardboard megaphone to shout comments and instructions after each scene in the performance. The Director's shouts should use adjectives to describe how the actors are to revise their acting, for example 'Not sad enough – be melodramatic', 'Too sad – be happier, laugh hysterically', 'Too happy – be thrilling, scream with terror'. Draw students' attention to gender roles and rework the play as *Mr Polly had a Baby* . . . The doctor could be male or female. Add ambulance officers, with lines like 'This sick baby needs to go to hospital.' This type of dramatising also provides opportunities to explore film genres such as comedy, melodrama, tragedy and horror. There's a range of well-known stories to perform in this manner, including *Jack and Jill Went up the Hill, Tikki Tikki Tembo* and any of Aesop's fables.

Epilogue

An epilogue asks students to predict what happens beyond the end of a narrative. Students need an understanding of characterisation, time frames and issues in the narrative to create an epilogue.

Have students write an epilogue for a class novel or work in groups to create a performance that shows what could happen after the end of a novel. Compare and discuss the validity of each epilogue presented. Students could also create prologues. A prologue would include events that took place before the start of the story, underpinning character behaviour and events in the story. A prologue would provide background information.

Games

1. **Verb/Adverb Improvisation** List adverbs that tell how *(slowly, painstakingly, carefully, swiftly, happily)* on pieces of cardboard and place in a container. List verbs *(eat, discussed, ran, jumped, whispers, sing)* on cardboard and place in a separate container. Have students play in teams. Have each team pick a word from each container and create an improvisation to illustrate both words together. Students themselves can create the word cards.

2. **Alphabet Challenge** Ask students, playing individually or in pairs, to write the following headings across the top of columns on paper: proper noun: place, common noun: place, verb, adjective, adverb, girl's name, boy's name (see below). Randomly select a letter of the alphabet and tell students to write a word starting with this letter in each column, and shout 'Stop!' when they are finished. As soon as a team shouts 'Stop!', have all students stop and compare their answers. Every correct unique answer scores two points. If another team has the same answer, score one point only for that answer. The team who finished first gets a bonus point if all their answers are appropriate.

proper noun: place	common noun: place	verb	adjective	adverb	girl's name	boy's name
Sydney	shopping centre	skip	smart	slowly	Suri	Sam

3. **What's Your Answer?** Create a deck of cards with grammar terms written on them. For example: *a saying verb, a doing verb, a proper noun in your school, a proper noun for a place in Australia, a descriptive adjective for a tree, a descriptive adjective for a person, a noun group with a determiner, a simple sentence* and so on. Place the deck face-down on a table. Have students play in groups. Students take turns to turn over a card. If they answer correctly they win the card. If they answer incorrectly the card goes to the bottom of the deck. The student with the most cards when the deck is finished is the winner.

4. **Quiz** Have older students create quiz sheets for younger classes. For example, a proper noun quiz has all proper noun answers. Allow students to use atlases, maps and other reference material to find their answers. Questions could include: *What is the capital of Tasmania? Name a town in central Queensland that begins with L. Where can you find polar bears? Name a river in Victoria. Name a desert in Western Australia. Which body of water is between Australia and New Zealand?*

5. **Findaword** Ask students to create grammar findawords for each other to solve. The findawords can focus on adjectives, common nouns, proper nouns, past tense verbs or adverbs.

6. **Label that Picture** Create a set of picture or photo cards from travel brochures, magazines, newspapers and so on. Create a set of grammar cards labelled *noun, noun group, noun group with determiners, verb, simple sentence with relating verb, adjective* and so on. Place cards in two piles face-down on a table. Have students take turns to turn over one of each card and give ten answers. For example, if they turn over a *noun* card, have them name ten nouns in the picture; if they turn over a card labelled *simple sentence with relating verb,* have them describe the picture in ten such sentences.

7. **Concentration** Have students play a game of Concentration by pairing a label card with a picture card. For example, one matching pair would be a card labelled *verb: eat* and a card showing a picture of a person eating. Shuffle the cards and place them in rows face-down on a table. Have students take turns to turn over pairs of cards. If the cards are a match, they keep the pair and have another turn. If the cards are not a match, they turn them face-down again. The student who has collected the most pairs at the end of the game is the winner.

8. **Noun Group Challenge** Write common nouns on pieces of paper and place in a container. Have students play individually or in pairs. Select a noun from the container and call it out. Tell students to write the longest noun group they can for the main noun that you called out. Noun groups can include adjectives, determiners, phrases and clauses. For example: *'desk' – teacher's desk, old wooden teacher's desk, old wooden messy teacher's desk, old wooden messy teacher's desk with the cracked surface, old wooden messy teacher's desk that is about to fall apart.*

9. **Memory Out Loud** Have students sit in a circle and take turns to list nouns taken on a picnic, seen at the zoo, bought at a shop, visible in the classroom, found in the home and so on. Each student needs to remember the items already listed and then add their own.

   I went to the zoo and I saw a bear.

   I went to the zoo and I saw a bear and a zebra.

   I went to the zoo and I saw a bear, a zebra and a hippo and so on.

   The game could also be played using verbs.

   I went to the park to play.

   I went to the park to play and run.

   I went to the park to play, run and sing . . .

Hot Seat

In Hot Seat, one student takes on the role of a character in a novel or a famous person in a historical recount, newspaper article, biography or autobiography. The rest of the class acts as interviewers or journalists and asks the student in the 'hot seat' questions about their thoughts, feelings and responses to events in their life. Hot Seat allows students to explore interview techniques and the structure of open-ended questions, point of view, modality and characterisation. Some answers will be based on evidence available to students in the text they have taken their character from. Some answers may not be readily evident but the person in the Hot Seat role should be able to extrapolate how their character would respond. The student in the Hot Seat will need to use thinking and feeling verbs to represent their point of view. Encourage them to vary the modality of their answers. Have students evaluate the effectiveness of their questions in exploring the character beyond what students already knew.

Improvisation

Improvisation involves students acting out a scene without rehearsal or script.

A useful improvisation game is 'Three-part sentence'. Have students work in groups, and have each group write one sentence including a noun group for a character, a verb or verb group and a setting (a prepositional phrase that tells where).

Rawley with his spiky hair and nose ring /excelled/ at Summerville High School.

Cut the sentences into grammatical components and place in three containers. Student groups randomly pick one piece of paper from each container and then create an improvisation based on the sentence components that they get.

Improvisation could also be based on quoted (direct) speech. Have groups write quoted speech on separate pieces of paper and place them into a container. Groups take one (or two or three for extra challenge) from the container and create an improvisation where characters have to say the speech. When doing 'Three-part sentence' improvisation for quoted speech the improvisation should end with one of the lines being spoken. Students can announce their lines before they start so that the audience can listen out for them during the improvisation or they can ask the class to tell which were the lines, at the end of the improvisation.

Quoted-speech improvisation could include questions, statements and commands such as *'Thank goodness you've arrived', 'Where have you been?', 'That wig is Leon's', 'Get the paint', 'It won't eat', 'I'm sick of that!'*

Newspaper headlines could also be used as stimulus for improvisations.

A simpler improvisation could be based on a noun, an adjective and a verb.

Mime

Have students write verbs *(eating, jumping, singing, hopped, flew)* and prepositional phrases that tell where *(on a picnic, on the moon, in the shower, under an elephant)* on pieces of paper and place them in separate containers. Students can take turns to select a word or word group from a container and mime the scene. The rest of the class needs to guess the answer. These grammar words could also be used for improvisation or as stimulus for narrative writing.

Multi-voice Recitation

In Multi-voice Recitation, students use their voices individually, in pairs, small groups or large groups to recite poems. Individual words in the poem, or lines and stanzas, can be allocated to particular students. Some students can chant echoes or background noises such as onomatopoeic words. Individual voices can recite softly, groups can recite loudly and so on. Sections of the poem can be recited as a 'round'. Have students work in groups to determine how they will present their poem, or organise a whole-class recitation for performance.

Play Scripts

Use published play scripts to discuss dialogue, stage directions, quoted speech and so on with students. Students can use published play scripts as models for their own writing of plays and radio plays. Point out to students how to use their voice for questions, statements, commands and exclamations and have them experiment with the following vocal elements.

Intonation – such as rising inflection where the tone of the voice rises at the end of a question *(Where's the can opener?)* or a falling tone contour, which indicates finality *(It's in the drawer where it's kept)*.

Pitch – how high or deep the voice sounds. Use of pitch affects meaning in speech. High pitch sounds excited. A lower pitch can sound sad or despondent.

Pace – how fast you speak. Faster pacing sounds excited. Slower pacing sounds bored or unenthusiastic.

Pause – allows the speaker to gather their thoughts or creates a moment of emphasis for listeners to think about what was said. Deliberate pauses can emphasise certain points in the speech, especially if eye contact is used for effect on an audience. Speakers often fill pauses with 'ums'. As students practise oral presentations they should learn to speak formally, using pause rather than 'um'.

Emphasis – is where a word or word group is emphasised to give it importance. How speakers emphasise certain words in their speech impacts on meaning.

Give that to me.

Give that to me.

Give that to me.

Stress is the way syllables in words are stressed to affect meaning.

The content of the will was a shock.

He was content to sleep through the day.

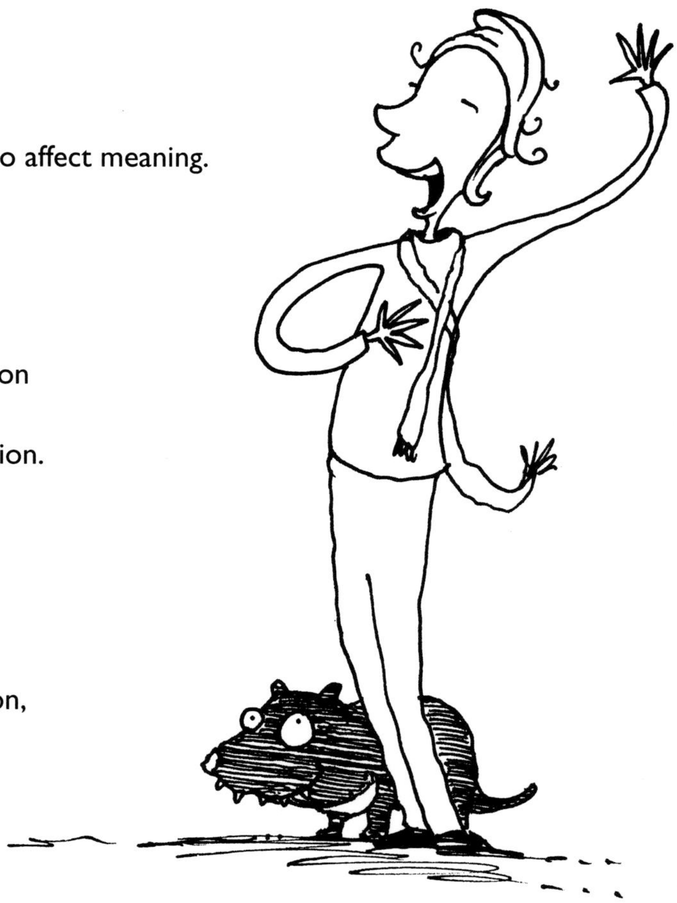

Poetry

Different forms of poetry are useful for focusing on different aspects of grammar. For example, Dylan Thomas Portraits are useful for teaching description. Focus on noun groups and adjectives.

Have you ever seen a Tasmanian Devil?

Wet spotted nose, short legs, powerful teeth, endangered species.

Ezra Pound Couplets can also focus on description, as well as the figurative language of metaphor.

A spider balancing on a web.

A tightrope artist suspended on a rope.

Readers' Theatre

Readers' Theatre is useful to teach students about speech marks, quoted speech, saying verbs and narrators. Have groups choose sections of dialogue in a novel and allocate which character's dialogue each student will read. Have them decide whether or not to use a narrator or to use a character's alter ego as narrator. Readers' Theatre can be useful to demonstrate the voice of the narrator. The narrator can also be a character so that character has two parts in the Readers' Theatre. If the author is the narrator, discuss third person narrative.

Role-play

Have students role-play interactions in various situations between various people. Role-playing provides students with opportunities to use spoken language in different contexts with different audiences and purposes. They can role-play classroom or school-based situations, pretend to be at the shopping centre requesting help from shopkeepers, making purchases, on the telephone with ambulance officers in an emergency, requesting and giving directions, offering assistance, interviewing for television and so on.

Students can take on the roles of story characters and build on their roles in different situations where they interact with others.

Role-play allows for exploration of the use of vocatives (distant, formal, polite, friendly). Students can also explore the use of body language and facial expression in varying situations and how use of these non-verbal cues is affected by the relationships between the language users (tenor).

Students can explore audience and relationships using puppets.

Storyboard

A storyboard is a shooting script for a film or video. It is like a cartoon version of a story, with the story divided into frames. Have students work in groups to create a storyboard, deciding whether the frames show close-ups, mid shots or long shots, based on what is significant in that part of the story.

Students can create storyboards for poems, play scripts and narratives. Storyboards allow students to explore point of view, time frames (connectives and adverbs), dialogue (quoted and reported speech/ speech bubbles), setting (prepositional phrases and noun groups), and characterisation (noun groups, thinking and feeling verbs).

Students can also present their storyboards as **freeze frames**. These are a series of depictions in which the scenes are presented in sequence. Students create a scene, freeze, then move into position for the next scene and freeze. The audience needs to close their eyes during the transitions between scenes so that the images they see are frozen depictions.

Story Map

Have students draw a map based on a story read together in class. Story Maps allow students to visually represent the setting for a narrative. Students need to consider, in particular, prepositional phrases that tell where, descriptive adjectives, noun groups, and connectives that show time or cause.

Sculptures

Have students create a sculpture using their bodies to depict an abstract noun such as *peace, cooperation, tranquillity, purpose, responsibility, global warming, pollution*. Students in middle primary will tend to find it easier to represent concrete nouns. Students operating at more advanced stages (or students who are bodily-kinaesthetic learners) will sometimes find more figurative or abstract and creative ways to represent words. Fluid sculptures add movement to the sculptures. Usually the movement is repetitive.

This Is Your Life

This form of role-play works well with narratives, biography or autobiography. Have students choose a character and then organise guests from the character's past to speak about the character. Tell them to consider the chronological order of events in the person's life and quoted speech. They can present the role-play as a spoof or parody.

Have fun with grammar!

- use it and play around with it
- make fun of it
- distort and exaggerate it
- play games with it
- enjoy it as a subject worthy of your students' time

There is no need for grammar to be onerous, so take care with your own attitude. Remember: Grammar is fun!

Annotated Models for Different Types of Texts

The following pages include text models taken from the *Grammar Rules!* student books. The models are annotated to show aspects of grammar relevant in the various types of texts.

Imaginative – Narrative

Social purpose

- To entertain, enlighten and/or to teach a lesson or moral

Forms

- Picture books, novellas, novels, storytelling, puppet shows, play scripts, ballads, storyboards

Visual elements

- Photos, drawings, illustrations in print media
- Gestures, facial expression and body language in film, and other oral presentations

Structure

- Orientation: the scene is set for events; characters and settings are introduced
- Complication: a problem is introduced for characters to deal with
- Series of events in the plot occur
- Resolution: characters resolve problems (either solve them or deal with them in some other way) and grow from the experience
- Comment or coda

adverb to tell when

prepositional phrase to tell how

Through the Doorway

Ronnie looked out her window at the blinding light that was coming from the neighbourhood park. She grabbed her jumper out of the closet and snuck out the back door without a sound. She wheeled her bike onto the street, then climbed on and headed down the road to the park.

Ronnie was astonished to see that all the light was coming from a small shoe-sized box. She knelt down next to it and lifted the lid. Inside was a remote control. Ronnie picked it up. A red light in the centre started flashing. Without thinking, Ronnie pushed the red button. Bang! An ear-splitting noise shattered the night. She jumped back quickly and before her eyes the remote turned into a gigantic doorway. Ronnie peered inside.

doing verbs

3rd person personal pronouns

prepositional phrase to tell where

short, simple sentence to support the speed of the events

onomatopoeia to add atmosphere

noun group with descriptive adjectives

Extract from *Grammar Rules! Student Book 5*, page 18

Informative – Description

Social purpose

- To describe people, places, animals or things

Forms

- Narrative poetry, conversations, scientific reports, information reports

Visual elements

- can include diagrams or photos with labels

Structure

- Orientation: introduction to the topic
- Logical sequence of descriptions about aspects of the topic
- Conclusion: summing-up statement
- Judgement or evaluation (optional)

adverb

evaluative language

emotive word

relating (being or having) verbs

prepositional phrase to tell where

reference chain of nouns and pronouns

compound-complex sentence

figurative language – simile

noun group with adjectival phrase

Green Sea Turtles of the Great Barrier Reef

The Great Barrier Reef is a magnificent habitat and nesting area for the critically endangered green turtle. The adult green turtles love to eat the tasty seaweed and algae found in the warm waters of the Pacific Ocean. These gentle plant eaters are olive-green in colour with perhaps some brown, reddish-brown or black markings. Each turtle has quite distinctive face markings. The shell is a cross between circular and heart-shaped and might grow to a metre long. It is a creamy colour underneath. Green turtles have oar-shaped flippers to pull themselves through the water like a canoe, and their heads and nostrils make them look like little aliens when they rise above the surface of their watery tropical paradise.

Extract from *Grammar Rules! Student Book 6*, page 8

Persuasive – Discussion

Social purpose

- To explore different points of view on a topic

Forms

- Newspapers and magazines, journals, talkback radio, panel discussions, polarised debates, conversations

Structure

- Orientation: introduction to the issue
- Opinion for one side of the issue supported by reasons
- Differing opinion supported by reasons
- Summing up
- Recommendation or judgement (optional)

thinking and feeling verbs

relative pronoun to link clauses

Top Wonder

There are two incredible natural wonders in the world that are so vast they can be seen from outer space. They are the Great Barrier Reef off the coast of Queensland, Australia, and the Grand Canyon in the United States of America. Which of these is the most spectacular?

Many people believe the Great Barrier Reef is the best natural wonder. At 2300 kilometres in length, it is the world's largest coral reef system. Colonies of tiny coral polyps have built the reef over thousands of years. It is truly a miracle of nature.

Other people think that the Grand Canyon deserves the title of best natural wonder in the world. The canyon was carved out by the Colorado River over two billion years. The canyon is around 445 kilometres long and 1800 metres deep at its deepest point – that's almost two kilometres.

Both these wonders were created by nature and continue to evolve, but in my opinion the Great Barrier Reef is a truly beautiful and precious part of this planet and it gets my vote for best natural wonder of the world.

noun group with phrases

evaluative language

relating (being or having) verb

superlative adjectives

Extract from *Grammar Rules! Student Book 6*, page 60

connectives

high modality

Informative – Explanation

Social purpose

- To tell how or why things work or how or why things are the way they are

Forms

- Science journals, textbooks, reference material

Visual elements

- Flow charts, cycle diagrams and other types of diagrams and illustrations

Structure

- General statement about the topic (could include a how or why question)
- Sequence of information – usually in cause and effect sequence or time order
- Concluding statement (optional)

logical order/number sequence

How Does the Alarm Bed Work?

1. An alarm clock, attached to the head of the bed, rings when it is time to get up.

2. Once it rings the sleeper has five minutes to get out of bed because that alarm starts a five-minute timer in the mattress springs.
3. If the pressure on the mattress springs has not changed when the five minutes are up (in other words, if the sleeper is still in the bed) then a latch at the head of the bed is released. This causes the mattress and bed base to catapult forward.
4. This, in turn, causes the sleeper to be ejected from the bed.

present tense

connectives to show time and cause

nominalisation

noun group with phrases

doing verb

technical terminology

Extract from *Grammar Rules! Student Book 3*, page 60

Persuasive – Exposition

Social purpose
- To present a strong point of view on a topic

Forms
- Speeches, letters to the editor, editorials, talkback radio, parliamentary and polarised debates, television current affairs interviews

Structure
- Position statement
- Arguments presented in logical order with supporting reasons
- Restatement of position/summing up
- Recommendation (optional)

thinking and feeling verbs

relative pronouns to link clauses

VOTE AGAINST SCHOOL SWIMMING

I do not think that swimming should be a compulsory school sport. Firstly, I believe that anyone in Australia who wants to swim or who likes swimming will swim outside of school anyway, so why waste school time doing things that everyone can already do? A second reason for voting against compulsory swimming in schools is the risk of skin cancer in Australia. We should not be expecting school children to spend any time in the sun at swimming pools. In addition, I feel that the time spent at swimming would be better spent doing other more important indoor activities like spelling and grammar.

relating (being or having) verb

logical sequence

high modality

1st person personal pronoun

Extract from *Grammar Rules! Student Book 4*, page 70

Persuasive – Advertisement

Social purpose

- To persuade people to buy a product or to take a course of action

Forms

- Leaflets, catalogues, brochures, posters, magazines, radio, television, cinema, newspapers, billboards

Visual elements

- Visual elements are significant in all advertising except radio. Visual elements include slogans and icons, colour, font, design, layout, photographs, images of famous people and places.

Structure

- Opening question/s or statement to capture attention
- Sequence of claims about the product. Arguments to support claims.
- Restatement of position: call to action

Wiz Bang 3000 Kitchen Hand!

Have you ever needed a spare hand in the kitchen?
Do you often run out of time to chop your food?
Do you ever run out of time to cook your food?
Do you ever run out of time to clean up the mess and do the dishes?
Do you ever wonder if you will have enough time to eat your food?

We now have the answer for you:

The WIZ BANG 3000 KITCHEN HAND!

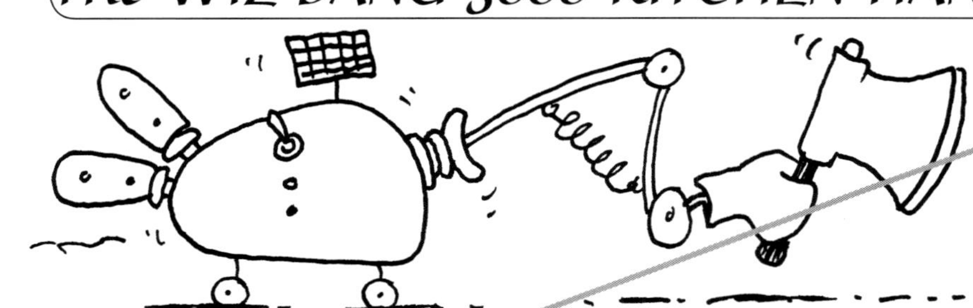

It chops, cooks, cleans and also feeds you your food.
Just ask for a meal from your WIZ BANG 3000 KITCHEN HAND and it will do everything.
But be quick, because THE WIZ BANG 3000 KITCHEN HAND has almost sold out.
So hurry and get this amazing invention today!

Don't miss out! Buy now!

doing verbs
question
thinking verb
voice of experts
present tense
high modality
noun group with adjective
emotive language
command

Extract from *Grammar Rules! Student Book 3*, page 36

Social purpose

- To provide information about a general class of thing

Forms

- Articles, reference material, journals, internet, encyclopedias

Visual elements

- Diagrams, graphs, photographs, charts, illustrations

Structure

- General opening statement: introduction to the topic
- Information about aspects of the topic, in a logical sequence
- Paragraphs based on topic sentences
- Reorientation or finishing-off statement (optional)

classifying adjective

3rd person personal pronoun

Cane Toads

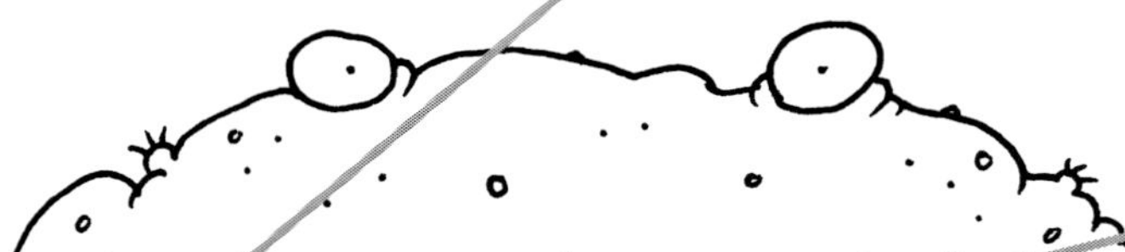

Cane toads were imported to Australia from Hawaii in 1935. They were introduced to Queensland sugar cane farms to eat the cane beetles that were destroying sugar cane crops. Cane toads have now successfully spread across the top of Australia, covering an area of more than one million square kilometres.

Cane toads eat anything they can swallow. Australian indigenous animals, such as snakes, lizards and water birds, are poisoned and killed when they attempt to eat the cane toad. Cane toads have no predators in nature.

passive voice

doing verbs

technical terminology

reference chain

extended noun group

relating (being or having) verb

Extract from *Grammar Rules! Student Book 4*, page 58

Informative – Procedure/Recipe

Social purpose

- To tell someone how to do something

Forms

- Recipes, cookbooks, directions, instructions, rules, cooking shows, gardening shows, manuals, conversations, 'how to' demonstrations

Visual elements

- Photographs and diagrams

Structure

- Statement of goal or purpose
- List of ingredients and/or equipment
- Method or steps in logical sequence as commands
- Caution/warnings (optional)

noun group with number adjective

noun group with descriptive adjective

Wart, Fester and Carbuncle Remover

INGREDIENTS

- 1 cup milk
- 100 g grated candle wax
- 1 tablespoon very hot chilli powder
- 10 mL nail polish remover
- 2 cups vinegar

METHOD

1. Mix all ingredients to a paste.
2. Apply a thin film of paste over affected areas.
3. Bandage affected areas.
4. Avoid water for four weeks. (This means no baths or showers.)

Extract from *Grammar Rules! Student Book 3*, page 58

noun group with classifying adjectives

logical order/ number sequence

doing verb in theme position

prepositional phrase to tell where

command

prepositional phrase to tell when

Informative – Recount

Social purpose

- To retell a series of events

Forms

- Letters, emails, diaries, biography, autobiography, newspaper articles, conversations, television news and current affairs programs

Structure

- Orientation
- Series of events in chronological order
- Summing up or reorientation
- Personal comment or judgement (optional)

past tense doing verb

connective to show <u>cause</u>

3rd person personal pronoun

past tense saying verb

reference chain

1st person personal pronouns

thinking and feeling verb

prepositional phrase telling <u>with whom</u>

Dear Timmy,

Last weekend I went fishing with my grandparents. We fished from the end of the jetty not far from where they live. My grandma caught the first fish. It was only small so she threw it back. I caught the second fish. My grandma shouted, "Way to go, Milly!" My fish was too small to keep so I kissed it and let it go. My grandpa didn't catch anything but he didn't mind. We bought fish and chips on the way home. I like going fishing with my grandparents.

From Milly.

Extract from *Grammar Rules! Student Book 4*, page 6

Persuasive — Response

Social purpose

- To respond to something, such as an event, an artwork, an issue or an aspect of nature. This text presents the writer's response to a nature tour.

Forms

- Book, film and art reviews; excursion reviews; diaries and journals; conversations; poetry

Structure

- Introduction or orientation to establish the context
- Exploration of different aspects of the topic: an outline of events, descriptions, thoughts, feelings
- Conclusion: judgement, opinion or recommendation

SEA LION ENCOUNTER

I recently went on a fantastic tour to Seal Bay on Kangaroo Island, in South Australia. Seal Bay is home to a large breeding colony of Australian sea lions. We were taken right down onto the beach by the park's interpretive officer to get an 'up close and personal' look at the sea lions. She advised us to stay at least six metres from the sea lions, but they came close to us and we had to slowly back away. The sea lions did not seem to care about us, though, and continued behaving naturally, which for the adults was sunbaking on the beautiful white sand while the pups played around, close to the water's edge, chasing the seagulls. Altogether, I had a lot of fun on the tour. The male sea lions were huge, the females were very protective and their pups were really cute. I would recommend the tour to everyone.

- doing verb
- emotive language
- evaluative language
- high modality
- 3rd person personal pronouns
- 1st person personal pronoun
- noun group with adjectives

Extract from *Grammar Rules! Student Book 6*, page 14

Assessing Grammar

The purpose of assessment is to find out what students know and understand, and to use this information to plan further learning opportunities. Assessment strategies include gathering evidence in a wide variety of ways and making judgements about teaching and learning, based on the evidence.

Formative assessment processes assist teachers to monitor ongoing teaching and learning. Formative assessment makes use of teacher-student interactions, observation of students as they are involved in tasks, analysis of work samples, peer assessment, and student self-assessment and reflection.

Summative assessment processes include analysis of work samples and other evidence of student learning, with a view to using these to inform further planning for teaching and learning.

Samples of students' written texts can be photocopied, analysed and stored in student portfolios to monitor progress and determine areas of need. Anecdotal records can be made about students' spoken texts, or spoken presentations can be filmed or recorded. Students' reflection and self-assessment can also be taken into account.

Revision Units are included in the *Grammar Rules!* student books at Units 6, 12, 18, 24, 30 and 35. These can be used as revision or for testing purposes. Each Revision Unit deals with aspects of grammar covered in previous units. Student performance on these units will show whether further revision is required.

Grammar assessment is one aspect of assessing how students construct written and spoken texts. You will need to examine the structure of the text and the grammar relevant for the purpose and audience. In spoken texts, you will also consider body language, facial expression and speech patterns. In written texts, you will also consider spelling and handwriting.

During **writing conferences**, discuss the purpose of the writing and the appropriate type of text and text form to achieve the social purpose. Discuss the structure of the text, the cohesion of the text as a whole (for example, use of connectives and reference chains), use of paragraphs and visual elements, and grammar at the sentence or clause level, and the level of word groups, phrases, words and word parts.

Finding time to engage in writing conferences with every student about every piece of writing is a challenge. Parent helpers can be of some assistance as long as they are trained in what to look for, what to suggest and how to assist students.

Peer conferences can also be useful as long as students are provided with specific criteria to focus on in each other's work. Students can be taught to firstly examine text structure and content to see if it matches purpose and audience. Next they should examine whether the text is effective grammatically. Then they can consider the finer details of punctuation and spelling.

Student self-assessment supports student autonomy and self-management. Encourage students to reflect on their own learning, effort and achievements. Students can use personal journals to record evaluations of their strengths and needs, as well as their responses to classroom activities. Reflection activities have been added to units in student books 1–4, to support self-assessment.

Each *Grammar Rules!* student book includes a pull-out section with a Student Writing Log. The pull-out section can remain in the student book for safekeeping or it can be easily removed and stored in students' writing folders. The Writing Log provides a way for students to keep track of the types of texts and text forms they are writing, and the grammar they are attempting to use in the context of their writing. The log includes a column where students rate their own writing, as well as a 'Where to next?' column for them to write their aims. Teachers can also include their comments and suggestions. The Writing Logs are a useful tool to refer to in conference with your students. They also support students' independence and encourage students to develop responsibility for their own writing tasks and grammar learning.

Samples of students' written texts are included on the following pages. They have been annotated to demonstrate for teachers how to assess students' grammar in written texts.

Analysis of Student Work Samples

Narrative Work Sample

Context

Students had explored fairytales and folktales. They had discussed the structure of a narrative text. They were reminded about the functions of the orientation, complication, events and resolution in narratives and were asked to write a tale about an imaginary creature. The student's writing below contains the orientation and complication.

> **A Mermaid Tale**
>
> Once upon a time there lived three children they were best friends and lived 2 minutes away from the beach. They would walk to the beach every day after school to go for a swim and a play on the sand. Until one day something strange happened something very weird. The children meet at the school gate as they did every day after school to walk to the beach together. Once they got there the water looked more welcoming than it ever did before. The children raced done to the water. Time had past when Freddy saw something in the water it wasn't anything that he had ever seen before it had scales that shimmered in the sunlight it was a mermaid. Freddy tried to tell his friends but they just laughed and said that he was imagining things until the mermaid popped its head out of the water "hello" she said "I am shelly but you can call me shell" the three children looked in amazement "this cant be happening" said Alfie as he rubbed his eyes . . .
>
> Work sample from 11-year-old student (typed by teacher with student's spelling)

- appropriate reference chains in the 3rd person narrative
- time words
- not explained
- descriptive noun group
- connectives
- quoted (direct) speech
- proper nouns

Assessment Comments

Structure

The student begins this 3rd person narrative with *Once upon a time* . . . and then introduces the main characters and sets the scene for events. The complication arises when the story characters meet a mermaid. The student continues the story (not included in the sample text above) to describe the children playing with the mermaid and then going home, after promising to meet the mermaid again the next afternoon.

The complication is not developed in the story: there is no problem for characters to resolve and no issues to overcome, so the story lacks interest and drive.

Why *the water looked more welcoming than it ever did before* is not explained.

Why the mermaid appears in the first place and what the mermaid is doing there is not explained.

The *strange and weird* happening is the appearance of the mermaid, but the story does not include any strange or weird events involving the mermaid.

Language Features

The student uses connectives appropriately to link events in time and through cause and effect.

There is consistent use of 3rd person personal pronouns and correct use of noun/pronoun reference chains.

The student makes appropriate use of past tense verbs, including a variety of thinking and feeling verbs, saying verbs, doing verbs and relating verbs.

There is some effective use of descriptive noun groups.

Prepositional phrases are used to establish where and when events occur.

The student needs to learn how to punctuate quoted speech in a narrative. The student needs support recognising sentences and paragraphs.

The student uses an apostrophe for the contraction *wasn't* but not for *cant*.

Description Work Sample

CONTEXT

Students were asked to write a description of an animal that they are personally familiar with, such as a pet.

My Dog

My dog is a Shih Tzu–Maltese cross. Her name is Turtle because my dad likes to watch the Three Stooges and he think it's funny when Curly says turtle because he says it like 'toitle'. Turtle is black and white. She is very fluffy and her fur keeps growing so we need to get her clipped quiet often. Sometimes her fur grows over her eyes. She has floppy ears. She has little pointy teeth like a vampire and when she growls and her lips curl back her bottom teeth stick out further than her top teeth and it looks really funny. She knows we are laughing at her and it makes her cranky. Turtle barks when anyone comes to the house. She thinks she is a good guard dog but she's really a big chicken. She is a really funny little dog and I love her.

Work sample from 12-year-old student (typed by teacher with student's spelling)

- effective use of reference chain
- relating (being or having) verb
- commonly confused word: *quite*
- complex sentence joined with too many *ands*
- metaphor
- overuse of *really*
- thinking and feeling verb
- noun group with adjectives

ASSESSMENT COMMENTS

Structure

The student has included an orientation or opening statement, a series of descriptions about aspects of the topic (name of the dog, its colour, fur, teeth and how it barks) and a conclusion that involves a judgement or evaluation.

The student shows interest in presentation of written work and includes visual elements.

Language Features

The student has used a reference chain (of nouns and pronouns for the dog) effectively.

The student has written an awkward complex sentence consisting of clauses linked with *and, when, and, and.* The sentence should be split and reworked to clarify meaning and connect ideas more appropriately.

The student overuses the modal adverb *really* and needs to develop use of other adverbs to show modality, such as *extremely, positively, definitely, totally*.

Other comments

The student needs to learn the difference between *quiet* and *quite*.

Discussion Work Sample

Context

The class engaged in a polarised debate. After the debate students were asked to write a summary of the discussion in their journals. They were reminded of the structure of discussion texts and they were told to write their recommendation or judgement about the topic in the conclusion.

Our school canteen should not sell any junk food.

Our school canteen are deciding whether or not to sell junk food. Junk food means pies, sausage rolls, flavoured milks, and chips.

Some people in my class think that junk food should be banned from school because they are making children fat and unhealthy.

Some people in my class think that eating these foods once a week is not going to make you fat so they should not be banned from the canteen. They say you can have some bad foods every now and then and if you exercise it's Ok to have treats. The teacher says that the canteen likes to sell junk foods because they make more money to give to the school for things they need like computers.

I think they should sell junk food at school because they don't have to buy it. They can have sandwiches.

Work sample from 8-year-old student (typed by teacher with spelling corrected)

inappropriate verb

overuse of *because*

overuse of *think*

students in the class

the canteen

the school

students

students

Assessment Comments

Structure

The student has included an orientation or opening statement to establish the topic. The student has included an opinion in favour of one side of the issue introduced by *Some people* . . .

An alternative opinion is introduced by the phrase *Some people*. . . This opinion should have been introduced differently from the first opinion, for example *Other people*. An additional argument is introduced by *The teacher says* . . .

There is a concluding statement that presents a judgement and recommendation.

Language Features

The student uses connectives appropriately to join points of view with reasons (although they do need to learn some alternative connectives to use instead of *because*).

The student uses *canteen are* because he or she is referring to people on a committee. A canteen cannot decide anything so the student should state *The Canteen Committee is* . . .

The thinking and feeling verb *think* is used three times. The student needs to develop a more extensive repertoire of thinking and feeling verbs.

The student's use of pronoun reference is very confusing. *They* is used to refer to the school, students and the canteen. The student also uses *you* to refer to students. Overuse of pronoun reference makes it difficult for a reader to connect the reference chains and make sense of a text.

Explanation Work Sample

CONTEXT

Students were asked to provide a spoken explanation to present to the class to explain how a leech sucks blood. Students used diagrams to support their presentations.

no apostrophe for possession

confusing construction

extended noun group

connectives to show time and cause

Explanation of how a leech sucks blood

Leeches suck blood from people and animals that are called the hosts.

A leech has a sucker at each end of its body. First of all it sticks onto a host with its rear sucker. Then it sticks on with its mouth sucker. So now it is stuck on its host at both ends. It then uses its sharp teeth to cut the host's skin. This makes blood flow out for it to suck up. The leeches saliva contains an anaesthetic so that the host cannot feel the leeches bite or know it is sucking blood. The leeches saliva also contains a chemical to stop the host's blood from clotting so that the blood keeps running otherwise it will clot and become a scab and the leech cannot suck it anymore.

The leech keeps sucking up blood until it is full and then it drops off the host onto the ground and it won't need another meal for a few months.

Work sample from 12-year-old student (typed by teacher with student's spelling)

ASSESSMENT COMMENTS

Structure

The student shows understanding that explanations present a sequence of phenomena.

The explanation needs an orientation, such as *Leeches are small worms*, to classify what a leech is before explaining how it lives.

Language Features

Complex sentences are created using appropriate connectives.

The student uses connectives appropriately to link through time and through cause and effect: *first of all, then, so, then, so, so, otherwise, until* and *then*.

Technical terminology is used appropriately.

The student uses a possessive apostrophe in *host's* but not in *leeches*.

There is some confusion in the grammar *on its host at both ends*. This sounds like both ends of the host rather than both ends of the leech. The explanation could be reworked to state *So now both ends of the leech are stuck on its host.*

Advertisement Work Sample

Context

Students examined advertising leaflets and then wrote an advertisement of their own to sell products of their choice to classmates.

Book worm school supplies

Back to school sale!

Buy all your school needs, now.

Get paper and pencils half price.

Free pencil case with every backpack purchased.

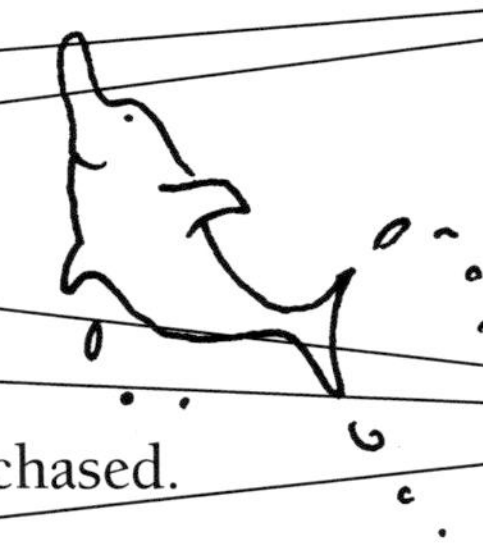

Spend $10 and go in the draw to-

Win a holiday to Sea World on the Gold Coast.

Be Quick!

Sale ends Sunday.

Work sample from 10-year-old student (typed by teacher with spelling corrected)

correct homophones

commands with doing verbs in theme position

emotive language

Assessment Comments

Structure

The student shows understanding of high modality and the use of gimmicks and prizes to attract customers. The advertisement is directed at school-aged peers and so appeals to their school needs as well as their likely interest in a holiday destination. Giveaways are well-aimed at the target audience. The advertisement is brief and to the point.

Language Features

The student uses the correct homophones for *buy* and *sale*.

The student uses high modality effectively to persuade the readers.

Doing verbs are placed appropriately in theme position in commands. Commands include ellipsis for 'you' – the reader.

Emotive language is used to sound persuasive and to ensure that the reader/purchaser hurries because the sale will end on Sunday. Perhaps the student could have used some more emotive language to elaborate on the prize trip to Sea World, and to entice readers to spend multiples of $10 to get extra tickets in the draw.

The student could have used verbs that appeal to the senses to persuade the reader that the trip is an exciting prize. Aspects of transport and accommodation included with the prize could also have been described.

The student could have included an address for the Book Worm store, and perhaps a telephone number or web address, along with store opening hours.

Perhaps the student could have listed specific items to lure the reader to make extra purchases other than paper and pencils; *all your school needs* could include items that students might want but not necessarily need. The writer would be familiar with all the latest 'fashion' items and gimmicks that attract age-peers to stationery items. These could be described using noun groups and emotive language.

Information Report Work Sample

Context

Students were required to work independently to research an animal of their choice and construct an information report.

appropriate use of noun group for topic in theme position

contraction used inappropriately

inappropriate gender term for lioness

inappropriate colloquial language

awkward pronoun reference

inaccurate spelling for contraction

awkward construction

inappropriate personal comment

The African Lion

The African lion is the biggest cat in Africa. Males are larger than girl lions. It has browny-yellowy fur. This colour blends in with the grass and sand on the plains of Africa. It's fur can look pretty matted and not sleek like a tiger or a cheetah. Lions like to sit on top of rocks. They can look all around them. Lions like to sleep under trees during the day. Lions live in large groups called a pride. Lions are a carnivore. Thats a meat eater. The lioness does most of the hunting for the pride. They hunt for antelopes, zebras, baby elephants and baby hippos, or sick or old animals that might be not so fast and easier to catch. Lions only hunt when they are hungry. I would like to be a lion.

Work sample from 11-year-old student (typed by teacher with student's spelling)

Assessment Comments

Structure

There is a general opening statement and then information about aspects of the topic. Most information is well-grouped for the information report: where the lion lives/what lions look like/what they do/what they eat. There is a reasonable balance to the types of information.

The student could be taught to use paragraphs or subheadings.

The personal comment as a conclusion is inappropriate in an information report.

Language Features

There is appropriate use of nouns and pronouns for the topic in theme position, but inconsistent use of plural and singular forms of those nouns *(males/it; lioness/they)*.

The student uses inconsistent gender terms to refer to the lions, *male* and *girl.*

The student uses mainly simple sentences with the connective *and* and one connective to contrast, *or*, in one complex sentence.

The student could have used connectives that show cause and effect, for example *Lions like to sit on top of rocks so they can look all around them.*

The informal or colloquial language is not suitable in an information report.

The student uses the contraction *it's* incorrectly for a possessive adjective.

The student uses *thats* instead of *that's* to define *carnivore.*

Procedure/Instructions Work Sample

CONTEXT

Students were required to write a procedural text for a familiar task. They had examined examples of instructions and were familiar with the structure and grammar required.

(Note: The student's spelling mistakes have been included in the typed copy below.)

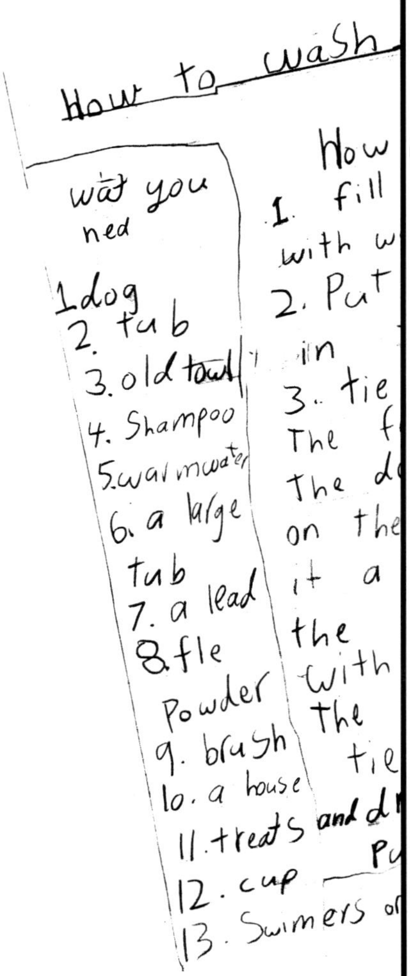

How to wash a dog

Wat you ned
1. dog
2. tub
3. old towl
4. Shampoo
5. warm water
6. a large tub
7. a lead
8. fle powder
9. a brush
10. a house
11. treats
12. cup
13. swimers or rancoat
14. a carm voice

How to do it
1. fill the tub with worm water
2. Put the dog in the tub
3. tie the dog to the fense
4. carm the dog
5. put shampoo on the dog wol giving it a treat
6. rince the shampoo of with a house
7. get the dog out and tie it up agen and drie it down and put the fle bouda on the dog and give it a lote of treats

superfluous to needs

upper case s

not mentioned in method

method written as a series of commands with doing verbs in theme position

off

should be separate steps

Work sample from 8-year-old student

ASSESSMENT COMMENTS

Structure

The student shows understanding of the structure and logical sequence required in procedural texts. The student lists the method and equipment required, although a number of items in the equipment list are not used in the method: swimmers, raincoat, cup, brush, old towel. The method is written in number order and is logical, comprehensive and well-sequenced.

Language Features

The student writes the method as a series of commands using doing verbs in theme position.

The final instruction, number 7, needs to be separated out into individual commands.

The student uses upper case and lower case inconsistently.

There are no punctuation marks in the method, although the student uses a full stop after each number.

Spelling mistakes are phonetically or visually plausible, for example 'carm', 'fle', 'fense'.

Procedure/Recipe Work Sample

Context

Students examined recipes and were given a model of a magic potion that advised how to turn a frog into a handsome prince. Students were asked to write a magic potion of their own based on the model provided.

Magic Potion for making a frog turn into a princess

To make a frog turn into a princess you need

1 strand of princesses hair.

1 pinch of a fairys glitter.

3 rose petals.

1 of Hanzel and Gretals breadcrumbs.

Snow whites poisoned apple.

1 wicked witches toenail.

Mix all of the ingredients together in a glass of milk.

Drink it all up.

Once you have drunk it wait for just 1 minute.

Then you will be a princess.

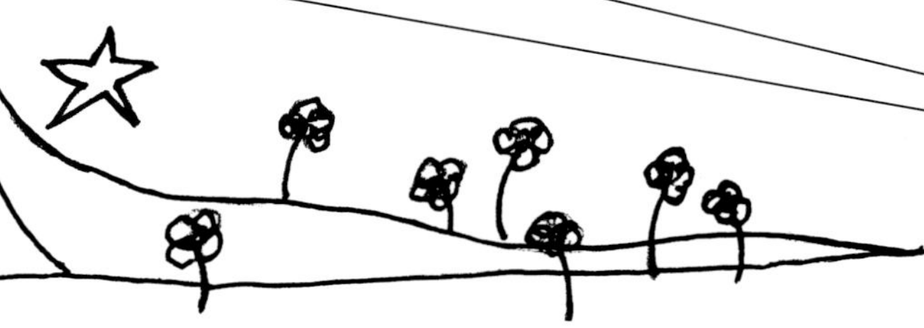

Work sample from 9-year-old student (typed by teacher with student's spelling)

a colon needed here

number adjectives

confusion with plural nouns

apostrophe needed to show possession

connectives to show time sequence

Assessment Comments

Structure

The student shows understanding of the structure of a recipe and lists ingredients as well as the method, although the glass of milk included in the method has not been listed with the ingredients. The method is written in logical order.

The text shows confusion about who the recipe is for, writing *Once you have drunk it . . . Then <u>you</u> will be a princess*, while the recipe's stated goal is to turn a frog into a princess, not 'you'. Perhaps the student is confused because the ingredients list what 'you' need to make the potion.

The student shows knowledge and understanding of other related texts and fairytales. (This is called intertextuality).

The student uses fairytale vocabulary effectively.

Language Features

There is appropriate use of number adjectives in the noun groups.

The student shows no understanding of the difference between plural nouns and possessive nouns. There is no awareness of apostrophes to show possession.

Time connectives are not usually appropriate in a recipe.

A colon is required after *To make a frog turn into a princess you need*

Recount Work Sample

Context

The class was taken on an outing across the road from the school for organised activities and games in a park. Upon returning to the classroom students were required to write recounts to tell what they did on the outing, commencing with "We left the school and crossed the road excitedly."

We left the school and crossed the
rowed exitedly Tim and Jon cared the parisut
we walked pust the netball cortes and
Sat on the the grownd ^ write a fuw notes.
Then we went acros the brig and had a look
at the loogn it was discusting i dowint now how
the ducks live We hate to line up in a
Singl line becus a lady and her dog come pust
Then we played folow the leder throw a small
forest we played a game with a parishut called
fishermen then we went to a different Spot and
whrot down all the things we cald here
Then we came backe to school

We left the school and crossed the road excitedly Tim and Jon carried the parachute we walked past the netball courts and sat on the ground and write a few notes. Then we went across the bridge and had a look at the lagoon it was disgusting I don't know how the ducks live. we had to line up in a single line because a lady and her dog come past Then we played follow the leader through a small forest we played a game with a parachute called fishermen then we went to a different spot and wrote down all the things we could hear then we came back to school

Work sample from 10-year-old student (typed by teacher with spelling corrected)

incorrect tense

proper nouns

limited use of punctuation – only two full stops

personal judgement with evaluative language

over-reliance on *then* as a time connective

appropriate connective to show cause

Assessment Comments

Structure

The events are recounted in chronological order. The recount ends when the student came back to the school rather than with a summing up, or a personal comment.

The student makes a personal comment 'it was disgusting I don't know how the ducks live.' The student uses evaluative language.

Language Features

Tim and Jon are spelled correctly, with capital letters for proper nouns.

The student uses the connective *because* to give a reason for making *a single line*.

The student uses two full stops appropriately but needs further work on recognising sentences in a text.

The student uses past tense appropriately for all verbs except *write*.

The student uses *then* four times to sequence events. The student needs to learn about alternative time words to help with sequencing in recounts.

Response Work Sample

CONTEXT

The teacher read the class a book of short stories and then asked students to write a book review. The teacher listed the title, author and illustrator of the book for the class to copy. Students were reminded to include a brief description of the book's contents in their reviews and to give their opinions about the book.

no variety in relating (being or having) verbs

evaluative language

overuse of *very funny* as a description

1st person personal pronoun

thinking and feeling verbs

Book Review

The ~~teacher~~ read us a book called The Cat on the Mat is Flat. The author is Andy Griffiths. The illustrator is Terry Denton. The book is nine funny stories. The words rhyme. The book is easy to read. Everyone in my class enjoyed the stories. They are very funny. ~~The teacher showed us~~ the pictures. The pictures are very funny ~~too I like~~ this book. I like ~~the~~ pictures. I think ~~everyone will like this book. even adults.~~

Work sample from 9-year-old student (typed by teacher with spelling corrected)

ASSESSMENT COMMENTS

Structure

The student uses an introduction or orientation to establish the context then different aspects of the topic (the story and the illustrations) are explored.

There is a concluding statement with a judgement and recommendation.

Language Features

The student uses 1st person personal pronouns *I* and *us* appropriately.

The student uses evaluative language to present opinions: *enjoyed, funny, like.*

Thinking and feeling verbs are also used to represent opinions *I like, I think*.

There is limited use of descriptive words: *funny* is repeated three times.

The student uses simple sentences throughout the review with no attempt to link clauses or use connectives.

The statement *The book is easy to read* needs to be qualified to state exactly who might find the book easy to read, for example, most students in Year 3.

Student Book 3

Scope and Sequence

This scope and sequence chart is based on the requirements of the Australian Curriculum.

Unit	Unit name/ Type of text	Clause to whole text level			Word and word group level		
		Sentences and clauses	Cohesion: theme, pronouns, lexical chains, connectives	Mood and modality, language and vocabulary	Nouns and noun groups	Verbs and verb groups	Adverbs and prepositional phrases
1	**Museum Visit** Recount				proper and common nouns	doing verbs; past tense	
2	**A Tasty Invention** Recount	sentences			proper and common nouns	thinking and feeling verbs	
3	**Dear Nana and Pop** Response/Email	simple sentences; clauses	1st and 2nd person personal pronouns: *I, me, we, us, you*			thinking and feeling verbs	
4	**The Case of the Missing Robots** Narrative		personal pronouns: *she, he, him, her, they, them, it*		noun groups with adjectives		
5	**Inventing Potato Chips** Response/Film review			fact and opinion		saying verbs; thinking and feeling verbs	
6	REVISION						
7	**My Special Place** Narrative/Poem	phrases			noun groups with adjectives		prepositional phrases
8	**Nintendo** Information report		personal pronouns	technical words	proper nouns	relating verbs	
9	**Penicillin** Recount			questions and statements			time words and phrases
10	**Molly's Discovery** Narrative		conjunctions (connectives)		singular and plural nouns	subject/verb agreement	
11	**Search for the Lost Valley** Narrative			exclamations; onomatopoeia			adverbs to tell how
12	REVISION						
13	**Trampolines** Discussion/Conversation	quoted speech; speech marks		evaluative words; apostrophes for contractions		saying verbs	
14	**The Thing Inside** Narrative			modality; emotive words			
15	**Where to Find the Hidden Treasure** Procedure/Directions			commands		doing verbs	prepositional phrases and adverbs
16	**Wiz Bang 3000 Kitchen Hand!** Advertisement		personal pronouns	emotive words; modality (modal verbs, modal adverbs)			
17	**Discovery: A New Species** Description				noun groups; articles; comparing adjectives		
18	REVISION						

Unit	Unit name/ Type of text	Clause to whole text level			Word and word group level		
		Sentences and clauses	Cohesion: theme, pronouns, lexical chains, connectives	Mood and modality, language and vocabulary	Nouns and noun groups	Verbs and verb groups	Adverbs and prepositional phrases
19	**Voyagers** Description/Poem			simile; idiom	apostrophes for possession		
20	**Everyone Should Recycle** Exposition/Speech		connectives	fact and opinion			
21	**Professor Snodgrass Fails Again** Narrative/Comic strip	quoted speech		stereotypes			
22	**Dinosaur Found at Local School** Recount/Newspaper article	reported speech		emotive words; sensationalism	concrete and abstract nouns		
23	**The Jacket** Narrative			time words		past, present and future tense	adverbs and prepositions
24	REVISION						
25	**The Best New Invention** Discussion		connectives	modality	noun groups		
26	**Breakfast Inventions** Description/Poem		lexical chains	metaphor	descriptive adjectives		
27	**Wart, Fester and Carbuncle Remover** Procedure/Recipe			commands	number adjectives (quantifiers)	doing verbs	adverbs to tell how
28	**How Does the Alarm Bed Work?** Explanation		connectives	technical language; evaluative language	nouns	doing verbs	
29	**How to Use the Drolley (or Dog Trolley)** Procedure/Instructions			evaluative language	noun groups; classifying adjectives		
30	REVISION						
31	**My Home** Narrative/Poem		personal pronouns	evaluative language	collective nouns		
32	**Trying to Negotiate** Discussion/Conversation	quoted speech	synonyms	statements; questions; commands; exclamations			
33	**Dear Diary** Response/Diary	quoted speech; speech marks	lexical chains; synonyms	evaluative language			
34	**The Invention of Money** Information report	commas in noun lists	personal pronouns	homophones	noun groups; commas in noun lists		
35	REVISION						

Grammar Focus: Nouns, doing verbs
Type of Text: Informative – Recount

Student Book 3
Unit 1

Establish a context for *Museum Visit* by asking students about their experiences of museums. If students have never been to a museum, explain the concept to them.

Read *Museum Visit* with students. Show them the location of Canberra on a map of Australia. Decide where the writer of *Museum Visit* might live if they had to drive two hours to get to the museum.

Discuss the way time is sequenced in recount texts. List the words in *Museum Visit* that tell the time sequence: *7 am, 10 am, after lunch, five o'clock*. Jointly construct a timeline for the events in the recount.

Talk to students about proper and common nouns. Brainstorm things in the classroom that are proper and common nouns. Make lists for display. Make a list of nouns for things a visitor might see in a museum.

Discuss the rule about doing verbs. Make sure that students understand that the form of the verb changes to show that actions happened in the past.

Discuss actions that students did yesterday. Begin a sentence with *Yesterday we ...* and have each student add a past tense doing verb. For example, *Yesterday we read, ran, jumped, walked, sat, looked, listened, played ...* Create a word bank of past tense doing verbs that students can refer to for spelling and writing.

Jointly construct a class recount. Make sure students recognise the words that organise the recount in a time sequence. Time order can also be called chronological order. Gifted students could investigate other words with the prefix *chrono*, which means 'time', and present their findings to the class.

Have students independently construct recounts. Assess their use of nouns, doing verbs and time order.

Grammar Focus: Nouns, thinking and feeling verbs
Type of Text: Informative – Recount

Student Book 3
Unit 2

Read *A Tasty Invention* with students. Point out that the first few sentences of the recount are used to give background information. Tell students that an earl is a British nobleman and that Sandwich was the name of the place where Montagu was an earl.

Discuss the way events described in the recount are written in time order: first this happened and then that happened and then the next thing happened.

Remind students that sentences start with a capital letter and end in a full stop, question mark or exclamation mark. Ask individual students to present an oral reading of the text, reading one sentence at a time per student, to clearly mark the end of each sentence.

Remind students that proper nouns start with a capital letter. List the days of the week and the months of the year on charts for classroom use.

Point out the capital letters for these proper nouns. Use a 'proper' (or very formal) accent and have students try out different 'proper' accents to read the proper nouns in the class lists and charts. They can imagine they are earls and they can use these accents to have fun with 'proper' nouns.

Reinforce students' understanding of thinking and feeling verbs by having them say what they *think* of the Earl of Sandwich and his invention and how they *feel* about sandwiches. Have them use their 'proper' accents.

Create a class list of thinking and feeling verbs to display in the room. Interested students or students who need extension in English could use a thesaurus to expand the list. Words on the list could be grouped with synonyms or antonyms.

Have students write personal recounts and then present these to the class as spoken texts.

Grammar Focus: Clauses, personal pronouns
Type of Text: Persuasive – Response/Email

Student Book 3
Unit 3

Read the email with students. Point out that the writer is responding to something she has learned by telling her grandparents about it. She is also responding to the news that she will be visiting her grandparents soon.

Point out the three types of sentences used in the text: statement, question, exclamation. Discuss the function of each in the email and the punctuation marks applicable to each. Remind students about verbs and discuss the sentence rule that specifies that every sentence must contain at least one verb.

Have students suggest which words are the verbs in individual sentences in the email. They should readily recognise doing verbs *(visit),* saying verbs *(says)* and thinking and feeling verbs *(think, love).* They might have difficulty recognising relating (being or having) verbs *(am, are).* They might also have difficulty recognising verb groups with auxiliaries *(can visit, can come, was painted).*

There is no need for students to identify every verb in the text at this stage.

Write the word *pronoun* and point out the word *noun* inside *pronoun*. Tell students that the way to remember a *pronoun* is to think of it as a little word that stands for a noun. Talk to students about pronouns that they use to refer to themselves *(I, me, us, we)* and that they use to refer to people they are talking to, or writing to *(I love you).* Ask students what pronoun could be used in the email to refer to the archaeologists and the Aboriginal people who discovered Australia *(they, them).*

Have students write emails that give their responses to something. They might, for example, write emails to a book character commenting on something the book character has done. Or, they might write to their own grandparents or relatives. Remind students to check their emails for correct punctuation of sentences.

Grammar Focus: Personal pronouns, adjectives
Type of Text: Imaginative – Narrative

Student Book 3
Unit 4

Talk to students about the structure of narratives (orientation, complication, series of events, resolution). Remind them that narratives involve characters and that something happens to the characters that makes a story interesting. Point out that *The Case of the Missing Robots* is the beginning of a narrative. It introduces the characters, sets the scene and also introduces the complication (an explosion). Have students brainstorm ideas for the rest of the story.

Tell students that narratives are often told about other people or things. These can be referred to by the pronouns *they, them, he, she, it, him, her.* Use picture books and novels to find examples of narratives told in the 3rd person with these 3rd person personal pronouns.

Tell students that narratives usually include words to describe characters, places, animals and things. These words are called adjectives or describing words and are very useful because they help readers imagine exactly what people, places, animals and things look like or feel like; without adjectives stories might not be as interesting.

Choose a character in a class novel or picture book and ask students to brainstorm adjectives for that character. Display the list with a picture of the character.

Read the first sentence of the story *The Case of the Missing Robots* without the adjectives *peaceful* and *clever*. Then read the sentence using different adjectives such as *horrible* and *cruel*, or *magic* and *crazy*. Ask students what effect the adjectives have on the meaning in the sentence and how they imagine the island and the inventor.

Grammar Focus: Saying verbs, fact and opinion
Type of Text: Persuasive – Response/Film review

Student Book 3 **Unit 5**

Tell students that *Inventing Potato Chips* gives the writer's response to a movie. Read the text with students. Divide the class into groups and have each group devise and then perform a dramatisation about the invention of potato chips. Ask students for their responses to each dramatisation: whether they enjoyed it, what aspects were funny or entertaining, and so on.

Brainstorm a class list of saying verbs, for example: *yelled, whispered, twittered, argued, cackled, shouted, screamed, demanded, shrieked, squealed, barked*. Give students a sample sentence such as, *These fries are too thick*. Have students use their voices to express the sentence according to each saying verb on the class list. Discuss the difference made to the meaning of the sentence by the saying verb used.

Talk to students about the difference between fact and opinion. Give them an example of a fact, such as *I am allergic to peanuts*. Ask students to write facts about themselves.

Give students an example of an opinion such as *I love peanut butter*. Discuss the way opinions about the same topic can vary from person to person. Remind students that opinions are often presented using thinking and feeling verbs: *I hate peanut butter*.

Play a game where a student makes a statement and the rest of the class has to decide whether it is fact or opinion.

Read a picture book or chapter of a novel to the class and then ask each student to write a sentence about the book that gives an opinion. Have them write their sentences on coloured paper or cardboard and display the sentences with the book. The school's teacher/librarian may wish to have the display in the library.

Grammar Focus: Prepositions, adjectives
Type of Text: Imaginative – Narrative/Poem

Student Book 3 **Unit 7**

Play a game of 'Simon Says' or 'Simone Says' using prepositions and prepositional phrases to tell students where to put their hands. For example: *Simone says put your hands in the air*. Focus attention on the where words (the prepositions that tell where).

Brainstorm a class list of prepositions that tell where, for example *in, on, under, at, beside*.

Note: Other types of prepositions can tell when (*after a few weeks*), how (*with a sword*) or with whom (*with her mother*). These other types will be introduced later in the *Grammar Rules!* program.

Play an instruction game where students listen to three or four instructions in a sequence and then have to follow the instructions. Include prepositional phrases in the instructions. For example, *Go to the back of the room and collect a yellow cube. Take the cube towards the front of the room. Put the cube under the nature table. Sit on the floor*.

This is a listening comprehension game as well as a game that focuses on prepositions and phrases. Simplify the instructions for children not able to remember, or process, a series of three or four instructions. Students who need a greater challenge could create instructions for other members of the class.

Read *My Special Place* with students. Ask students to point out the prepositions.

Remind students that adjectives are describing words. Talk to students about their own special places. Suggest that a special place could be their bedroom, their kitchen at home, the home of a grandparent, or a place they went on a holiday. Ask them to describe their special place and use prepositions and prepositional phrases to tell where the special place is located. Have students write their own special place poems and then provide time for publication of the poems. Display them in the room with illustrations.

Grammar Focus: Relating verbs
Type of Text: Informative – Information report

Student Book 3
Unit 8

Read the information report with students. Discuss the meanings of the technical terminology. Tell students that information reports often include terminology that's relevant to the topic. Discuss the meaning of *child-friendly* and what the storyline of 'Beauty and the Beast' might include. Ask if students are familiar with the Pac-Man character. Discuss students' use of electronic games, the types of games played by students and the home rules for use of these games.

Read through the relating verb rule with students. Relating verbs are probably the most difficult for children to understand. Relating verbs relate nouns to other nouns or parts of themselves. They are simply about **being** *(I am a girl)* or **having** *(The boy has black hair)*. Tell students that every sentence has to have at least one verb. If they can't find a doing verb or a thinking, feeling or saying verb then they must be able to find a relating verb.

Tell students that information reports often include relating verbs because information reports tell about what things are or what they have.

Review personal pronouns with any students who need revision. Make sure students understand that personal pronouns relate to gender and number. For example, *he* and *him* are used for a single male; *she* and *her* are used for a single female; *they* and *them* are used for two or more people or things. *It* is used for things that don't have a gender, such as a table, a chair or a tomato. *It* is also used for animals when the gender is not known.

Provide time for students to create information reports of their own. Make sure they use relating verbs appropriately.

Grammar Focus: Questions and statements, time words
Type of Text: Informative – Recount

Student Book 3
Unit 9

This recount tells a series of events in time order. Tell students that recounts always tell about things that have happened already and that retelling the events in time order is the clearest way to retell what happened.

Read the following to students:

I arrived at school at 7.30 am. I had cereal and fruit for breakfast. I rode my bike to school before the traffic. I like cereal for breakfast to give me energy for bike-riding. It took twenty minutes to get to school.

Ask students what is wrong with the way this text is organised. Make sure that they recognise the importance of time words when sequencing events in recounts.

Time words can be prepositional phrases *(in the morning)*, adverbs *(early)*, or even noun groups *(tomorrow morning)*. At this stage students do not need to label the parts of speech. They only need to recognise that these are words that relate to time in a text.

Discuss the difference between statements and questions. Play a game of twenty questions. Have one student think of an animal and write the animal on a piece of paper to show you. Have other students ask questions to determine what the animal is. They are only allowed twenty questions altogether. Model for students the types of questions that are useful in this game, until the class understands how to play. The student who is 'in' is only allowed to answer yes or no. For example: Is it a mammal? Does it live on land? Does it eat meat? Does it live in Australia? If twenty questions are asked and the animal is not guessed then the person who is 'in' is a winner.

Grammar Focus: Conjunctions, singular and plural nouns
Type of Text: Imaginative – Narrative

Student Book 3
Unit 10

Read *Molly's Discovery* with students. Tell students that this is the orientation for a narrative. An orientation tells who the main characters are and it sets the scene for the events in the story. Ask students to name the main characters in *Molly's Discovery*. Ask them to discuss what could be in the casket. Brainstorm a list of possibilities. They might make use of this list if they write the rest of the story.

Discuss the concept of conjunctions ('joining words'). Tell students that some words function to join or link ideas in a text. Tell them that the way ideas are linked is very important to the meaning, so they need to be careful when they choose conjunctions. Make sure students understand the ramifications of using the different conjunctions in questions 2 and 3 on page 24. Read out correct and incorrect choices and discuss the differences in meaning.

Make sure students have access to dictionaries so they can check their spelling of singular and plural nouns. Teach them the spelling rule: change *y* to *i* and add –es, for words like *baby* → *babies*. Point out that most nouns change their spelling in some way to become plural, even if it's just to add a suffix –s.

Verbs and nouns need to match in number. The anomaly in present tense English is that a plural noun has a verb that looks singular *(the children run swiftly)* while a singular noun has a verb that looks plural *(the child runs swiftly)*. We can call this 'matching' nouns and verbs to simplify the concept for students. Focus students' attention on matching nouns and verbs that sound 'right' in texts that you are reading with the class.

Grammar Focus: Exclamations, adverbs
Type of Text: Imaginative – Narrative

Student Book 3
Unit 11

Explain to students that this text is the orientation of a narrative. It introduces the main character and uses onomatopoeia, exclamations and adverbs that tell how, setting the scene for events.

Explain the definition of an exclamation to the class. Tell students that exclamations are often said loudly. Divide the class into small groups and have students role-play some scenes where they use exclamations.

Create a whole-class poetry recitation using onomatopoeia to add sound effects to the recitation. Find some poems with the potential for sound effects. These could be rain or storm poems, jungle poems, animal poems and so forth. Your school's teacher/librarian should be able to provide suggestions. Have a number of students recite the lines of the poem either individually or as a group. Have other groups of students chant onomatopoeia words as a background chorus.

These onomatopoeia words can either be words used in the poem or words created to add to the atmosphere of the poem, such as *Drip, drip, drip* for raindrops and *Smash! Clang! Crash!* for a thunderstorm. Point out the exclamations and have the students chant them loudly. Students might also enjoy adding percussion instruments and body percussion (clapping, stomping, finger clicking) to enhance the sound effects.

Students can perform their recitation for another class or for a whole-school assembly.

Play students some rainforest music and discuss the way the sounds of the rainforest have been represented by the musical instruments.

Tell students that onomatopoeia can be an effective strategy to hook a reader's interest at the beginning of a narrative.

Grammar Focus: Evaluative words, quoted speech
Type of Text: Persuasive – Discussion/Conversation

Student Book 3 **Unit 13**

Organise a Readers' Theatre presentation of *Trampolines* (see page 18 for instructions). Allocate one student to say Henry's lines and another student to say Dad's lines. Have another student or the rest of the class read the narrator's lines. These will be all the text that is not actually spoken by the two characters. Talk to students about the speech marks and the way they function to mark what characters are actually saying.

Point out the quoted speech in Big Books available in your school. Point out the saying verbs that tell how each character is saying their speech. Brainstorm a word bank of saying verbs to display in your classroom. Students can refer to this list when they are writing their own texts.

Tell students that in discussions people present their opinion or points of view. Ask students to compare Henry's opinion about trampolines with Dad's opinion. Ask for volunteers to continue the discussion between Henry and Dad.

Suggest that Henry and Dad discuss other inventions about which they might have different opinions such as televisions, hand-held electronic games, war toys, skateboards and so on. Make sure that students recognise that opinions include evaluative words. Evaluative words give a valuation or judgement about something.

Point out that people are entitled to evaluate things differently and have different opinions and that it is important to listen politely to the opinions of others and then make up your own mind. Give examples that are relevant to your students. Tell students that it is also OK to change your own opinion after listening to the opinions of others.

Grammar Focus: Point of view, emotive words
Type of Text: Imaginative – Narrative

Student Book 3 **Unit 14**

Tell students that the sample text *The Thing Inside* is a narrative in which the characters try to change each other's minds about an issue. They try to sound very convincing so that they win the argument. Explain how body language, tone of voice and gesture can be used in arguments to make them seem even more persuasive. Talk to students about the words used by Deni and Amy, as well as the way the words are spoken using voice and gesture. Words and phrases such as *Don't be a chicken* and *It will be fun* are emotive. Emotive words are used in arguments to sound more persuasive.

Point out the name-calling by Deni and ask students whether this is a fair or appropriate thing to do in an argument. Discuss why people call each other names in an argument.

Choose students to present *The Thing Inside* as a Readers' Theatre (see instructions on page 18). Point out the question marks and the exclamation marks as well as the speech marks. Point out the saying verbs *(argued, fumed, explained, announced, asked)* that will tell the readers how to say their speech.

Have students use substitute saying verbs in *The Thing Inside* and repeat the Readers' Theatre activity. For example, instead of *argued Amy* in the first paragraph, students could substitute *whined Amy*. Discuss the differences made by the saying verbs.

Have students work in groups to create frozen sculptures for emotive words in *The Thing Inside*, such as *trespassing, fumed, treasure*.

Grammar Focus: Commands, prepositional phrases
Type of Text: Informative – Procedure/Directions

Student Book 3
Unit 15

Tell students that this text is a set of commands that give directions for finding a hidden treasure. Tell students that commands often start with a doing verb *(Go to your chair.)* and that sometimes commands end with an exclamation mark *(Stop!)*.

Have students work in pairs and have each pair work together to give and follow commands. One person in each pair can start by giving the commands and partners can swap roles. Tell students to use doing verbs at the start of each command.

Point out the numbers used in *Where to Find the Hidden Treasure* to help sequence the directions. Ask students why directions are sometimes numbered. Ask what would happen if these directions were placed in a different order. Tell students that numbers help to sequence directions in the same way that time words help to sequence events in a recount or a narrative.

Jointly construct a map to accompany the directions in *Where to Find the Hidden Treasure*. Have students work independently or in pairs to draw maps for the directions in question 4 on page 35. Display and compare their maps. They could also draw some treasure on their maps and draw X to mark the spot.

Tell students that some words and phrases tell where, for example *there, here, in the garden, under the bed*. Find and examine with students other examples of directions and look at the words and phrases that tell where. Have students complete the **Try it yourself!** and independently write directions to find a treasure or secret place.

Grammar Focus: Emotive words, modality
Type of Text: Persuasive – Advertisement

Student Book 3
Unit 16

Tell students that the advertisement for the Wiz Bang 3000 Kitchen Hand is similar to an exposition text because it is trying to convince you to accept a point of view about the object: the kitchen hand. Read the text to students and then discuss the words that are emotive *(Don't miss out!)* and the words that show high modality *(Buy now!)*.

Discuss with students whether they would like to buy a kitchen hand. Ask them to give reasons why or why not.

Modality is an important concept for students to recognise in exposition texts such as arguments and advertisements. Discuss modality in terms of statements that express certainty or obligation, such as *You will buy one, You must buy one*.

Discuss with students the difference between:

buy now and *maybe buy now;*
so hurry and *if you could possibly hurry;*
be quick and *you might like to be quick.*

Point out the ways to express certainty or uncertainty (high modality and low modality).

Jointly construct a whole-class poem of words that express high modality such as those in the tip on page 33 and the rule on page 37 of the Student Book. Write the poem as a collection of high modality words with opposite meaning, for example:

Yes, no, must, mustn't, do, don't,
Absolutely definitely, positively not

Will do, won't do, can do, can't,
Must go, won't go, shall go, shan't.

Perform the poem in two parts. Have students stand in two lines on opposite sides of the classroom facing each other. Students chant in groups to 'throw' the words across the room with their voices as in a ping pong match, 'batting' words back and forth.

Grammar Focus: Articles, comparative (comparing) adjectives
Type of Text: Informative – Description

Student Book 3
Unit 17

Read the description *Discovery: A New Species* to students. Discuss the text. Point out to students that noun groups play an important role in descriptions. Noun groups need to describe the people, things, animals and places in texts. Adjectives and articles form part of the noun group.

Noun groups can include:

articles: *a, an, the*

demonstrative pronouns: *these, those, that*

possessive adjectives: *my, your, his her, their, our, its*

You might like to use this opportunity to tell students how to use *a* and *an* in front of nouns. The indefinite article *a* is used in front of single nouns beginning with consonant sounds *(a puppy)*. The indefinite article *an* is used in front of nouns that begin with vowel sounds *(an igloo)*. *A* and *an* generalise their nouns. The definite article *the* is used in front of particular things such as *the school concert, the team.*

Adjectives change form when used for comparison. They are often called comparative (comparing) and superlative adjectives, but students do not need to learn these terms at this stage. They do, however, need to learn how to form comparative adjectives appropriately. Comparative forms compare two things by adding *–er* or using *more (prettier, more spacious)*. Superlative forms compare more than two things by adding *–est* or using *most (prettiest, most spacious)*.

Make a class book of things at your school. Have each student write a noun group that includes a determiner and an adjective, for example *The beautiful old gum tree*, or *Our fabulous concert*. Have students illustrate their noun group and create a class book.

Grammar Focus: Ownership
Type of Text: Imaginative – Description/Poem

Student Book 3
Unit 19

Read *Voyagers* to students. Discuss the meanings in the poem. Ask students what language features they notice in the poem. Point out the possessive apostrophes *(wind's, waves', ship's, Jones's)*, simile *(like a cork)*, alliteration *(ship's sails strain/where, winds, waves)*, and contraction *(we're)*.

Make sure students understand the difference between the possessive apostrophe and the apostrophe used in contractions when a letter is left out. Teach them that the possessive adjective *its*, as in *its foot,* does not get an apostrophe for possession. An apostrophe does belong in *it's* for *it's hot (<u>it is</u> hot)*.

Idiomatic expressions are used in all languages. Ask students for whom English is a second language to ask parents and grandparents for examples of idioms from their own cultural backgrounds, for example, the Chinese characters literally translated to mean *may you always have leftovers at dinner* idiomatically mean *be prosperous*.

Students learning English as a second language need to develop an understanding of idiom in order to be fully competent in English.

Make a class collection of idioms and have students create posters to illustrate their literal or idiomatic meanings. Students could have fun illustrating, for example, *a leopard can't change its spots; not enough room to swing a cat; straight from the horse's mouth; put a sock in it; turn a blind eye; you are what you eat.* There are many websites that have examples of idioms for teacher reference.

Simile is another way to illustrate language use. Once students learn about simile they will start to notice similes in all forms of language. The meanings of similes are mostly easier to work out than the meanings of idioms, which have a stronger link to culture; however, similes can be based on stereotyping and this aspect should be discussed with students.

Grammar Focus: Fact and opinion, connectives
Type of Text: Persuasive – Exposition/Speech

Student Book 3
Unit 20

Everyone Should Recycle is an exposition text. It presents one point of view with reasons to support the point of view. Connectives link ideas in an exposition text usually through cause and effect *(I think 'point of view' because of 'reason')*, or through contrast *(I believe 'point of view' although I recognise other 'point of view')*.

Teach students how to structure an exposition. Point out the opening statement in *Everyone Should Recycle*. It introduces the topic and outlines the speaker's opinion about the topic. Exposition texts then present the arguments in logical order, such as in a number order. They can use connectives such as *firstly, secondly, thirdly* and *finally* to assist their ordering. They also use connectives such as *because, therefore, so that, otherwise, however, also, as well as*. Expositions end with a summing-up statement. The speaker or writer often makes a recommendation or urges you to act in a certain way. This is referred to as a 'call to action'.

It is useful for students to understand that persuasive texts can use facts and opinions to support arguments and reasons.

Point out that *Everyone Should Recycle* speaks about recycling in general rather than a specific instance of recycling at the school or in someone's home. This way of addressing topics is used in reports and explanations to talk about general classes of things, such as wombats or evaporation. Understanding how to write about general classes of things is a step towards students effectively using abstract nouns, nominalisation and passive voice.

Grammar Focus: Quoted speech
Type of Text: Imaginative – Narrative/Comic strip

Student Book 3
Unit 21

Share examples of comic strips with students. Point out that comics are narrative texts because they tell a story or part of a story. *Professor Snodgrass Fails Again* is a narrative comic strip. It has an orientation, a complication and a resolution. The resolution isn't an ending or a solution to the problem faced by the professor: he merely 'resolves' to keep trying. Discuss these aspects of narrative structure with students. Point out the speech balloons and the use of the text box to give a time frame for the comic. Have students explore these features in other comic strips. Tell students to also examine comic strips for use of thought bubbles and text boxes with various kinds of information including setting information *(back at the lab/on another planet/in another lab)*. Discuss these phrases that tell where or when or give different information.

Have students examine the drawing of the professor character in the comic strip. Talk about the professor as a stereotype and why this is funny in a comic strip.

Explore other comic strips for stereotyping. You might like to look at television cartoons with the class to further explore the concept of stereotyping and the use of narrative structure. Television cartoons also sometimes use text boxes and thought bubbles.

The concept of stereotyping could be extended to cover television shows that students watch. Discuss for example the view of a family, or gender roles presented in the shows. Compare these television families with students' real-life families. Make a class chart with headings *Like my family* and *Not like my family*. Students could brainstorm in groups or pairs before contributing to a class discussion.

Use Big Books to demonstrate the use of speech marks in narrative.

Grammar Focus: Reported speech, emotive words
Type of Text: Informative – Recount/Newspaper article

Student Book 3
Unit 22

Before students read *Dinosaur Found at Local School*, write the headline on chart paper or the board. Ask students to suggest what the newspaper article could be about. Write their suggestions. Read the article to the class and compare the article with students' suggestions. Tell students that the goal of a headline is to attract attention and make people want to read the article. Also point out that newspaper articles and headlines often use emotive words to make the news more interesting. Emotive words were dealt with in Unit 16.

Cut out examples of emotive or sensational headlines from newspapers. Do not read the articles with students yet. Divide the class into groups and distribute the headlines amongst the groups. Ask each group to create a dramatisation to illustrate their headline, or ask each group to jointly construct a newspaper article to accompany their headline.

Allow time for students to present their group work to the rest of the class and then read the actual articles to them. Discuss and compare students' work with the articles.

Tell students that the newspaper article *Dinosaur Found at Local School* is a recount. It presents events in time order. Ask students to summarise the four main events in the article and discuss their time order (chronological order).

Show students how to represent what people say as reported speech. Reported speech is not included in speech marks but will be prominent in newspaper articles as well as narratives, some recounts and also argument texts where experts are quoted. Point out examples of reported speech in any Big Books available in the school.

Provide a further selection of attention-grabbing headlines and have students work in pairs or independently to write the articles to accompany the headlines.

Grammar Focus: Tense, time words
Type of Text: Imaginative – Narrative

Student Book 3
Unit 23

Read *The Jacket* with students. Point out that the text is the orientation for a narrative. It sets the scene for events and introduces the main character. Tell students that whatever Ella finds in the pocket of the very small jacket will lead to the complication in the narrative. The complication involves a problem for the character. It is important for students to understand complication as something having to happen in a story otherwise their stories are likely to be boring.

Read picture books to students and have them identify the characters and setting in the orientation and the problems faced by the characters as the complication. Sometimes students end their stories by simply writing 'the end' when they feel they have written enough rather than thinking about a suitable ending or resolution to the characters' problems. Discuss the resolution in narratives.

Some students might recognise that narratives do not always begin with an orientation. Narratives might begin with a prologue or the complication and then introduce the characters. Narratives can also include a series of complications for characters. The resolution is not always happy for the characters but the characters will have learned from their experiences. More complex plot structures in narratives will be dealt with in upper primary Units.

Ask students to identify the words and phrases in *The Jacket* that help sequence the events in time *(every year, one night, after, until morning, the next morning, eventually)*. Note: These words are adverbs, prepositional phrases and noun groups.

Verb tense also helps to establish a time frame for events. Teach students how to recognise past tense (useful in narratives and recount), present tense (useful in information reports for things that happen continually, for example *Koalas eat leaves*) and future tense.

Grammar Focus: Modality, connectives
Type of Text: Persuasive – Discussion

Student Book 3 **Unit 25**

The Best New Invention is a written discussion. It presents opposing views about the winning inventions in a competition. It begins with an introduction, includes opinions and reasons and then ends with a final recommendation. Read *The Best New Invention* to students and point out the noun groups that introduce the two opposing arguments and the final recommendation: *Many people, Other people* and *Every child.* Teach students how to write discussion texts and connect the opinions with reasons using connectives that link through cause and effect.

Have pairs of students role-play high modality discussions between two people where each person must absolutely convince the other person to change their mind. Topics to argue about could include: the best take-away food, dogs are smarter than cats, computer games are better than game consoles, or any topic that is relevant to the children in your class. Discuss the words (high modality), gestures, facial expressions and body language that are used in the texts to make them sound more persuasive.

Have pairs of students undertake role-plays of low modality discussions using the same topics. Before they begin, write some low modality words and phrases on the board or chart paper for students to refer to during their discussion. Tell students to acknowledge each other's points of view but not change their minds about their opinion. Suggest they use words and phrases such as *maybe, possibly, I wonder if, I see your point, I think perhaps, I know what you mean but . . .* Talk to the class about the ways opinions were presented in the high modality discussions and the low modality discussions.

Ask students to reflect on how they felt using high modality compared to low modality.

Grammar Focus: Lexical chains, adjectives
Type of Text: Imaginative – Description/Poem

Student Book 3 **Unit 26**

Each stanza of the poem *Breakfast Inventions* is a cinquain. Lines two and five are synonyms for line one in each stanza.

Tell students that metaphor is when things are said to be the 'same' as each other. Give examples such as: a car can be a lemon; a person can be a couch potato, a night owl, or the top dog. Ask students what the toaster is called in *Breakfast Inventions.* Make sure they understand the metaphor. Remind students that they learned about simile in an earlier unit (Unit 19). Make sure that students understand the difference between simile and metaphor. In simile things are said to be 'like' each other.

Teach students about content strands or lexical chains in a text. A lexical chain for the toaster can be all the words that are to do with the toaster: *toaster, kitchen hero, working, making, champion.* A lexical chain for toast would be *hot, crispy breakfasts*. Understanding lexical chains is useful for when students make notes.

In note-making students need to learn to write the content words only. Often poems only consist of content words. Connectives and other words required for textual cohesion in a narrative or information report, for example, might not be needed in a poem.

Read students picture books, but omit the adjectives as you read. Reread the stories with the adjectives. Make sure students understand the function of adjectives in different types of texts. In arguments, narratives and poetry, adjectives can show bias or opinion. For example, a bull terrier might be described as *a vicious brute* or *a great pet* depending on the speaker or writer's experience of bull terriers.

Have students write their own cinquains using adjectives. They could choose an invention, an appliance or food, or write one about themselves.

Grammar Focus: Number adjectives, commands
Type of Text: Informative – Procedure/Recipe

Student Book 3 **Unit 27**

Read the recipe with students. Discuss the ingredients and make sure students understand that the recipe is a joke.

Tell students that number adjectives are part of noun groups. They describe aspects of number and they can be precise and exact, or vague and inexact. In recipes it is important for number adjectives to be exact or the recipe will not work out. Show students examples of recipes. Ask them to bring copies of recipes from home. Make a class display of the recipes. Organise some cooking activities so that students have an opportunity to measure out ingredients and focus on number adjectives. Make an uncooked modelling clay using the following recipe (make sure you handle the boiling water yourself, rather than having students use it):

Ingredients: 8 cups plain flour, 4 cups salt, 16 tablespoons cream of tartar, 8 cups boiling water, 8 tablespoons cooking oil, powder paint or food dye, glitter

Method: Be extra careful with the boiling water!
Mix all ingredients into a smooth dough.
Add colour and glitter to suit.
Store in the fridge.

Point out the structure of recipes and the use of commands in the method sections. Make sure students notice the doing verbs at the beginning of the commands. Look out for any commands that begin with adverbs that tell how, such as *carefully, quickly, slowly*.

Make a class number book of noun groups that include number adjectives (such as *one lonely puppy, one hundred football fans, a thousand stars*). Each member of the class could illustrate a page. Numbers could include 1–10 and then 20, 30, 40 to 100 and then 1000. Some children could volunteer to illustrate two pages. Point out any descriptive adjectives that students may use. Assemble the book and present it to a lower primary class at your school or to the library.

Grammar Focus: Connectives
Type of Text: Informative – Explanation

Student Book 3 **Unit 28**

How Does the Alarm Bed Work? provides an explanation of how an invention works. The explanation uses connectives to show a time sequence and to show cause and effect. Point out that explanations often have diagrams or flow charts to help explain the process. Explanations also often include technical language or terminology that is specific to the subject.

Read the explanation to the class. Ask students what they notice about the structure and the language features. Explanations are probably the most difficult texts for students to read, write or understand. Students often confuse explanations with procedures. Procedures do not include connectives to show cause. Explanations do not include commands. Recognising these two important aspects will help students learn the difference between procedure and explanation.

Jointly construct a simple explanation on a topic such as how a classroom item works. It could be a door, a window or a biro.

Make sure you include connectives that show cause. Use a simple format such as *this causes this, which in turn causes this and so then this happens*. If you start with a three-step process and then expand or clarify the steps, then students will begin to understand the structure and grammar of explanations.

Your school's teacher/librarian might be able to find a selection of simple explanations that students can examine.

Grammar Focus: Classifying adjectives
Type of Text: Informative – Procedure/Instructions

Student Book 3 **Unit 29**

How to Use the Drolley is a procedure in the form of a set of instructions. Tell students that instructions tell how to use something. The Drolley instructions are not written strictly as commands. Talk with students about instructions for using a piece of school equipment, how to cross the road, how to complete a classroom activity, or instructions from home or television. Brainstorm a list and display it in the room.

Adjectives tell more about a noun. Some adjectives function to describe and some adjectives function to classify. The job of a classifying adjective is to classify a noun, or tell what category of thing it belongs to. Students can learn to think about the way the adjective is functioning in the text. Ask them whether the adjective is describing a quality of the noun such as its colour, shape, texture or size, or whether the adjective is telling what category of things the noun belongs to.

Students can also tell the difference by trying to add *very* before the adjective. *Very* cannot be used in front of classifying adjectives:

a very tall tree (makes sense because *tall* is a descriptive adjective)

a very gum tree (does not make sense because *gum* is a classifying adjective).

Play a game with students. Divide the class into groups of four. Provide all students with dictionaries. Give students a list of ten nouns, and have groups work together to find and write descriptive and classifying adjectives for each noun. When the first group is finished, all groups must stop work and compare their answers. All correct adjectives earn two points for a team; however, if another group has the same adjective the groups only score one point. Teams add up their points to see who wins the game.

Grammar Focus: Collective nouns, pronouns
Type of Text: Imaginative – Narrative/Poem

Student Book 3 **Unit 31**

Read *My Home* with students. Discuss the meaning of the poem and the voice of the narrator of the poem; that is, talk about who is speaking in the poem. This will not necessarily be the poet. Discuss the point of view presented and ask students to suggest alternative points of view.

Talk to students about the personal pronouns *I, me, us, we, you*. Tell students that we use *I* and *me* to refer to ourselves and *you* to refer to the person or people being spoken to. Make sure students don't use *yous* (tell them *ewes* are sheep). Tell students that *you* means one person or a whole audience of people. It is singular **and** plural. Remind students about 3rd person personal pronouns: *he, him, she, her, they, them, it.*

Read students a paragraph from a novel or picture book. Then read the text again but replace the pronouns with the noun they refer to. This will make the text more difficult to follow and will demonstrate the function of pronouns to replace nouns and make texts flow better.

Make sure students understand that collective nouns are singular. They stand for one collection of things.

Grammar Focus: Types of sentences
Type of Text: Persuasive – Discussion/Conversation

Student Book 3 **Unit 32**

Trying to Negotiate is a discussion text. It includes various points of view on the issue of packing up. The mother presents the opening and closing statements and the children offer arguments and reasons. The text includes statements, commands, questions and exclamations. Remind students about the punctuation marks used for each type of sentence. Teach students how to use their voices to ask questions, make statements, commands and exclamations. Ask students to identify the saying verbs and the quoted speech of each person involved in the discussion in *Trying to Negotiate*. Select four students to perform the text as a Readers' Theatre – Mum, Aggie, Billy and a narrator (see page 18 for instructions on Readers' Theatre).

Explore the concept of synonyms with students. Tell them synonyms don't have to mean exactly the same thing. They just need to have similar meanings. Use examples of students' own written texts to highlight when to use synonyms.

Students often use *said* continually in their narratives. Other favourites are *got*, and *and then*. You might like to teach students how to use a thesaurus.

Work with students to jointly construct a text on the board or chart paper. Use the word *got* frequently, or other overused words such as *and*. For example:

I walked to the shop and got some milk. When I got home I got into trouble for losing the change. I got my brother to make me a banana smoothie. Dad got one too. Then Mum got me to walk the dog. I got a lot of exercise that day.

Ask students for suggestions for more interesting or accurate words to replace *got* in the text. Create word banks of synonyms for words your students overuse in their texts.

Grammar Focus: Lexical chains, evaluative words
Type of Text: Persuasive – Response/Diary

Student Book 3 **Unit 33**

The text *Dear Diary* is a girl's response to her little brother's interference with her property. It tells the writer's thoughts and feelings about the little brother and the situation. Read *Dear Diary* to the class. Have volunteers take on the role of Katy and read the diary using voice (pitch, tone, pace, intonation) and facial expression to enhance meaning. Have volunteers take on the role of Katy to describe how she feels about her brother's actions.

Have volunteers take on the role of Ben and give his point of view about events described in the diary. Have students in character as Ben tell his friends at school what he did to annoy his sister and how he feels about the events.

Discuss siblings with students in your class. Ask students' opinions about older or younger siblings, step-siblings or being an only child. Discuss the advantages and disadvantages of each. Ask students to use evaluative words to present their opinions.

Remind students that lexical chains are chains of content words in a text. Content words in *Dear Diary* include words for mice, and words for Ben and what he did.

Talk to students about the meaning of the idiomatic expressions *screaming blue murder* (complaining very loudly) and *laughing his head off* (laughing vigorously). Ask students what difference these expressions make to meaning in the text. Ask students if their families use these expressions or others. Make a class list.

Grammar Focus: 3rd person personal pronouns
Type of Text: Informative – Information report

Student Book 3 **Unit 34**

The Invention of Money is an information report. It presents information about the history of the development of money. Talk to students about the factual information included and how it is different from opinion texts such as *Dear Diary* in Unit 33.

The Invention of Money includes subject-specific terminology that should be discussed with students. Discuss the concept of trading with students. Ask them to consider things that they own that they don't need or want or use anymore and what they would like to trade these items for. You could show them examples of advertisements that offer goods for trade.

Remind students of the 3rd person personal pronouns: *he, him, she, her, they, them, it*. Have students write 3rd person narratives about characters they create and use 3rd person personal pronouns in their narratives.

Remind students that information reports usually involve common nouns to discuss general classes of things such as *money, gold, a farmer*. Ask students to suggest a noun for each category of common noun, for example *the money I have in the bank; the gold in my grandad's tooth; Andrew Dobbs, the local farmer who grows blueberries.*

Have students create homophone posters to illustrate the different meanings of the words and their spellings. Homophones are pairs of words that sound the same, but have different meanings. Make a class list to include, for example, the following homophones that students should be made aware of: *poor, pour, paw, pore; to, too, two; wait, weight; waste, waist; their, there, they're; threw, through; by, buy, bye; right, write; one, won; whole, hole; you, ewe; eight, ate; road, rode, rowed; four, for.* Add to the list as students discover extra homophones.

Other word pairs are spelt the same but have different meanings, for example:

- trip: either a journey or to stumble
- grave: either a place where a person is buried or a description for a serious matter
- bat: equipment for playing baseball or a small animal

Have students create sentences or improvisations based on the sets of homophones.

Commas are used to:

- separate items in a list: *I need eggs, flour, baking powder and sugar.*
- introduce quoted speech in a sentence: *Rhys said, "I'd like a banana."*
- indicate a pause in a sentence so that it makes sense: *I'll eat Dad before my flight. I'll eat, Dad, before my flight.*
- separate a name from the rest of a sentence: *Would you like a banana, Jarrod?*
- separate phrases from the rest of a sentence: *All the children, even Grace, had a terrific time.*
- separate embedded clauses: *The children, who haven't completed their work, will need to stay behind.*
- separate descriptive adjectives in a sentence: *The big, red ball bounced over the fence.*
- separate adverbs after a verb in a sentence: *The ball rolled maddeningly, annoyingly slowly into the hole.*

Teach students the use of commas as appropriate for their writing needs.

Student Book 4

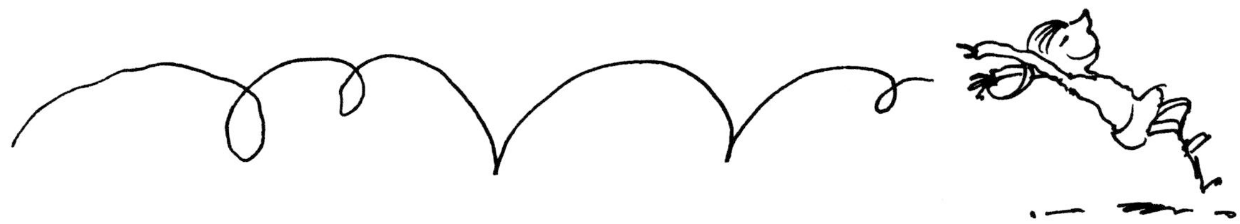

Scope and Sequence

This scope and sequence chart is based on the requirements of the Australian Curriculum.

Unit	Unit name/ Type of text	Clause to whole text level			Word and word group level		
		Sentences and clauses	Cohesion: theme, pronouns, lexical chains, connectives	Mood and modality, language and vocabulary	Nouns and noun groups	Verbs and verb groups	Adverbs and prepositional phrases
1	**Dear Timmy** Recount/Email				nouns	past tense doing verbs	
2	**My Day at the Beach** Recount				proper and common nouns	past tense saying verbs	
3	**The Big Catch** Narrative		conjunctions (connectives): *so, but, because*			thinking and feeling verbs	
4	**Dear Diary** Recount/Diary		personal pronouns: *me, I, we, us*		noun groups		
5	**A Tale of Little Fish** Narrative		personal pronouns		noun groups		
6	REVISION						
7	**Kakadu Seasons** Description/Poem				noun groups; descriptive adjectives		
8	**Our New Dam** Recount		personal pronouns: *we, I*		noun groups including number adjectives, singular and plural nouns, collective nouns		
9	**Dear Mum** Recount/Email		possessive pronouns		possessive adjectives; apostrophes to show possession		
10	**Australia's Mightiest River System** Information report	simple sentences		technical vocabulary		relating verbs (being and having verbs): *is, belongs, equals, was, had, are*	
11	**The Driest Place on Earth** Information report	clauses	conjunctions (connectives): *and, so, because*	questions and statements; technical vocabulary; question words			
12	REVISION						
13	**Under the Sea** Description/Illustration						prepositions: *in, on, under, over, beside, off, with, near, during, after, at, before, from, inside;* prepositional phrases
14	**Frog Potion** Procedure/Recipe			commands	noun groups with prepositional phrases	doing verbs	prepositional phrases
15	**How to Catch a Fish** Procedure/Instructions			commands		doing verbs	adverbs to tell how
16	**Sun Safety** Procedure/Instructions				noun groups	verb tense	
17	**Directions to the Olympic Pool** Procedure/Instructions			commands	proper nouns	doing verbs	
18	REVISION						

Unit	Unit name/ Type of text	Clause to whole text level			Word and word group level		
		Sentences and clauses	Cohesion: theme, pronouns, lexical chains, connectives	Mood and modality, language and vocabulary	Nouns and noun groups	Verbs and verb groups	Adverbs and prepositional phrases
19	**Super Crab** Narrative/Comic strip	quoted (direct) speech; reported (indirect) speech					
20	**Isabel Letham, Surfie Legend** Recount/Biography		theme	statements; commands			
21	**Recycled Water** Explanation			technical vocabulary		verb tense; verb groups; helping verbs	
22	**We Tank You** Advertisement		personal pronouns	commands		doing verbs in theme position	
23	**Lake Eyre** Information report	compound sentences	personal pronoun *it*; conjunctions (connectives): *however, so, and*	technical vocabulary	comparative and superlative adjectives		
24	REVISION						
25	**Sewage** Information report		lexical chains	technical vocabulary	commas in noun lists		
26	**How a Pearl is Made** Explanation		conjunctions (connectives to show cause and effect, to show time sequence)	technical vocabulary		verb groups; helping verbs; verb tense	
27	**Cane Toads** Information report		reference chains; theme position		classifying adjectives; proper nouns		
28	**What's Your Favourite Sea Animal?** Discussion/Interview transcript		conjunctions (connectives to show cause and effect, to compare and contrast)	question tags		thinking and feeling verbs	
29	**Daintree** Response/Travel review	compound sentences			noun groups with adjectives; subject-verb agreement	thinking and feeling verbs	
30	REVISION						
31	**Tsunami** Information report			technical vocabulary		verb groups; regular and irregular verbs	adverbs
32	**High Tide Sends Residents to the Roof** Newspaper article	direct (quoted) speech; indirect (reported) speech		modality; emotive language		modal verbs: *will, will not, might, might not, should, should not*	
33	**Vote Against School Swimming** Exposition		connectives: *firstly, secondly, in addition*	modality		modal verbs: *might, should, could, must;* thinking and feeling verbs	
34	**Bobby and the Quest for the Hidden Treasure** Narrative		varying themes				prepositional phrases to tell when and where; adverbs to tell how
35	REVISION						

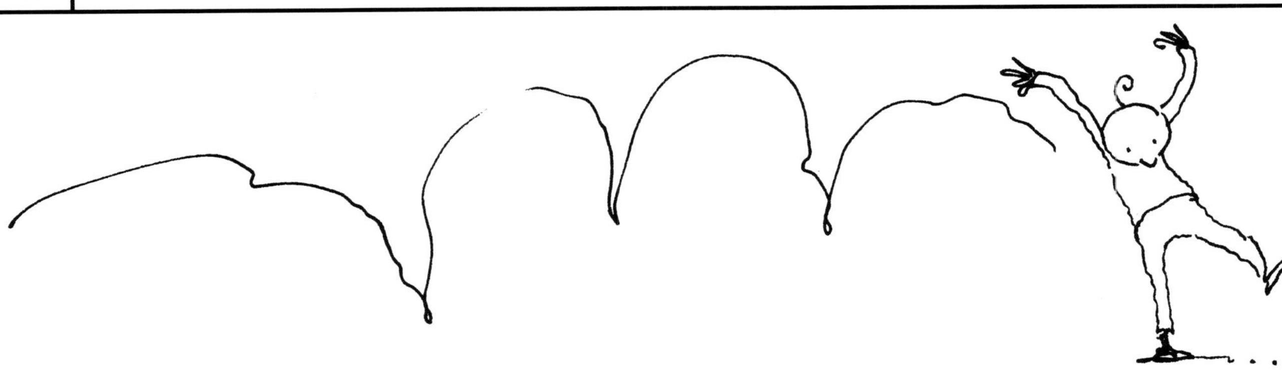

Grammar Focus: Nouns, doing verbs
Type of Text: Informative – Recount/Email

Student Book 4
Unit 1

Read *Dear Timmy* with students. Talk to students about the way the recount is structured. Point out that the opening sentence functions as an orientation to what the recount is about. Point out that the final statement functions as a conclusion: it gives a personal comment or judgement about the events. Make sure students recognise that events in the recount are sequenced in chronological (time) order. Ask students to identify time words *(last weekend)* and other words that help give a chronological order to events *(first fish, second fish)*.

Remind students that nouns are words for people, places, animals or things.

Discuss doing verbs with students. Remind students that doing verbs tell the actions. Ask students to suggest verbs for actions they can do in the classroom *(write, read, jump, cut, paste, look, listen)*. Focus their attention on the past tense forms of the doing verbs in *Dear Timmy: fished, caught, threw, kissed, bought.*

Tell students that verbs can also indicate that something is said. These verbs are called saying verbs. In the text Grandma shouted because she was excited. Ask students to suggest other verbs that could be used for the way Grandma said *Way to go, Milly! (yelled, screamed, whined, moaned, groaned, laughed).*

Have students act out each way of saying *Way to go, Milly!* trying out different voices. Help students to recognise that in *Dear Timmy* it is understood that Milly has a close relationship with the grandparents and so Grandma probably would not have groaned, whined or whinged unless as a joke.

Grammar Focus: Common and proper nouns, saying verbs
Type of Text: Informative – Recount

Student Book 4
Unit 2

My Day at the Beach is a recount. Ask students what they notice about the structure and grammar of the text (orientation, concluding statement, past tense, time words, chronological order).

Remind students that nouns are naming words for people, places, animals and things. Discuss the difference between common nouns and proper nouns. Tell them that proper nouns are very 'proper' or 'important' and need capital letters. Brainstorm proper nouns in your local area and make a list that is relevant to students: the name of the school, the principal, the suburb or town, the street, teachers' names and students' names, for example.

Remind students that saying verbs are verbs that tell how something is said. Have students act out the verbs in question 4 and decide which ones are vocal and therefore saying verbs.

Have students act out the saying verbs they write for question 5 and the sentences they write for the saying verbs suggested in question 6. Have them read their answers out loud around the room using appropriate voices for the saying verbs.

Make a class word bank of saying verbs and have students recite a nursery rhyme such as *Twinkle Twinkle Little Star* in the manner suggested by the saying verbs. They could for example 'chuckle' the rhyme, 'groan' the rhyme, 'sob' the rhyme and so on.

Point out the words in *My Day at the Beach* that tell when things happened: *last Saturday, as soon as, after a while, when.*

Make sure students recognise the reference to ice-cream: *mine*.

Grammar Focus: Thinking and feeling verbs, conjunctions
Type of Text: Imaginative – Narrative

Student Book 4 **Unit 3**

The Big Catch is the beginning of a narrative. Revise the usual structure of narratives with students: orientation, complication, series of events, resolution. In *The Big Catch* readers are introduced to the main character, Joe, and told of his desire to go with his uncle to tag and release a great white shark. Have students brainstorm the sorts of complications that could occur in this narrative.

Ask students to identify the words in the text that tell readers Joe's thoughts and feelings: *was excited, desperately hoped*. Tell students that it is important in narratives to describe characters' thoughts and feelings because that is how readers come to know and understand the characters. It is how readers empathise with the characters. We need to be able to put ourselves 'in a character's shoes'. Read extracts from narratives to students where characters' thoughts and feelings are included.

Set students the task of finding picture books that use thinking and feeling verbs to represent how characters are thinking and feeling. Or, create thinking and feeling verb labels for illustrations in picture books. Provide time for students to share extracts from the books they have found in groups or as a whole-class activity.

Review saying verbs with students and ask students to identify the saying verbs in *The Big Catch: had agreed, had been nagging, had always claimed*. If appropriate, point out the helping verbs (auxiliary verbs) that are part of each verb group.

Point out the conjunctions *because* and *but* that are used to link ideas in sentences in *The Big Catch*.

Have students work individually or in pairs to write the rest of the story *The Big Catch*. Provide time for pairs to read their stories to the rest of the class. Discuss the complication and then resolution for each story.

Grammar Focus: Noun groups, personal pronouns
Type of Text: Informative – Recount/Diary

Student Book 4 **Unit 4**

Ask students to identify aspects of the structure and grammar of recounts that they have learned in earlier Units.

Remind students that nouns are people, places, animals and things in a text. Speakers and writers often need more than one word to build up a complete picture of the noun. For example, a speaker may use a single noun to talk about dogs: *I saw dogs*. Or, the speaker may use a noun group to describe the dogs more accurately: *I saw Rennie's cute, little, snub-nosed dogs* or *I saw Rennie's huge, old labrador dogs*.

Ask students to close their eyes. Say the word *cat* to students and have each student imagine a cat. Then ask a number of students to describe the cat they imagined. Point out that everyone will form a different image unless the cat is described accurately by a noun group such as *a sleek black cat with green eyes*. Write a number of nouns on the board or chart paper *(house, car, teacher, school, tree, plant)* and ask students for suggestions to build up noun groups around those nouns.

Teach students about personal pronouns *me, I, we* and *us*. The writer of *Dear Diary* also uses *my* and *our* in noun groups such as *our school* and *my first event*. Students may identify these as pronouns but more accurately they are possessive adjectives. They are part of the noun group and they function to tell more about the noun. Students will learn more about these in later Units. At this stage they only need to recognise these words as part of the noun group.

Grammar Focus: Noun groups, personal pronouns
Type of Text: Imaginative – Narrative

Student Book 4
Unit 5

Read *A Tale of Little Fish* with students. Focus their attention on the noun groups and the way these establish the characters and setting for the narrative.

Revise narrative structure and features with students. Point out the starting words to the story, *A long time ago . . .* Examine a number of novels and picture books with students, focusing on how they begin. Students should be able to find a great variety of interesting story starters. Make a class chart of the most interesting and have students refer to them or use them as models to start their own narrative texts in intriguing ways.

Remind students of the function of personal pronouns in texts. They are words that replace nouns for people and things. Using personal pronouns makes a text easier to follow and understand because you don't have to keep repeating the noun or people's names.

If appropriate for your students, help them identify when and how to use 1st, 2nd and 3rd person personal pronouns. Tell them that narratives are often written about other people and so use 3rd person personal pronouns to refer to them. Diaries are written about yourself, so diaries include 1st person personal pronouns. Tell students that when they refer to their listener or their reader in a text they refer to that person or those people as *you*. Ask students to discuss the sorts of texts they create and when they would use 1st, 2nd or 3rd person personal pronouns. Discuss the gender aspect of personal pronouns.

Revise thinking and feeling verbs and ask students to discuss how the characters in *A Tale of Little Fish* might feel or what they might think about their circumstances. This will be useful when students complete the **Try it yourself!** activity.

Grammar Focus: Noun groups, adjectives
Type of Text: Imaginative – Description/Poem

Student Book 4
Unit 7

Kakadu Seasons is written in two stanzas, which are both cinquains. Point out the structure of the cinquains to the class.

The poem is useful to demonstrate to students how an understanding of grammar helps when analysing poems. The poem uses noun groups to build descriptions of Kakadu in two seasons, dry and wet. The noun groups include descriptive adjectives. Help students identify the main nouns in the poem and then the noun groups. Point out to students the noun at the end of each line in stanza one, including *wetlands* and *profusion*. Point out the three nouns in stanza two: *drylands, air, landscape*. The second stanza ends with a verb, *waiting*. Ask students why they think the poet used this verb to end the poem and what effect that verb has on the meaning of the poem. Use of the verb *waiting* reinforces the ongoing nature of the process. You could also discuss the construction of *drylands* and *wetlands* as compound nouns rather than using *wet* and *dry* as adjectives in front of the noun *lands*.

Have students perform the poem as a Multi-voice Recitation (see page 17 for an explanation of Multi-voice Recitation).

The poem would also be suitable as stimulus for a visual arts activity. Divide the class into ten groups. Allocate each group one line of the poem. Provide each group with one large sheet of chart paper or poster-sized cardboard. Provide art and craft materials including paint, oil crayons, charcoal, scissors, coloured paper and glue. Tell groups to draw, paint and collage abstract images to represent their line of the poem. Print out or write the poetry lines and then display the paintings in sequence as a series of panels with their matching lines of the poem.

Grammar Focus: Nouns, number adjectives
Type of Text: Informative – Recount

Student Book 4 **Unit 8**

Discuss the sequence of events in the recount *Our New Dam* with students. Point out the words that help to sequence the recount in time: *Last June, after a few weeks, since then, the past eight months.*

Ask students to identify the nouns in the text. Tell students that the noun groups include descriptive adjectives *(deep, wide)* as well as adjectives that tell number *(second, eight)*. Words in a noun group such as cardinal and ordinal numbers are called number adjectives. Number adjectives can tell an exact number or order *(second, one, first)* or an approximate number *(some, many, few)*.

Also in the noun groups in *Our New Dam* are possessive adjectives: *'our new dam', 'my parents', 'our herd of cows', ' my mum', 'our vegetables'*. Ask students to identify these in the noun groups in the text.

Talk to students about singular and plural nouns. The rule on page 21 of the student book gives some information on how to make nouns plural.

Here is some more detailed information:

- Most nouns form plurals by adding –s *(houses, schools, teachers)*.
- Nouns that end in *x, s, sh, ss* or *ch* add –es to form plurals *(boxes, fusses, lunches)*.
- Most nouns ending in *f* change the *f* to *v* and add –es *(loaf → loaves)*.
- Nouns ending in o usually add –es; however, many can also be spelt correctly by adding –s or –es *(mangoes/mangos, potatoes, volcanoes)*.
- Nouns ending in *y* change *y* to *i*, then add –es *(babies)*.
- Some nouns change their middle vowels *(man → men, foot → feet)*.
- Some nouns do not change at all *(fish, sheep)*.
- Some nouns have different ways of forming plurals *(child → children, appendix → appendices)*.

Grammar Focus: Possessive pronouns, possessive adjectives
Type of Text: Informative – Recount/Email

Student Book 4 **Unit 9**

This unit deals with three ways to show ownership in texts.

1. Using possessive pronouns: *theirs, his, hers, yours, mine, ours.*

   That hat is mine.

2. Using possessive adjectives. These always form part of a noun group.

   That is my hat.

3. Using an apostrophe in the noun.

   That is Colin's hat. (singular noun not ending in s → add 's)

   The albatross's wing was broken. (singular noun ending in s → add 's)

   The children's hats are on the shelf. (plural noun not ending in s → add 's)

   The twins' hats are here. (plural noun ending in s → add ')

Students should learn to differentiate between the ways of showing ownership. The most difficult aspect is learning how to place apostrophes. Students learned about singular and plural nouns in Unit 8 and need to use that knowledge here to determine where to place apostrophes.

Make sure students realise that the possessive adjective *its* does not have an apostrophe. *Its leg is sore.*

You might need to teach students about the apostrophe that shows a letter has been left out in words such as *it's (it is)* to help them decide whether the apostrophe shows ownership or a missing letter. They can also use context to determine meaning. *It's a hot day = It is a hot day.*

Extend students' knowledge about noun groups, if appropriate. Tell students that as well as possessive adjectives, noun groups can include words that point out (demonstrative pronouns). *That is Toby's hat.*

Grammar Focus: Simple sentences, relating verbs
Type of Text: Informative – Information report

Student Book 4
Unit 10

Students are introduced to information reports in this unit. Read *Australia's Mightiest River System* with students. Help students recognise the categories of information included in the report, starting with the Murray River and concluding with the problems faced by the Murray–Darling River System. Show students the location of the river system on a map of Australia. Further, current information about the river system is available on the internet.

Information reports often include subject-specific terminology that students might need to examine further, using dictionaries or other means, so that they can fully comprehend the meaning in the text.

Relating verbs are possibly the most difficult types of verbs for students to recognise. They are not as easily discernible as doing verbs or saying verbs.

Tell students that relating verbs are simply about **being** or **having**. They function to tell what things are or what they have.

Killer whales are mammals.

Killer whales have teeth.

Point out to students that every sentence must have at least one verb. Some sentences are quite long and contain a number of verbs.

Some whales have teeth and some whales have baleen. (two relating verbs)

Israel ran to the shop and bought milk and cookies to share with his friends. (three doing verbs)

Tell students that simple sentences only have one verb. (A simple sentence is a clause.)

Killer whales have teeth. (one relating verb)

Make sure students understand the concept that a sentence needs to make sense. It must have a verb or it cannot make sense. Some sentences only contain one word and that word must be a verb.

Stop! (doing verb)

Note: The subject of the command *Stop!* is 'you'. 'You' is implied, as in *You, stop!* or *Stop, you!*

Grammar Focus: Questions and statements, clauses
Type of Text: Informative – Information report

Student Book 4
Unit 11

The Driest Place on Earth is an information report. It includes technical or subject-specific terminology. It provides statements of information about the topic – Antarctica. Point out to students that sentences can be statements, questions, commands or exclamations and each type of sentence has a specific punctuation mark: full stop, question mark or exclamation mark. Show students an example of each type of sentence. For example:

Statement: *It is raining.*

Question: *Is it raining?*

Command: *Wear your raincoat.*

Exclamation: *I'm soaked!*

Tell students that information reports usually only include sentences that state facts. These are statements. Read *The Driest Place on Earth* to students and pause at each full stop, making sure students focus on each statement of fact in the report.

Teach students the six question-starter words: *who, what, when, where, why, how*. These questions can provide a format for students to use when they are writing newspaper articles or narratives.

Play a 'Celebrity Head' game, where one student has a headband that states who she or he is – a famous person in the local community, history or the media. The person with the headband has to ask members of a panel questions to discover her or his identity. The panel only answers *yes* or *no*. This game gives students opportunities to practise asking the types of questions that can help solve puzzles or problems.

Teach students that a sentence can be made up of one or more clauses. Clauses are joined together to form sentences. Teach students that conjunctions (connectives) function to join or link clauses in sentences.

Grammar Focus: Prepositions, prepositional phrases
Type of Text: Imaginative – Description/Illustration

Student Book 4 **Unit 13**

Prepositions are words that tell where or when. They are always used with a noun, noun group or pronoun because they don't carry any content meaning on their own. Brainstorm a list of prepositions with students, such as *in, on, under, over, beside, against, near, of, off, round, about, between, with, without, within, around, till, until, underneath, during, at, by, beyond, behind.*

Point out to students that they can use these prepositions with nouns to be specific about where or when in texts: *in a minute, under a log, beside the seaside.* These are prepositional phrases. Prepositional phrases are especially useful in directions, recipes, narratives and descriptions, but students will recognise them frequently in a variety of texts.

Note: Some prepositions also function as adverbs depending on how they are used in a text.

(adverb) *The handle has come off.*

(preposition) *He fell off the bed.*

(prepositional phrase)
He fell off the bed.

It is simpler to call these adverbs and prepositional phrases 'words that tell where or when'.

Have students brainstorm, and then chant, rhymes focusing on the prepositional phrases: *Jack and Jill went up the hill; Humpty Dumpty sat on the wall; Little Jack Horner sat in a corner; Little Miss Muffet sat on a tuffet; She sells seashells by the seashore.*

Ask students to work in pairs to investigate folktales and fairytales. Tell them to choose one to paint and label with a prepositional phrase. For example, they could paint Rapunzel throwing her hair out the window/of the tower.

Grammar Focus: Doing verbs, prepositional phrases
Type of Text: Informative – Procedure/Recipe

Student Book 4 **Unit 14**

Read the recipe *Frog Potion* with students. Make sure students notice the structure of the recipe: the goal, ingredients and method. Make sure they notice that the ingredients are nouns or noun groups and that each ingredient starts with an amount. Make sure students notice that each step in the method is a command. Commands start with verbs to tell the reader or listener what they need to do. Point out that most of the commands in this recipe start with a doing verb.

Examine further examples of recipes with students. Ask them to bring sample recipes from home to discuss and display in the classroom. Engage in a cooking or making activity. There are recipes that require mixing without cooking if you do not have access to an oven. Ask for parent helpers for your cooking session. It might be especially relevant to have some recipes from the cultural backgrounds of the students in your class and to also try to ensure that the foods are healthy or that you point out that some foods are for special occasions – not every day.

Jointly construct a recipe with students. It can be a magic potion recipe and follow the model of *Frog Potion.* Decide with students what the goal of the recipe should be, then create a list of magical ingredients and list the steps in the method in logical order. Display the recipe on chart paper in the classroom.

Make sure students notice that recipes do not include words such as *please, if you like, maybe, possibly.* This discussion will help them with question 6 before they attempt it on their own. Some students might benefit from working in pairs to complete this particular question.

Grammar Focus: Commands, adverbs
Type of Text: Informative – Procedure/Instructions

Student Book 4 **Unit 15**

Point out to students that *How to Catch a Fish* is a different type of procedure text from the recipe in Unit 14. This text is a set of instructions. Instructions tell how to do something. Instructions begin with a goal or statement of aim, the same as a recipe. Then the steps to achieve the goal are listed in logical order.

Make sure students notice the doing verbs at the beginning of each line. The doing verbs make each line a command. Commands tell you what to do.

Tell students that sometimes commands end in an exclamation mark. Exclamation marks are used when something is said loudly or in anger or surprise. Commands as exclamations can be found on signs and notices as well as in narratives.

Instructions do not usually have exclamation marks unless it is for a command such as 'Beware!'

Explain to students that some kinds of adverbs add meaning to verbs. Present them with a mnemonic to help them remember the term *adverb*. An adverb can <u>*add*</u> meaning to a <u>*verb*</u>.

Adverbs that tell <u>how</u> end in *–ly*. Examples of adverbs that tell <u>how</u> include *swiftly, slowly, loudly*. Instructions sometimes make use of adverbs that tell <u>how</u> to ensure people follow instructions carefully.

Jointly construct a class set of instructions for using a piece of classroom equipment such as a pair of scissors, a computer or a chair.

Grammar Focus: Noun groups, verb tense
Type of Text: Informative – Procedure/Instructions

Student Book 4 **Unit 16**

Sun Safety is a procedure text. It provides instructions for staying safe in the sun. Each instruction starts with a command. These instructions are not written in any particular order, such as chronological order. They do not need a sequence.

Questions 1, 2 and 3 ask students to build up noun groups and recognise extended noun groups, such as noun groups with phrases. Point out to students that noun groups include a head noun or main noun as well as adjectives and other words that combine to represent the noun accurately. To help work out the whole noun group students can ask: Who or what is it about? For example:

The cat that has four white feet is outside.

Ask: What is the sentence about? The sentence is about *the cat that has four white feet*; *the cat that has four white feet* is the noun group.

It is useful for students to have some understanding of past, present and future tense.

Verb tense represents time as past, present or future.

Past: *We <u>ate</u> lunch at 12 o'clock.*

There are two main forms of present tense:

We <u>are eating</u> lunch now. This form of the verb shows that the action is currently happening.

The following present tense example implies the activity is timeless or always happening. This is sometimes called 'timeless present' tense. It is very common in information reports, explanations and descriptions.

Fish <u>swim</u> in the ocean.

Emperor penguins <u>live</u> in Antarctica.

Future tense: *We <u>will eat</u> lunch at 12 o'clock.*

Point out to students the helping verb (auxiliary verb) *will*. It forms part of the verb group.

Grammar Focus: Commands, doing verbs, proper nouns
Type of Text: Informative – Procedure/Instructions

Student Book 4 **Unit 17**

Directions to the Olympic Pool is another kind of procedural text that gives instructions. These are directions. Directions help you to get somewhere. Directions start with a stated goal and then include commands in logical sequence. Tell students that a logical sequence is very important in directions. Remind students that commands usually begin with verbs. In this case, all the commands begin with doing verbs.

Create a display of maps and street directories for your classroom. Include telephone books or online directories to show students the way addresses are written. Find your school's address in a telephone directory. Find your school in a street directory or map. Use the internet or scan a street directory page into a computer to show the location of your school. Discuss the location of the school and any local landmarks. Point out that street names, and the names of suburbs and towns, are proper nouns and require capital letters.

Jointly construct a set of directions to tell how to get to your school library or canteen from your classroom, or to get to a location in your local area from your school gate. Discuss with students the logical sequence required in directions and the use of doing verbs in the commands.

Demonstrate to students the importance of logical sequence in directions by using directions as jigsaw cloze activities. Refer to the explanation of jigsaw cloze on page 14.

Have students work in groups to create maps of the school and playground. Have each group then construct a set of directions for another group to follow to find their way from one point on the map to another.

Photocopy local area maps for students to practise giving oral directions to each other to reach secret locations on the maps.

Grammar Focus: Quoted and reported speech
Type of Text: Imaginative – Narrative/Comic strip

Student Book 4 **Unit 19**

Display a variety of examples of comic strips in your classroom for students to explore.

Discuss the comic strip *Super Crab* with students. Point out to students that the speech balloons contain the speech spoken by the characters. Point out the structure of narrative texts: orientation, complication, events, resolution. Point out that the crab rescuing the little fish was an initial resolution to a complication but a second complication followed. Have students work in pairs to draw some extra cells for the comic strip to show what could happen next. Make sure they write any speech in speech balloons.

Tell students that when characters in narratives speak what they actually say is called quoted speech. Quoted speech is usually recorded in speech marks or inverted commas *(Freddie said, "Hello.")*. Full stops, question marks and exclamation marks go inside the speech marks. In comic strips quoted speech is mostly contained in speech balloons so inverted commas are not needed.

Reporting what someone else has said is called reported speech *(I told him Freddie said hello.)*.

Ask two students to improvise a one-minute conversation about a topic of their choice. Demonstrate for students how to write that conversation using speech marks. Invite a different class member to orally report that conversation. Make sure the report includes what each student said in their conversation. Record the conversation using reported speech. Point out the difference in the ways to record speech.

Grammar Focus: Theme
Type of Text: Informative – Recount/Biography

Student Book 4 **Unit 20**

Isabel Letham, Surfie Legend is a recount text. It presents information about a person's life. The events are retold in chronological order. Tell students that a recount about a person's life written by someone other than the person is a biography. Tell them that when you write a recount about events in your own life history it is called an autobiography.

Demonstrate the construction of your own autobiography (or the biography of someone you know or a character that you can pretend to know) in front of students.

Theme is the first grammatical component of a clause. The theme is often all the words up to the verb or the verb itself.

Go to your classroom. (The verb in theme position highlights a command.)

Carefully chop the carrots. (The adverb highlights a how instruction for safety.)

Grandpa will be happy to see us in the morning. (The noun highlights who will be happy or who is the focus for the events.)

The results of the spelling test were important to the students. (The noun group in theme position highlights the test results.)

Question 1 in *Isabel Letham, Surfie Legend* asks for students to identify the theme at the beginning of each of the six sentences rather than the theme of each clause because identifying the clauses within the sentences will be too difficult for most students at this stage. Students will identify Isabel's name or a pronoun for Isabel at the start of each sentence. Other recounts that students come across will use time words as theme. Using time words as theme assists with sequencing and chronological order. It focuses the reader or listener's attention on the importance of time in the text.

Grammar Focus: Helping verbs, verb tense
Type of Text: Informative – Explanation

Student Book 4 **Unit 21**

Explanation texts often make use of technical terms or subject-specific terminology to explain a process or phenomenon. Demonstrate the use of a dictionary to find meanings for technical terms such as *condenses* and *evaporates* in *Recycled Water*.

Explanations can include connectives that show cause and effect *(because, so)*, and connectives that show time order *(then, after)*. Explanations usually start with an introduction that introduces the topic or makes a general statement about the topic. An explanation might have a concluding statement. Ask students to identify aspects of the structure and features of explanations in *Recycled Water*.

Point out that explanations are often accompanied by diagrams and illustrations. These help to explain difficult concepts in a visual manner. Ask students to work in groups to create a diagram or flow chart that shows the way water is recycled on earth. Display and compare their drawings.

Unit 16 dealt with verb tense and introduced students to the concept of helping verbs (auxiliary verbs). Remind students that a helping verb with a main verb is called a verb group. Helping verbs help give the verb a tense. Sometimes a verb needs more than one helper. For example *I would have liked a swim but it was getting late.*

Revise the way time is represented in a text. As well as helping verbs indicating a time frame for events, other time words in a text also function to show whether events have happened, are happening now, always happen or are predicted to happen in the future.

We ate lunch at 12 o'clock. (past tense) *We have eaten lunch already.* (past tense)

We are eating lunch now. (present tense)
We will eat lunch at 12 o'clock.
(future tense)

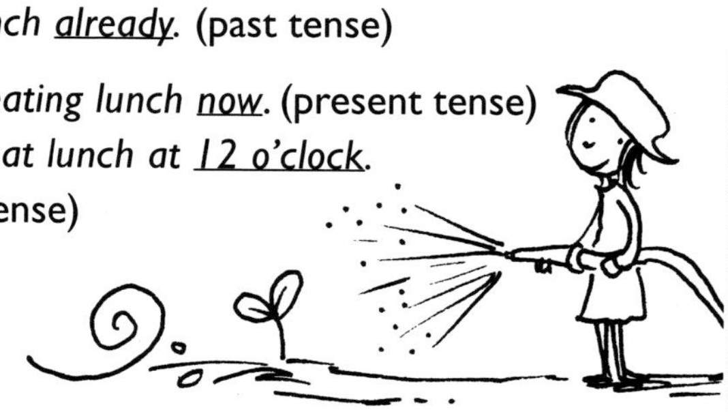

Grammar Focus: Theme, personal pronouns, possessive adjectives
Type of Text: Persuasive – Advertisement

Student Book 4
Unit 22

This advertisement is a persuasive text that uses commands to tell the reader what to do. Ask students what they notice about the grammar of the text. Students should be able to identify noun groups including the possessive adjective *your*. They should point out the verbs in theme position in the clauses and be able to articulate why the verbs are in theme position (ie to act as commands).

Remind students about the types of words that can generally be found in theme position in particular texts. For example, commands in directions or recipes usually have doing verbs as theme. Information reports and descriptions often have nouns as theme. Repeating a noun or pronoun for a noun in theme position in the clause reinforces the topic and allows new information to be added about the topic.

Revise personal pronouns with the students. Ask them to identify the personal pronouns in *We Tank You*. Addressing the reader as *you* and the workers who provide the tank as *we* makes the advertisement seem more personal. Have students search through magazines and newspapers for advertisements. Particularly see if they can find examples of advertisements that use personal pronouns. Discuss other language features of the advertisements. Create a display in the classroom. Create labels to attach to the display. For example:

This ad addresses readers as 'you'.

This ad uses verbs in theme position to give commands.

This ad uses adjectives to make the product sound really good.

Point out other features of advertising such as expert recommendations (scientists, dentists, movie stars, doctors); recommendations by everyday people (children, parents); emotive words that might make people buy the product *(great value, on sale now, limited time only, special deal)* and aspects such as eye-catching use of colour or design.

Grammar Focus: Conjunctions, comparative adjectives
Type of Text: Informative – Information report

Student Book 4
Unit 23

Read *Lake Eyre* with students. Remind students that clauses and sentences can be joined or linked by conjunctions. Teach students the different meanings created by the different types of conjunctions described in the rule on page 50 of the Student Book. In *Lake Eyre* the conjunction *however* is used to point out the contrast between the lake at its fullest and the dry salt pan. The conjunction *so* is used to show when one thing causes, or leads to, another (what causes the way the Lake Eyre dragon walks).

Remind students that *it* is a pronoun. It is used to refer to places, animals and things in a text when they have already been mentioned. It saves having to keep naming the thing again and helps the flow of meaning.

Most adjectives can have three forms to show degrees of comparison. These are called positive, comparative and superlative.

The **comparative** form is used when comparing two things:

- Add *–er* to the end of most adjectives with one or two syllables.
- Use the word *more* for most adjectives longer than two syllables.

Some adjectives are **irregular** because they don't follow this pattern.

The **superlative** form is used when comparing more than two things:

- Add the suffix *–est* to the end of most adjectives with one or two syllables.
- Use the word *most* for most adjectives that have more than two syllables.

Again, **irregular** adjectives do not follow any pattern.

For example:

large → *larger* → *largest*

ridiculous → *more ridiculous* → *most ridiculous*

good → *better* → *best*

Some adjectives do not have comparative or superlative forms: their meaning is absolute. They can't be compared. For example, *dead*. You can't be *deader, deadest, more dead* or *most dead*. Other examples include: *full, live, perfect, right, wrong*.

Grammar Focus: Lexical chains, commas in a list
Type of Text: Informative – Information report

Student Book 4
Unit 25

Read *Sewage* with students. Tell them that the words that make up the main content of a text are called the lexical words. These words form lexical chains. They are all the important 'meaning' words. Texts can have more than one content strand. A content strand or lexical chain can include noun groups, verbs, phrases and adverbs.

Dictagloss is a useful activity for establishing an understanding of content words with students. Engage students in Dictagloss activities with other examples of information reports. Focus their attention on noting the important words from the text as you read it aloud to them. Dictagloss is explained on page 14.

Poetry is also useful for helping students understand content words because poems are condensed for meaning and often only include content words.

Don't be too pedantic about students' labelling of the lexical chains in a text. At this stage students just need a general understanding of the importance of content words and their function to carry the different strands of meaning in a text.

Help students recognise when to use commas in their own writing and what commas signify when they are reading texts. Teach them, for example, that commas are used in lists to separate each item in the list. For example: *toilet, kitchen sink, washing machine, dishwasher, bathroom sinks, showers and bathtubs*. The word *and* is usually used before the final item in the list. This can help prevent ambiguity, as in the following sentence: *I wore a coat, boots, beanie and scarf, and I took an umbrella.*

Commas are also used to separate quoted speech in a text.

Ali said, "I'm hungry."

"Have an apple," said Dad.

For further examples of when to use commas, see page 57.

Grammar Focus: Verb groups, conjunctions
Type of Text: Informative – Explanation

Student Book 4
Unit 26

Read *How a Pearl is Made* with students. Ask students what grammatical features they notice in the explanation. Have them use dictionaries to explore the technical terms used.

Ask for volunteers to draw a flow diagram with labels to show the process of making a pearl. Display and discuss the diagram. Ask students to predict what might eventually happen to the pearl and the pearl oyster. Show students jewellery store catalogues that contain images of pearls. Point out that people now farm pearl oysters and implant tiny grains inside the shells so that the oysters will grow pearls. Some oysters can live for six to nine years, and grow three pearls in their lifetime.

Discuss the verbs and verb groups in the explanation. Point out the helping verbs (auxiliaries) included in some of the verb groups to help establish tense.

Remind students that conjunctions can link clauses in a text through time and through cause and effect. You might like to refer to conjunctions as joining or connective words, or connectives. 'Connective' is a broader term than 'conjunction' and it also refers to the function of the word or word group in the text as a whole, not just within a sentence, and is therefore a useful term. Students do not need to label the different kinds of connectives. They just need to be aware of the function of the connective in the text and the way the connectives link parts of the text. Time connectives include: *after, meanwhile, when, until, as long as, at first, now that, while, since*. Cause connectives include: *because, therefore, so that, in case, however, unless*.

Question 1 in the student book asks for verb groups. Be aware that some students might include single verbs in their answer, which is acceptable.

Grammar Focus: Reference chains, classifying adjectives
Type of Text: Informative – Information report

Student Book 4 **Unit 27**

Read *Cane Toads* with students. Discuss the structure and features of the information report.

Teach students that words that refer to the same person, place, animal or thing throughout a text form a chain. This is called a reference chain. In the following example, words in the reference chain are all in theme position in the clauses.

The students at our school are very clever. They enjoy reading and writing. They especially enjoy 'Grammar Rules!' activities. Our fabulous students deserve medals.

In the following example, words in the reference chain are not all in theme position in the clauses. *The students at our school are very clever. 'Grammar Rules!' especially excites them and they enjoy all reading and writing activities. We are going to give them medals for being such good students.*

Students can easily confuse references in their own writing and, to fully comprehend texts they are reading, they need to be able to follow the references.

Have students work in pairs to find sections of text in novels that include pronoun reference. Have them rewrite a section of the text without the pronouns – writing the nouns in full instead of using the pronouns. Have them read their efforts to the class. Point out how much more complicated the texts seem when there are no pronouns.

Daisy started to eat her dinner. She had sardines in her bowl and she licked until they were all gone.

Daisy started to eat Daisy's dinner. Daisy had sardines in Daisy's bowl and Daisy licked until the sardines were all gone.

Teach students about words that classify the noun in a text. These words are called classifying adjectives and they form part of the noun group: *tropical storm, tennis match, leather shoe.*

Grammar Focus: Question tags, verbs, conjunctions
Type of Text: Persuasive – Discussion/Interview transcript

Student Book 4 **Unit 28**

This discussion text presents differing points of view on a subject. Point out the introduction or orientation to the discussion as well as the concluding statement. Point out to students the way each point of view is presented with reasons. Tell students that discussions often include thinking and feeling verbs because people are presenting what they think or feel about issues. Examples include: *think, feel, hope, believe, wonder, trust, rely, expect, agree.*

In a discussion, questions can be asked to gain further information or to clarify opinions. Remind students about the question words: *who, what, where, when, how, why*. Point out that when you ask a question your voice rises at the end. This is called a rising inflection and it enhances meaning. In spoken language the voice can go up to indicate a question even if the structure of the written text is not grammatically a question: *You're coming?*

Point out the questions that Ben and Ali both ask in *What's Your Favourite Sea Animal?*

The structure of these questions is that of a statement with a question tag at the end. Adding a question tag indicates that an answer or response is expected. Ask students to suggest a statement and add a question tag to it. Often the person asking a question with a question tag has an expectation about the response: *You've done your homework, haven't you?* implies that the questioner expects that the homework has been done. This is different from *Have you done your homework?*, which implies that the questioner does not know whether the homework has been done or not.

Grammar Focus: Noun groups, adjectives, subject-verb agreement
Type of Text: Persuasive – Response/Travel review

Student Book 4
Unit 29

Demonstrate the construction of a book review for the class. Read a picture book to review or review a book or novel that the class has already read. Write the review on chart paper or the board. A suggested structure for response texts is included on page 29.

If possible, display or examine other examples of reviews. These could be book reviews written by students in other classes or internet reviews of books, films, CDs, computer games and so on. Discuss the structure and features of the reviews.

Daintree is a travel review. It presents the writer's opinions about the Daintree as a holiday destination and includes some noun groups with adjectives to describe that destination. Read *Daintree* with students. Ask students to compare this review with other reviews they have experienced. Point out the orientation, the concluding judgement or recommendation, and the thinking and feeling verbs.

Review singular and plural nouns with students. Remind students about the importance of using correct verb forms with singular and plural nouns. Explore verbs and singular and plural nouns. Students need to focus on the verb and its helping verb (auxiliary) to make sure they write the correct verb forms.

	Singular noun	Plural noun
Present tense	*The cat licks its paws.*	*The cats lick their paws.*
	A cat is a mammal.	*Cats are mammals.*
Past tense	*The cat licked its paws.*	*The cats licked their paws.*
Present tense with helping verb	*The cat is licking its paws.*	*The cats are licking their paws.*
Past tense with helping verb	*The cat was licking its paws.*	*The cats were licking their paws.*

Grammar Focus: Verb groups, verb forms
Type of Text: Informative – Information report

Student Book 4
Unit 31

Read *Tsunami* to the class. Discuss the concept of a tsunami. Tell students that a tsunami is a big wave but not a tidal wave because tsunamis have nothing to do with tides. Tell them that, in deep water, a tsunami can travel as fast as a jet aeroplane.

Note the technical terms in the information report and ask for volunteers to look for these words in a dictionary and share their meanings with the rest of the class.

Interested students might like to find out why the north-west coast of Australia is the most likely place on Australia's coast to be hit by a tsunami. Provide time for the student or students to complete their research and then present their findings to the class.

The Unit deals with regular and irregular verb forms. Tell students that regular verbs have a base form and then suffixes are added to the base form to change the tense of the verb.

Regular verbs need the suffix *–d* or *–ed* or *–ing* to change their tense.

walk → *walked* → *walking*

skate → *skated* → *skating*

There are associated spelling rules for adding suffixes to words. Tell students that when verbs:

- have a short vowel sound before a single final consonant, the final consonant is doubled before adding the suffix.
  stop → *stopped* → *stopping*
- end in *y* they will need to change the *y* to *i* and then add *–ed*. *spy* → *spied* → *spying*
- end in –e after a consonant and a preceding long vowel sound the final e is dropped when adding *–ing*. *rake* → *raked* → *raking*

Irregular verbs change in a different way to show tense, often by changing their middle vowels.
I am flying. I flew. I have flown.

Grammar Focus: Speech, modality, emotive words
Type of Text: Informative – Information report/Newspaper article

Student Book 4
Unit 32

Read the newspaper article with students. Ask students to identify aspects of structure and grammar such as quoted and reported speech, saying verbs and noun groups.

Tell students that newspaper articles need to be interesting so that people will read them. They also need to have attention-grabbing headlines and photos. Tell them that newspapers include words that will appeal to people's emotions: these are called emotive words. In *High Tide Sends Residents to the Roof* the words *forced to abandon their homes* are used to ensure readers empathise with the residents. A newspaper article might say a person was *attacked by a dog* rather than *bitten by a dog* because *attacked* is more emotive.

Select a number of students to take on roles of Bilkington residents for a television current affairs interview. This interview could take the form of a panel Hot Seat activity (see page 16 for instructions on Hot Seat). Other students could take on roles of interviewers or journalists. The rest of the class becomes the program's audience.

The degree of certainty a speaker or writer has about a topic is called modality. Being very certain or definite is high modality. Being unsure or uncertain is low modality. *Must, must not, will, will not* are considered high modality because they are very definite. *Might, maybe, could* and *possibly* are words that convey lower modality because the speaker or writer is not so certain. Modality is about certainty, usualness and obligation.

Point out that newspapers report about specific people, places and events rather than about generalised classes of things, as found in information reports in other sources.

Grammar Focus: Connecting arguments, modality
Type of Text: Persuasive – Exposition

Student Book 4
Unit 33

Speeches are exposition texts. Talk to students about the structure of the text *Vote Against School Swimming*. Make sure students realise the speech would have been written down, practised and then presented as a spoken argument or presented by a speaker in a debate. Ask students to read the speech using voice and body language to support the arguments.

Make sure students notice the way the speaker's opinions are strongly expressed in *Vote Against School Swimming*. The speaker is trying to convince others about a point of view. Modal verbs are helping verbs that represent the certainty or uncertainty of an argument. Modal auxiliaries include words like *must, should, would, might, will, can, should not, would, wouldn't.* Direct commands are high modality: *Shut the door.* The same requests can be expressed using lower modality: *Would you mind shutting the door?*

Point out that advertising uses high modality, too. Advertisers make definite claims about their products and use language to convince others of a point of view. The function of modal verbs is to add degrees of certainty or obligation to the verb, either making the verb higher or lower modality: *You might enjoy. You must try.*

Review theme in texts. Information reports and descriptions usually have nouns as theme. Repeating a noun (or a pronoun for that noun) in theme position in the clauses reinforces the topic and allows new information to be added about the topic.

Teach students how to engage in polarised debates and parliamentary debates (see page 14 for instructions), making use of modality.

Grammar Focus: Prepositional phrases, adverbs
Type of Text: Imaginative – Narrative

Student Book 4
Unit 34

Read *Bobby and the Quest for the Hidden Treasure* with students.

Divide the class into groups. Have groups create dramatisations about Bobby and his friends searching for treasure, commencing with the scene where they are digging under the willow tree. Have groups perform for the rest of the class.

Have students work in pairs or groups of three to write the conversation between Bobby's family members where they discuss a hidden treasure. Remind students to use speech marks, capital letters for proper nouns for peoples' names, and saying verbs to record the conversations. Have students present their written dialogue as Readers' Theatre (see page 18 for instructions.)

Have students work in groups to create storyboards or comic strips for the sequence of events in *Bobby and the Quest for the Hidden Treasure*. When students complete the **Try it yourself!** activity on page 73 of the Student Book, they can add to their storyboards or comic strips.

Talk to students about ways to use grammar to create interesting narratives. For example, it can be a good idea to vary the sentence beginnings so that the story is more interesting to read. Using different word groups in theme position can surprise a reader, make a story exciting or more interesting. For example 'After travelling for a while . . .' is used at the start of a sentence in *Bobby and the Quest for the Hidden Treasure* rather than 'They walked for a long time . . .'

Remind students that prepositional phrases are groups of words that provide information about where and when events occur in stories (circumstances of place or time). They consist of a preposition *(in, on, under, over, beside, after, before, during, while, later, past, near, across, between, through)* followed usually by a noun or noun group. Some prepositions can start phrases that tell when as well as phrases that tell where. For example:

I left before eight o'clock. (tells when)

Take the first turn on the left before the bridge. (tells where)

Remind students that the theme is the first part of the clause. Questions 4 and 5 require an understanding of theme.

Any text that students encounter provides an opportunity to explore the grammar and the impact of grammatical choices on meaning. *Bobby and the Quest for the Hidden Treasure* can be used to review any of the following grammatical features, if relevant for your students:

Noun groups with adjectives that describe, classify or tell number: *an enormous willow tree; one day*

Possessive adjectives in the noun group:
his friends;
his family

Synonyms: *huge/enormous*

Thinking verbs: *decided, remembered*

Doing verbs: *dig, hopped*

Proper nouns: *Bobby*

Compound nouns: *waterfall*

Homophones: *one/won*

Personal pronouns: *they, it*

Reference chains: *Bobby and his friends/they/they/they/the frogs/they*

Conjunctions to show cause: *so*

Conjunctions to show addition: *and*

Student Book 5

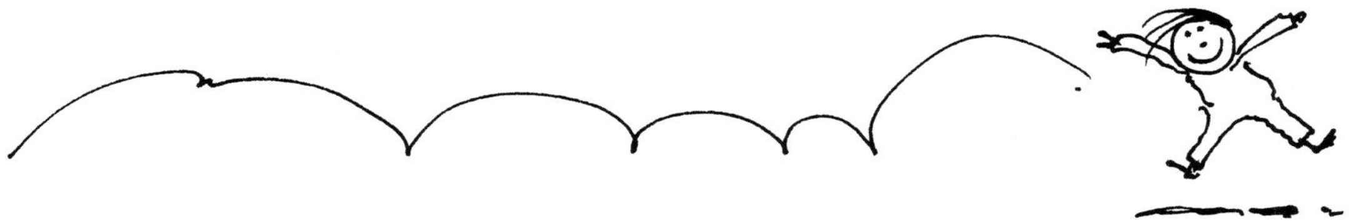

Scope and Sequence This scope and sequence chart is based on the requirements of the Australian Curriculum.

Unit	Unit name/ Type of text	Clause to whole text level			Word and word group level		
		Sentences and clauses	Cohesion: theme, pronouns, lexical chains, connectives	Mood and modality, language and vocabulary	Nouns and noun groups	Verbs and verb groups	Adverbs and prepositional phrases
1	**A Doggy Heroine** Information report	simple and compound sentences; clauses	conjunctions (connectives): *and, so, because, but, or, until*; personal pronouns: *she, her, he, him, it*				
2	**Battle for the Planets** Narrative				noun groups including adjectives; proper nouns; collective nouns	auxiliary verbs; subject-verb agreement	
3	**The Eagle has Landed** Recount/Newspaper article	clauses; simple sentences; commas	conjunctions (connectives): *as, and, while*			verbs	
4	**Glittery Moon** Narrative		relative pronouns: *who, whose, that, which*		noun groups; descriptive and classifying adjectives		adverbs and adverb groups
5	**A Movie Classic** Response/Film review			modality		verb groups; thinking and feeling verbs; saying verbs; auxiliary verbs	modal adverbs
6	REVISION						
7	**Through the Doorway** Narrative				adjectives; possessive adjectives		prepositional phrases; adverbs
8	**Valentina Tereshkova** Recount/Biography		theme			relating verbs (being and having verbs); doing verbs	
9	**Galactic Airways** Exposition/ Advertisement		theme; personal pronouns	commands; modality with positive and negative polarity		doing verbs; verb tense	
10	**The Columbus of the Cosmos** Recount/Biography	complex sentences; main clause and subordinate clauses	conjunctions (connectives); relative pronouns; possessive pronouns: *mine, ours, yours, his, hers, theirs*		apostrophes of possession		
11	**Amateur Astronomer** Recount					past tense; regular and irregular verbs	adverbs and prepositional phrases
12	REVISION						
13	**Save Planet Earth** Discussion/Interview transcript			modality		auxiliary verbs; thinking and feeling verbs	modal adverbs
14	**Earth Day** Information report	quoted (direct) speech			nominalisation; noun groups including possessive adjectives, articles, number adjectives, descriptive adjectives, classifying adjectives		
15	**The Black Hole** Narrative	ellipses; complex sentences; subordinate clauses	relative pronouns		noun groups; nominalisation; adjectives	verb groups	adverbs
16	**Does Life Exist on Other Planets?** Discussion		connectives: *or, similarly, however, on the other hand, because, although, unless, therefore, alternatively, likewise*	acronyms			
17	**Life on Earth** Information report		technical terms	statements and questions; question tags		relating verbs (being and having verbs)	
18	REVISION						

Unit	Unit name/ Type of text	Clause to whole text level			Word and word group level		
		Sentences and clauses	Cohesion: theme, pronouns, lexical chains, connectives	Mood and modality, language and vocabulary	Nouns and noun groups	Verbs and verb groups	Adverbs and prepositional phrases
19	**Cosmonaut Cookies** Procedure/Recipe		theme	commands	noun groups	verbs; present tense; past tense suffixes and auxiliaries	
20	**Film Review** Response/Film review			fact and opinion; evaluative language; modality; exclamations	adjectives		adverbs
21	**Dear Mr Armstrong** Response/Letter	addressing envelopes; commas		evaluative language	noun groups; descriptive and classifying adjectives		
22	**Alien** Description/Poem	colons	conjunctions (connectives): *or, and*	metaphor			adverbs and prepositional phrases
23	**Ecological Footprint** Information report	clauses; commas	relative pronouns: *who, whose, which;* conjunctions (connectives): *so, both, neither/nor, either/or, because*		nominalisation		
24	REVISION						
25	**Mass Panic – UFO Terrorises City** Information report/ Newspaper article	quoted (direct) and reported (indirect) speech		emotive language; gender inclusive language			
26	**Mars, the Red Planet** Description				noun groups; superlative and comparative adjectives; adjectival phrases	relating verbs (being and having verbs)	
27	**How is the Earth Magnetic?** Explanation			technical terms		past and present tense	prepositional phrases to tell how, where and when
28	**Who Needs Science?** Response/Letter to the editor		connectives to link arguments	modality; vocatives			
29	**Today's Debate** Exposition/Parliamentary debate			vocatives; emotive language			
30	REVISION						
31	**Dear Diary** Response/Diary			colloquial language; similes; metaphors	noun groups	thinking and feeling verbs; relating verbs; auxiliary verbs	
32	**What to Do if Aliens Land in Your Neighbourhood** Procedure/Instructions		conjunctions (connectives): *if*; theme	commands; tongue-in-cheek humour		verbs; present tense	
33	**Andy Thomas, Astronaut** Recount/Biography		connectives; reference chains	fact and opinion	adding suffixes to form nouns for people		
34	**The Cost of the Space Program** Discussion		connectives: *on the other hand, nevertheless, whereas, despite, however, yet, though*; lexical chains	point of view			
35	REVISION						

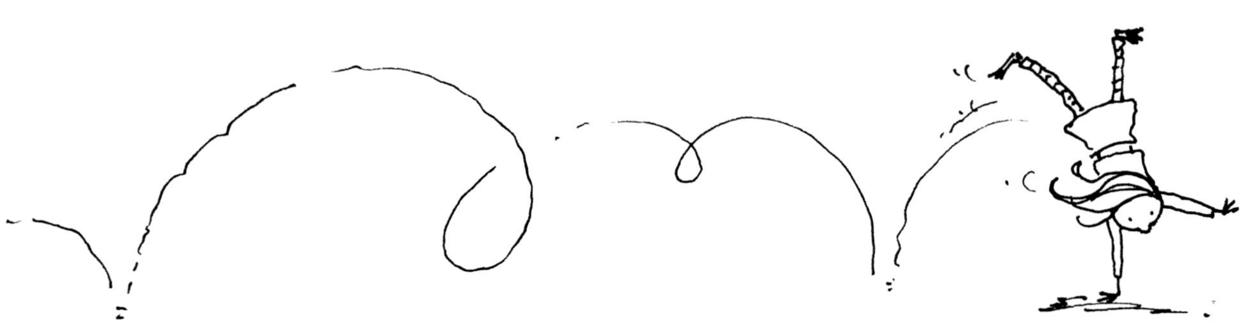

Grammar Focus: Sentences, pronouns
Type of Text: Informative – Information report

Student Book 5
Unit 1

It is useful for students to develop an understanding of the clause as a grammatical structure. Teachers are usually comfortable with the concept of a sentence but find the concept of a clause less familiar. A clause is a grammatical unit that expresses an idea. A clause must have a verb. A clause can be a simple sentence on its own. A clause that makes sense on its own is called an independent clause. A clause might not completely make sense on its own. It might depend on another clause for meaning and need to be attached to it. Then it is called a dependent clause. Clauses can be linked in a variety of ways.

I like the shirt / that Nana gave me. (an independent clause followed by a dependent or subordinate clause; the clauses are linked by the relative pronoun *that*)

A sentence is a word or a group of words that makes sense or is complete on its own. A sentence must have at least one verb. The simplest sentence is an independent clause.

Compound sentences consist of two or more independent clauses joined together using conjunctions (connectives) such as *and, but, or.* Complex sentences consist of two or more clauses joined together, with a mix of dependent and independent clauses.

Examples of types of sentences include:

Stop! (simple sentence as a single verb command)

How old are you? (simple sentence as a question)

Peggy is walking to school. (simple sentence as a statement)

I brought paper but I forgot my pencil. (compound sentence – two independent clauses joined by the conjunction *but*)

Discuss the role of personal pronouns in *A Doggy Heroine*. Personal pronouns replace, or refer to, nouns already used or implied in a text. Teach students the 3rd person personal pronouns *she, her, he, him, they, them, it.*

Grammar Focus: Noun groups
Type of Text: Imaginative – Narrative

Student Book 5
Unit 2

Talk to students about narrative structure. The extract *Battle for the Planets* introduces the setting and main characters in the narrative. It also introduces a complication for the Ferlings and sets the scene for a dangerous encounter with the Grimlies. Remind students that narratives need to have a complication or problem for characters to face and overcome.

Explain to students the definition and function of noun groups. Tell students that a noun group is a group of words based on a main noun that gives a description or extra information about that main noun. In some teacher reference material the main noun is called a 'head noun'. Noun groups can include adjectives *(gentle creatures)*, as well as embedded clauses *(kind and gentle creatures who roamed the planets)* and phrases *(the alien with three arms)*.

You may note the two prepositional phrases at the beginning of *Battle for the Planets:* In the deep wilderness / of space. The preposition in is linked to the noun group the *deep wilderness of space* to form a prepositional phrase that tells where. Prepositional phrases will be dealt with in later Units.

Tell students that some verbs need helpers. These helping verbs are called auxiliary verbs, in the same way that caravans can have auxiliary batteries or schools can have auxiliary staff. Auxiliary verbs need to match singular or plural nouns appropriately.

The child is going.	*The child was going.*
The children are going.	*The children were going.*
The child/children will go.	

If necessary, revise singular and plural nouns and their associated spelling patterns with students. See also the notes in this book for Unit 8 and Unit 29 in *Student Book 4* (pages 63 and 72).

Grammar Focus: Clauses, commas
Type of Text: Informative – Recount/Newspaper article

Student Book 5
Unit 3

Revise with students the concept of a clause and the ways clauses are joined using conjunctions (see the notes for Unit 1 on page 77).

Ask students to analyse the structure and features of the newspaper article. Make sure they recognise the function of a lead paragraph, photos, captions, quoted and reported speech and other aspects of newspaper articles. Sometimes articles are recounts. The main issue is summarised in the lead paragraph and then the events are presented in chronological order. Sometimes newspaper articles present information that is not a recount and therefore not written in chronological order. Display examples of newspaper articles in the classroom for students to examine in groups and identify aspects of structure and features.

Have students create lists of questions they would ask of any of the *Eagle* astronauts if they were to interview them after their space flight. Teach students the difference between open and closed questions.

Tell them that open questions are worded in a way that elicits more depth in the responses. The wording of closed questions can tend to elicit simple or single-word answers and close down communication.

Open question: *What things did you do at school today?*

Closed question: *Did you have a good day at school?*

Teach students the question starter words: *who, what, where, when, how, why.*

Newspaper articles can be used as the stimulus for a Hot Seat activity. Students can take on roles of characters in an article and sit for media interviews. See page 16 for an explanation of Hot Seat.

Grammar Focus: Adjectives, adverbs, relative pronouns
Type of Text: Imaginative – Narrative

Student Book 5
Unit 4

Make sure students understand that adjectives function to add meaning to a noun or pronoun. Ensure that students recognise the different functions of adjectives. Descriptive adjectives describe the noun. *(The girl was tall. The tall girl)* Descriptive adjectives are sometimes called describers. The word *very* can be used in front of a descriptive adjective. *(The boy was very tall. The very tall boy)*

Classifying adjectives function to classify or categorise the noun, rather than describe its qualities *(oak tree)*. It is not possible to use the word *very* in front of a classifying adjective. (You can't say *a very oak tree.* You can say *a very old oak tree*, as *old* is a descriptive adjective.) Some words can function as either a noun or a classifying adjective. *I love tennis.* (noun). *I saw the tennis match.* (classifying adjective).

Adverbs tell how, when and where. They function to add meaning to verbs, adjectives and other adverbs.

Adverb adding how meaning to an adjective: *very tall*

Adverb adding when meaning to an adverb: *before now*

Adverb adding where meaning to a verb: *come here*

Relative pronouns *who* (and *whom*), *whose, which* and *that* are used at the start of clauses to relate the clause to another clause. Like personal pronouns, relative pronouns refer to nouns already mentioned in a text.

The rocket went into space. The rocket was a Saturn V.

The rocket / that went into space / was a Saturn V. (*that* refers to *the rocket*)

Who and *whom* relate to people. *That* relates to people and things. *Which* relates to things. *Whose* shows possession.

Have students work in groups of three to write a resolution for the narrative *Glittery Moon*. Provide time for groups to share their work with the rest of the class.

Grammar Focus: Verb groups, modality
Type of Text: Persuasive – Response/Film review

Student Book 5 **Unit 5**

Review the four functions of verbs with students:

Saying verbs indicate something is being said. *(said, shouting, whispered)*

Thinking and feeling verbs represent mental activities. *(love, believed, hoping)*

Doing verbs represent actions. *(jumping, fly, skipped)*

Relating verbs show relationships, such as being and having; they relate what things **are** or what they **have** *(are, is, has, equals)*.

This unit of work focuses on saying verbs, as well as thinking and feeling verbs. It also introduces students to the concept of a verb group. It describes a verb group as a group of words that do the job of a verb. Verb groups can include:

- two verbs of equal value, for example *remembered feeling*
- auxiliary verbs, for example *is cooking, was going*
- modal verbs, for example *could eat, must go*

Modal verbs indicate the degree of certainty, usualness, inclination or obligation there is about the topic. Some adverbs also help to express modality *(absolutely, usually, definitely, very)*.

Response texts, such as the film review *A Movie Classic*, include opinions. Opinions can be expressed using thinking and feeling verbs, modal verbs and adverbs that express modality.

Work with the class to jointly construct a response to a book, a film, a concert, a song or a poem. Demonstrate for students how to express opinions using the aspects of grammar dealt with in Unit 5. Ensure that students understand that they are entitled to have differing opinions and are not obliged to agree with you, or each other. They need to learn how to justify their opinions with reasons. They also need to learn to accept the opinions of others.

Grammar Focus: Prepositional phrases, possessive adjectives
Type of Text: Imaginative – Narrative

Student Book 5 **Unit 7**

Through the Doorway is an orientation to a story. It introduces the main character, Ronnie, and sets the scene for the complication (what happens to Ronnie when she peers inside the doorway). Have students work in groups to write the complication, events and resolution for the story. Make sure students realise that complications allow characters to grow, solve problems and reveal aspects of their character. Make sure students use noun groups, as well as thinking and feeling verbs, to represent the character of Ronnie, and to tell how she is thinking and feeling. Thinking and feeling helps readers to empathise with characters.

Make sure students can identify prepositions. Examples of prepositions include *in, on, under, over, behind*. A preposition in front of a noun or pronoun makes a prepositional phrase: *in the spaceship; after sunset; with a remote control.*

Point out to students that prepositional phrases tell where, when and how. Prepositional phrases are important in narratives to set the scene for events. They provide the circumstances under which events occur.

Talk to students about the difference between an adverb and an adjective. An adjective adds meaning to a noun or pronoun. Give students the mnemonic, 'ad' to 'verb' equals *adverb*, to help their memories.

Revise noun groups with descriptive and classifying adjectives with students. Revise possessive adjectives as words in the noun group that show ownership.

Grammar Focus: Relating and doing verbs, theme
Type of Text: Informative – Recount/Biography

Student Book 5 **Unit 8**

Tell students the difference between biography and autobiography. Both are forms of recount texts. They retell events in a person's life, in chronological order. The prefix 'auto' means 'self' so autobiography means your life story written by yourself. Read *Valentina Tereshkova* with students and discuss any aspects of grammar they notice about the recount.

Doing verbs are probably the easiest verbs for students to distinguish, because they are 'action' words. We can see the actions or the processes occurring. Conversely, relating verbs are possibly the most difficult verbs to understand or recognise because you cannot see any action. Relating verbs show how a noun relates to itself or to its parts or some other aspect of its existence. Relating verbs represent what things **are** or what they **have**.

Theme is defined as the first grammatical element of a clause. Each type of text typically uses particular grammatical components in theme position.

For example, recounts often use time words and phrases as theme because time is significant in ordering events in a recount. Information reports often use topic nouns as theme to focus on the topic. Repeating the topic in theme position helps readers access, or unpack, the text. Procedures often use verbs in theme position.

In *Valentina Tereshkova*, theme is mostly nouns and pronouns referring to the topic: Valentina Tereshkova.

Help students recognise the theme of clauses in texts they encounter and the importance of theme in developing different types of texts in their own speaking and writing.

Suggest that students write autobiographies and illustrate their autobiographies with photographs.

Grammar Focus: Verbs, modality
Type of Text: Persuasive – Advertisement

Student Book 5 **Unit 9**

Advertising uses high modality to persuade readers and listeners to buy something or do something. Modality is evident in negative statements and positive statements. Sometimes students can get confused and only think that positive statements are high modality. *It will rain.* Negative statements also represent high and low modality. *It will not rain. It might not rain. It probably won't rain.*

Advertising sometimes makes use of commands with doing verbs in theme position. Using a doing verb in theme position highlights the action requested: *book now; buy now; try it today; enjoy the taste; feel the difference.*

Advertising can use technical terms to impress and to show expertise about the subject. Technical terms used in *Galactic Airways* assist in persuading the reader that flights are safe and that the company has a high knowledge of its field.

Students can use dictionaries to find definitions for the terms: *galactic, simulator experience, zero gravity, unparalleled safety features, fully compliant,* and then discuss the meaning of the terms as they are used in the advertisement.

The form of the verb tells the time frame for events. This is called tense and there are three basic tenses: past, present and future. Auxiliary verbs *(was, have been, will be)* and suffixes *(–ed, –en, –t, –d, –ing)* help to show tense.

Some types of texts are more closely linked to a particular tense. For example, information reports and explanations are usually in present tense because of the habitual nature of the processes they describe. *Birds fly. Water evaporates.*

Recounts are past tense texts.

Grammar Focus: Pronouns, conjunctions
Type of Text: Informative – Recount/Biography

Student Book 5 **Unit 10**

Possessive pronouns and possessive apostrophes are two ways to show ownership in texts. Possessive pronouns are easy to recognise but must not be confused with possessive adjectives. Possessive pronouns do not need apostrophes.

Possessive pronouns: *his, hers, theirs, yours, mine,* and *ours*

The ticket is <u>hers</u>.

Possessive adjectives:
his, her, their, your, my and *our*

<u>Her</u> ticket is for this flight.

Note: The words *his* and *its* actually work as both possessive pronouns and possessive adjectives.

Make sure students don't confuse the possessive *its* with the contraction *it's (it is).*

Apostrophes are used with nouns to show that the noun owns something. There are particular spelling rules associated with using apostrophes for possession, as shown in the rule on page 24 of the Student Book. Go over these with students.

Make a poster about the use of apostrophes to display in the room.

A complex sentence is any sentence with an independent clause plus one or more other clauses that add to the meaning of the independent clause. (Remember that an independent clause is a simple sentence that makes sense on its own.) Complex sentences can be formed using relative pronouns and conjunctions.

The astronaut, who flew to Mars and escaped from alien capture, is being interviewed on the news tonight.

Have students work in groups of four to construct biographies of someone they are learning about in a school subject. Provide time for students to present the biographies like episodes of 'This is Your Life'. One student can take on the role of the famous person (living or dead). Others in the group can act as host of the show, and friends or relatives. Students might also record messages such as 'Your aunt could not here tonight but sends this message from Islamabad'.

Grammar Focus: Past tense, telling when
Type of Text: Informative – Recount

Student Book 5 **Unit 11**

Recount texts retell events in chronological order. Time words and phrases are useful, along with past tense verbs, to provide a method of sequencing the events. *Amateur Astronomer* is a personal recount rather than a biography or an autobiographical recount.

Regular verbs need the suffix *–d* or *–ed* or *–ing* to change their tense.

There are associated spelling rules for adding suffixes to words. Tell students that when verbs:

- have a short vowel sound before a single final consonant, the final consonant is doubled before adding the suffix.
  stop → *stopped* → *stopping*
- end in *y* they will need to change the *y* to *i* and then add *–ed*. *spy* → *spied* → *spying*
- end in –e after a consonant and a preceding long vowel sound the final e is dropped when adding *–ing*. *rake* → *raked* → *raking*

Irregular verbs change in a different way to show tense, often by changing their middle vowels.
I am flying. I flew. I have flown.

Using an auxiliary also affects the form of the verb in the past tense. In some teacher reference material these verbs will be called past participles *(I was <u>flying</u>)*. To assist students' understanding of time in texts, focus on recognising the way time is represented in the verbs, and in time phrases and adverbs. This knowledge will help students represent time appropriately and coherently in their own written and spoken texts.

You may also want to point out to students the nouns in *Amateur Astronomer*. Nouns can be specific *(the Skywatch Observatory)* or general *(observatories)*. Personal recounts involve specific nouns. Information reports and explanations usually involve whole classes of things and so deal with generalised nouns (such as ants, water, drought).

Grammar Focus: Modality, thinking and feeling verbs
Type of Text: Persuasive – Discussion/Interview transcript

Student Book 5
Unit 13

Discussions deal with different points of view on a topic. In *Save Planet Earth*, the radio talkback host has invited calls from members of the public to express their views on a topic of interest. Explain to students how talkback radio works if they are unfamiliar with this media format.

Differing points of view are presented in the discussion. Opinions are supported by reasons or arguments. Thinking and feeling verbs are common in discussion texts because they represent how people feel about an issue or what they think.

Remind students that the function of modal auxiliary verbs is to help verbs represent the degree of certainty or uncertainty the speaker or writer has about a topic. Modal auxiliaries include words such as *must, should, might, will, can, should not, would, wouldn't.*

Modal adverbs also help to show degrees of certainty about a topic, for example *possibly, probably, never, always, definitely, absolutely, positively.*

Have a polarised debate on a topic related to *Save the Planet*. Choose a high modality debating statement such as:

'The government should ban all car use on weekends to help prevent global warming.'

An explanation of polarised debating can be found on page 14.

Make sure all students have opportunities to express their points of view.

Teach students how to use a thesaurus to find alternative thinking and feeling verbs for question 6 and to use in their own discussion texts in the **Try it yourself!** activity.

Grammar Focus: Noun groups, quoted (direct) speech, nominalisation
Type of Text: Informative – Information report

Student Book 5
Unit 14

Review noun groups as a way to build up complete descriptions of the noun. Noun groups are particularly useful in narratives, descriptions and information reports. Possessive adjectives or articles are often included in a noun group. Remind students that noun groups can include words that point out *(that, the, a)* ask questions *(whose, which)* and show ownership *(my, our)*.

The articles *a*, *an* and *the* are words that point out. *A* and *an* are indefinite articles. *Pass me a ruler* means any ruler or no particular ruler. *The* is a definite article. *Pass me the ruler* means a particular ruler.

Use *a* and *an* before singular nouns and collective nouns only: *a tiger; tigers.*

In general, use:

a before words beginning with a consonant sound and *an* before words beginning with a vowel sound: *a sock; an igloo; an hour.*

Number adjectives are another category of word that can be part of a noun group. Number adjectives can be cardinal numbers *(one, thirty)* ordinal numbers *(first, last)* vague amounts *(many, few)* or specific and precise amounts *(first, one)*.

Nominalisation is a form of abstraction. Speakers and writers can turn a verb into a noun. More noun groups can be included in a clause than verbs because a clause only has one verb or one verb group. Nominalisation is used in explanations and information reports to pack meaning into the texts. Nominalisation is actually a simple concept that seems difficult but is very useful for students to understand. Understanding the way nominalisation works in texts will help student comprehension. Further explanation of nominalisation is included in the notes for Unit 23.

Grammar Focus: Subordinate clauses, ellipses
Type of Text: Imaginative – Narrative

Student Book 5
Unit 15

When writing narratives, authors need to use subject-specific terminology to make their texts believable. They can write from their own background knowledge and they can also do specific research in the 'field' or subject area of the text. Focus students' attention on the space terminology used in *The Black Hole*.

Tell students that an ellipsis is when meaning is implied but not actually stated in words. For example, 'You' is implied, or understood, in the command *Read the question ([You] Read the question)*. Ellipsis can be represented in a written text by three dot points (. . .), which show that words have been left out. Meaning is implied by the dot points but not stated in words. Ellipsis dot points can also be used when recording speech to indicate hesitancy: *"I thought I told you . . . he isn't coming."*

Have students work in groups to brainstorm a plan to save the planet Onega. Have students write, draw or illustrate their plan and then present it to the rest of the class.

Have students work in pairs to create comic strips for *The Black Hole*. Or, they could create storyboards for a movie of *The Black Hole* (see page 19 for instructions on storyboards). The class could divide the particular scenes of the story between groups or pairs of students and then each group could focus on the smaller number of scenes to represent their section of the film. Remind students that storyboards use close-ups, mid shots and long shots, and that they need labels or captions to indicate the scene being shot. Display the storyboard in sequence. Discuss students' representations of the story events and characters.

Grammar Focus: Connectives, acronyms
Type of Text: Persuasive – Discussion

Student Book 5
Unit 16

The discussion *Does Life Exist on Other Planets?* starts with an opening statement or orientation, presents a number of points of view on the topic, and ends with a conclusion or summing up of the main issue. Discuss the structure of the text with students.

The differing points of view in the discussion are attributed to the following noun groups: *Some people; scientists; many people*. When presenting a discussion it can be useful to quote experts or scientists, or numbers of people and groups of people in this way, to support opinions or to introduce differing opinions. This helps to substantiate a point of view.

Discussions can express varying degrees of modality from certain to not so certain. *The majority of scientists at Monash University believe that . . .* sounds more authoritative than *Some scientists think that it's possible . . .*

Connectives help texts to hang together or cohere in logical ways. Connectives are words that function to connect one part of a text to another. They can add information, compare things, show cause and effect, show a time sequence and sequence arguments. Connectives include:

- conjunctions *(and, because, but)*
- adverbs *(finally, firstly, secondly)*
- phrases *(on the other hand, as well as, in contrast, if not . . . then)*

Use cloze and jigsaw cloze activities to teach students about connectives. An explanation of these activities is included on page 14.

Grammar Focus: Statements and questions
Type of Text: Informative – Information report

Student Book 5 **Unit 17**

Talk to students about the ways questions are formed. Questions usually have specific grammatical structures. They can commence with a question word *(who, what, where, when, how, why)* or a verb *(Is that my hat? Are you coming?)*.

Tell students that, in writing, questions end in a question mark, but in spoken texts we can use our voices to indicate a question even if the sentence is not structured as a question. When asking a question the voice usually rises at the end. This is called a rising inflection. Sometimes statements become questions due to rising inflection in the voice, for example: *You're having dinner with us?*

Have students play with sentences, using rising inflection, as well as body language and facial expression to ask questions while reading statements or speaking lines from familiar rhymes and poems.

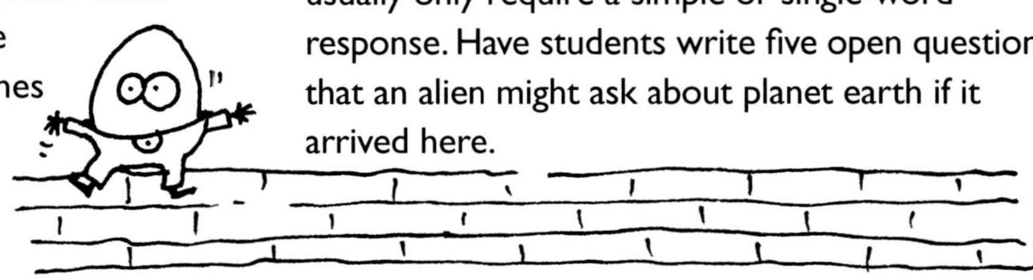

Humpty Dumpty sat on the wall?

Humpty Dumpty had a great fall?

Restructure the wording of the same rhymes and ask questions.

Why did Humpty Dumpty sit on a wall?

When did Humpty Dumpty have a great fall?

What happened to Humpty Dumpty?

Where was the wall?

Teach students about question tags at the end of statements as another way to form questions. Teach students the difference between open and closed questions and the types of response elicited by each. Open questions elicit a more detailed response than closed questions, which usually only require a simple or single-word response. Have students write five open questions that an alien might ask about planet earth if it arrived here.

Grammar Focus: Commands, verb tense
Type of Text: Informative – Procedure/Recipe

Student Book 5 **Unit 19**

Point out the structure of the recipe. It has a stated goal, which is expressed in the title *Cosmonaut Cookies*, a list of ingredients and then a method. Steps in the method are listed in logical or numbered order. Point out that each step in the method is written as a command with a verb in theme position in each clause. Ask students to discuss why recipes are written in this way.

Create dramatisations of television cooking shows. Ask whether students have seen cooking demonstrations on television, such as on any lifestyle programs. If not, it might be possible for you to record one of the cooking demonstrations and play it for the class. Brainstorm a list of things students noticed about television cooking shows, such as format, entertainment value, interaction with a show host or audience members, type of recipe, the way the cooking demonstration was organised with ingredients pre-prepared and so on.

Suggest students use the recipes written for the **Try it yourself!** to create their own cooking shows. Suggest that students organise who will act as the chefs, any costumes required and any props. Present the cooking shows to another class or a school assembly.

Question 5 requires students to recount the making of Cosmonaut Cookies. Make sure they understand the recount is in past tense and uses time words and time phrases *(the first thing we did was, then, after)* to retell a sequence of events that have already occurred.

Grammar Focus: Evaluative language
Type of Text: Persuasive – Response/Film review

Student Book 5
Unit 20

Film Review is a response text. It presents the writer's thoughts, feelings and opinions about a film. Opinions represent a judgement or an evaluation. Statements that present opinions may be positive or negative. *I liked it. I didn't like it.* Discuss the language used in evaluations: adjectives, modality and thinking and feeling verbs.

Adjectives can be used to provide favourable opinions as well as unfavourable opinions. Explore antonyms of adjectives, including the use of prefixes.

Tenor is concerned with the roles and relationships of the people involved in the language situation. Relationships take account of which person has power or authority over the other, who has more status, and how age and familiarity of the language users impacts on the language choices made. The tenor of any language situation is determined by the people involved: parent to child, speaker to formal audience, teacher to parent, teacher to student, police officer to suspect, employer to new employee. How we address the audience as listeners or readers is part of the tenor considerations of any text.

Have students write school reports for themselves using evaluative language. Discuss the tenor of the text. Make sure students recognise the way a principal and teacher would write on a report card. They can itemise subjects in a list and write a separate evaluation for each subject as well as an overall general comment from a teacher. The reports can be humorous and tongue-in-cheek or realistic. Tell students to write a principal's comment as well using the tenor of a principal evaluating a student.

Have students work in pairs to write report cards for each other. Discuss the less formal tenor of these texts, written about friends and for friends as the audience.

Grammar Focus: Evaluative language, commas
Type of Text: Persuasive – Response/Letter

Student Book 5
Unit 21

The letter *Dear Mr Armstrong* is a response text. It provides an introductory context, includes the writer's thoughts and feelings, and ends with an expression of thanks and an opinion. It uses evaluative language to give an opinion and to express the point of view.

Teach students how to form contractions. Contractions are shortened words that have an apostrophe where a letter or letters have been left out.

Verbs can be contracted:

- after a pronoun: *I will* → *I'll*
- after a noun: *the job is finished* → *the job's finished*
- after a question word : *What is the time? What's the time?*
- for a negative: *have not* → *haven't; would not* → *wouldn't; is not* → *isn't*

Make sure students understand the difference between *you're* (contraction) and *your* (possessive adjective). *<u>You're</u> late. Where is <u>your</u> hat?*

Make sure students understand the difference between *it's* (contraction) and *its* (possessive adjective).

<u>It's</u> a hot day. (It is a hot day.)
<u>It's</u> lost <u>its</u> wheels. (It has lost its wheels.)

Discuss the different uses of the comma explained in the rule on page 47 of the Student Book (in lists of nouns; to separate adverbs; to separate adjectives). There are a few more uses of the comma you may like to discuss with your class:

- after or before speech: *Dad said, 'When are we leaving?'*
- to separate phrases in a sentence: *Mum ran, with shoes in hand, to the front door.*
- to separate a person's name in a sentence: *Bobby, you can leave now.*

Grammar Focus: Adverbs, prepositional phrases
Type of Text: Imaginative – Description/Poem

Student Book 5
Unit 22

The poem *Alien* is in a modified cinquain form. Each stanza consists of four lines written in a one, two, three and then four or five word pattern. The poem uses metaphor to say that a person is an alien when they are new to a place. Ask your school's teacher/librarian to find examples of poems that use metaphor.

Review connectives and how they function to link ideas through cause, time, comparison or addition. Question 5 asks students to identify the difference made by the connectives *and* and *or*. *Or* is a connective that compares. The dictionary says an alien is someone strange *or* foreign. The poet says they feel strange *and* foreign on the first day at a new school. The connective *and* is used to emphasise that the poet feels both emotions.

Use extracts from literature to discuss the ways thoughts and feelings are represented.

Note: A brief description of colon use is given in the rule on page 48 of the student book. Here is a fuller list of how colons can be used:

- before a list of bullet points
- before a list of things *I bought: apples, oranges, bananas.*
- before the dialogue in a play script
- before a phrase *There were four tickets: not enough for all of us.*
- before a clause to make a different meaning more obvious *Joe believes in aliens: Belinda doesn't.*
- before a quotation *Grandma always said: Eat your crusts so your hair will go curly.*

Point out the colons in the poem, *Alien*. Tell students that poets often manipulate or ignore grammar rules to suit their purposes. Ask for a pair of volunteers to make a class poster about colons and display these examples in the room for student reference.

Grammar Focus: Nominalisation, joining clauses
Type of Text: Informative – Information report

Student Book 5
Unit 23

Information reports, like explanations, have technical subjects. Technical subjects require appropriate terminology. After students complete question 3, discuss the terminology used in *Ecological Footprint* to ensure students understand the subject matter.

Nominalisation was introduced in Unit 14. Nominalisation is when verbs are turned into nouns. Nominalisation allows more nouns, and therefore more concepts, to be built into a clause or sentence. Nominalisation makes texts appear more technical. Nominalisation is also often used in official writing. Texts can appear daunting to students when they have a great deal of nominalisation, but once students learn to 'unpack' the nominalised words they can more readily comprehend the texts. Students can also recognise the contexts in which texts are often constructed in such a way: journals, some newspaper articles, academic papers, scientific explanations, some government reports and so on.

Compare the following passages with students (verbs are underlined):

The dolphins were killed by fishing boats trawling for tuna. Conservationists are organising a mass protest.

The killing of the dolphins by tuna trawlers has led to the organisation of a mass protest by conservationists.

Remind students that sentences can be simple (one clause), compound (two equal clauses) or complex (two or more clauses of unequal value in a sentence). Complex sentences can be created by linking clauses using relative pronouns. Sometimes commas are needed to separate the clauses when using relative pronouns to prevent ambiguity or to help the 'flow' of the text.

The singer, who won the competition, is appearing at the shopping centre on Tuesday.

Grammar Focus: Emotive language, reported (indirect) speech
Type of Text: Informative – Information report/Newspaper article

Student Book 5
Unit 25

Read and discuss the events portrayed in the newspaper article with students.

Tell students that newspaper articles can include interviews with people. Their speech is sometimes quoted or sometimes reported. Teach students how to report what someone else has said using reported (indirect) speech. Have students work in pairs. Have one person in each pair whisper a sentence to their partner. Have the partners report it to the class, for example *Alexi said that he's hungry*.

Discuss the use of inclusive language with students. The term 'inclusive language' is used to describe language that does not exclude or discriminate against any particular group of people based on gender, disability, race, culture, religion or ethnicity. Tell students, for example, that it is sexist to presume people are male or female and to write about them as 'him' or 'her' unless you actually know their gender and it is relevant to the situation or context.

Question 3 asks students to write the reported speech of an army general to be quoted in the newspaper: *Include the reported speech of an army general to give the army's perspective on the UFO.* This is a gender inclusive way to construct the sentence. It would have shown bias to say: *Include the reported speech of an army general to give <u>his</u> perspective on the UFO.* This wording presumes an army general must be male. Another way to construct the question in a gender inclusive way would be to ask the army general for <u>*his or her*</u> *perspective* on events. This allows for both genders to be treated equally.

Grammar Focus: Adjectives, adjectival phrases
Type of Text: Informative – Description

Student Book 5
Unit 26

Description texts include an opening statement then a series of paragraphs describing aspects of the topic. *Mars, the Red Planet* is a scientific description. Scientific descriptions do not usually include value judgements or a final comment. They also do not usually contain emotive or evaluative language.

Have students compare literary descriptions found in narratives and poetry with scientific descriptions. Ask the school's teacher/librarian to find examples of descriptions in a variety of texts, including information reports, explanations, poetry and narrative texts, to share with the class.

Descriptions can include extended noun groups. Nouns can represent human and non-human participants. Scientific explanations mainly deal with natural phenomena and so include non-human participants: *Mars, the Sun, Earth, surface.*

Before students attempt the **Try it yourself!** activity display travel brochures in the classroom, or download travel brochures from the internet for students to read. Provide time for students to examine the language used in them. Discuss emotive language, high modality, evaluative language and use of descriptive adjectives. When students construct their own travel brochures help them use the same descriptions as *Mars, the Red Planet* but use them to persuade people to visit Mars, as tourists. Students will need to rework the scientific descriptions to create persuasive descriptions. Encourage students to explore synonyms for adjectives to make their writing more interesting and more precisely descriptive.

Display the Mars travel brochures in the classroom and discuss the effectiveness of each in persuading tourists to visit Mars. You might also like to have students work in groups to create a segment on Mars for a television travel show.

Grammar Focus: Prepositional phrases
Type of Text: Informative – Explanation

Student Book 5
Unit 27

Ensure that students recognise the structure and aspects of grammar relevant to explanation texts. Explanations explain how or why things are the way they are. Processes and phenomena are explained in a sequence. The sequence can be through time or through cause and effect. Explanations usually include technical terminology. Explanations are often accompanied by diagrams, such as flow diagrams or cycle diagrams, or other visual aids, to assist readers to understand potentially complex sequences or processes.

Connectives are usually significant in explanations to connect information across clauses. Connectives that link through cause and effect, or through time, are especially significant in explanations. A simple way to demonstrate for students how to create an explanation text is to provide the following structural example: 'This happens, which causes this, which causes that, and then this happens.' If students keep this format in mind as they create their own explanation texts they will create effective texts.

Another aspect of grammar particularly relevant in most explanation texts is the present tense. Because explanations deal with phenomena or processes that are ongoing, the texts are written in present tense to represent the ongoing or timeless nature of events such as evaporation, photosynthesis, aluminium smelting, recycling plastics, metamorphosis and so on.

Ensure that students understand the different purposes of an explanation, which is a 'what happens' text, compared to a procedure, which is a 'how to' text.

Grammar Focus: Modality, vocatives
Type of Text: Persuasive – Response/Letter to the editor

Student Book 5
Unit 28

Remind students that the social purpose of a persuasive text is to persuade others to adopt an action or a point of view. Responses link ideas using connectives such as *firstly, however, similarly, likewise, finally. Who Needs Science?* uses high modality and emotive language. Point out and discuss words such as *definitely, obviously doesn't realise, I'm happy, go back to your cave* and so on.

Before students attempt question 5, have them role-play with partners a conversation between Proud Scientist and N. Baines. Tell them to use low modality and discuss science in the classroom. Have students reflect on the benefits of low modality in an argument.

Remind students that the tenor of a situation is determined by the relationships between the people involved in the situation. Texts are constructed differently depending on the audience. The purpose and subject can be the same but the language can vary for different audiences.

For example, whether you are writing an article about the weather for a formal unknown audience or writing an SMS message about the weather to a friend will affect the language choices made.

Divide the class into groups of three or four students. Have one-third of the groups plan a speech for an audience of parents. Have one-third plan a speech for an audience of the younger children in your school, and have the final third prepare a speech for an audience of local government officials. Give the groups the same subject. Provide time for students to plan and practise their speeches. Have one member of each group present their speech. Discuss the different language choices made for the different audiences (ie discuss tenor).

Grammar Focus: Emotive language, vocatives
Type of Text: Persuasive – Exposition/Parliamentary debate

Student Book 5
Unit 29

Parliamentary debates involve two teams (called Affirmative and Negative) of three speakers. Speakers for each team take turns to present their arguments.

The text *Today's Debate* is the first speaker's prepared introduction for the Affirmative team on the topic 'Using animals in space experiments is wrong'.

Discuss with students the way the debate uses emotive language and vocatives to involve the audience and appeal to emotions. Discuss the amount of research into the topic that is represented in the debate. Sometimes students try to rely on their own knowledge in a debate and don't realise that they need to conduct research, analyse their research findings, and then synthesise the information to form their arguments. These are higher-level thinking skills. Also, students do not always realise that, as members of a debating team, they do not need to agree personally with the side to which they have been allocated. Teach students how to structure and connect their arguments for a debate.

Vocatives are words for people's names, or words used to address people in spoken and written texts. Vocatives demonstrate the relationship between the people in the situation. The relationship can be formal, polite, disrespectful, casual, unfriendly, professional and so on. Teach students to recognise the differences in the way people are addressed in different situations. This knowledge will help them understand how to make appropriate language choices in different situations.

Many examples of the language used in varying relationships can be found in literature. The school's teacher/librarian should be able to provide examples of conversations between different types of characters that demonstrate tenor, and/or use of vocatives.

Grammar Focus: Verb groups, noun groups
Type of Text: Persuasive – Response/Diary entry

Student Book 5
Unit 31

Dear Diary provides a young person's personal response to missing out on a camping trip. The response uses emotive language, descriptive adjectives, thinking and feeling verbs, and high modality. Ask students to identify these aspects of grammar in the text. Have students also explore the length of sentences in *Dear Diary*. Sometimes writers vary their sentence lengths to create particular effects. A series of short sentences, for example, can increase the pace and excitement of a text, while a long involved sentence can slow the pace of the text.

Leila ran! She ran swiftly. She didn't look back. She ran for her life.

Leila meandered slowly along the rocky path, kicking at pebbles, scuffing her shoes, thinking ponderous thoughts.

Help students understand the meaning of the terms 'colloquial language' and 'slang'. Read students extracts of conversations in novels such as Aidan Chambers's *The Present Takers* and Allan Baillie's *Hero*. Compare and discuss the use of slang to represent the characters in the novels. If these particular novels are not available in your school it does not matter. Any novel that uses slang in conversations between the characters will do. Ask your school's teacher/librarian to find extracts for students to explore. Also examine the thinking and feeling and saying verbs used in the dialogue to build readers' understanding of the characters and what motivates them.

Make sure students understand that diaries are examples of personal writing: the usual audience for the writing is the writer. Diaries provide writers with an opportunity to 'let off steam', to rant and rave, and write whatever they like. Often diary writing is like speech written down. Have students read *Dear Diary* out loud, as if they are talking to a friend.

Grammar Focus: Commands, conjunctions
Type of Text: Informative – Procedure/Instructions

Student Book 5
Unit 32

Instructions advise what is to be done under particular circumstances, such as mending a bike tyre, cleaning a fish tank or avoiding aliens. The goal or aim is often included as a heading: *What to Do if Aliens Land in Your Neighbourhood.* Instructions are usually written in point form as a series of steps or commands.

Read *What to Do if Aliens Land in Your Neighbourhood* to the class. Ensure that students recognise the humour in the instructions. Make sure they understand that the writer was not being serious, but is 'poking fun' at the topic or the situation. The writer used the structure and grammar of a procedural text and used it to make fun of the topic while making fun of procedural texts at the same time. Discuss each separate instruction in *What to Do if Aliens Land in Your Neighbourhood* and consider whether each is feasible in the event of aliens really landing in the neighbourhood.

Have students work in groups to create a set of tongue-in-cheek instructions. They can choose any topic they like. They could write instructions for keeping children entertained on a road trip, dealing with siblings, dealing with ghosts and so on. Tell them to include warnings and other safety advice in their instructions. Make sure they use the appropriate structure and grammar of procedural texts. Have them create posters to display their instructions. They can illustrate their posters. Discuss how they have demonstrated their understanding of the way tongue-in-cheek humour works in texts.

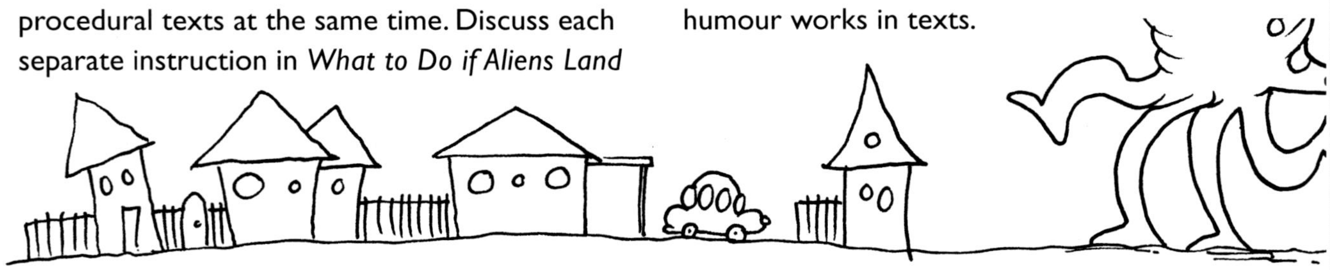

Grammar Focus: Connectives, reference chains
Type of Text: Informative – Recount/Biography

Student Book 5
Unit 33

Biographies are recount texts. Biographies retell significant events in a person's life. The biography *Andy Thomas, Astronaut* is written in time order after the opening, introductory paragraph. Information is presented in chronological sequence. *Andy Thomas, Astronaut* ends with a personal comment about the life of Andy Thomas. This is the only section of the text that moves away from fact and gives the writer's opinion. Ensure that students recognise the difference between fact and opinion in the text.

Have students summarise the main events in the recount. This will assist them to recognise the chronology of events.

Songs are often written about famous people. Have students work in groups to create a song about the life of Andy Thomas. Allocate students to mixed-ability groups and try to ensure that a student with musical-rhythmic intelligence is allocated to each group. Students should firstly choose a familiar tune. Tell them to work out their chorus. They can then sing aspects of the biography to the tune. They might consider arranging three verses and repeating the chorus three times. They might consider having half the group hum the tune while the rest of the group sings the words. Tell students their songs do not have to be factual. They can make up extra things about the astronaut such as *'he's a true blue Aussie – he eats Vegemite sandwiches before a space flight'*. Allow time for rehearsal then have groups sing for the rest of the class.

As an extra activity to explore biography and past tense, students could research another famous person and create a comic strip summary of the significant events in the person's life.

Grammar Focus: Connectives, lexical chains
Type of Text: Persuasive – Discussion

Student Book 5
Unit 34

The Cost of the Space Program is a discussion text. Discussions include a number of points of view on a topic or issue. In this discussion, the contrasting opinions are linked using connectives such as *nevertheless* and *on the other hand*. The discussion uses the opinions of experts to substantiate the points of view. The final paragraph provides a summing up of the discussion. Point out to students that it does not necessarily present the writer's opinion or judgement. Ask if they can tell what the writer's opinion might be. Is it evident in the text? Discuss the grammatical features of the text with students.

A text hangs together, or is cohesive, based on patterns of words that run through the text. This is a lexical chain or chain of content words. Any text can have a number of lexical chains. Lexical chains can include nouns and noun groups, verbs and verb groups and adverbs or prepositional phrases. Recognising lexical chains assists students when they are researching and need to skim through or scan texts to search for particular points of interest.

Dictagloss is a useful activity to assist students in making notes, recognising lexical words and learning to listen for key words and phrases in a spoken text. Instructions about Dictagloss are included page 14.

The Cost of the Space Program is an example of the type of text that could be used as a jigsaw cloze. In jigsaw cloze, texts are cut into paragraphs or smaller sections such as sentences. Students need to reassemble the sections in the correct order. The four paragraphs of this text have four distinct purposes structurally and therefore allow students to focus on structure to reassemble the whole text.

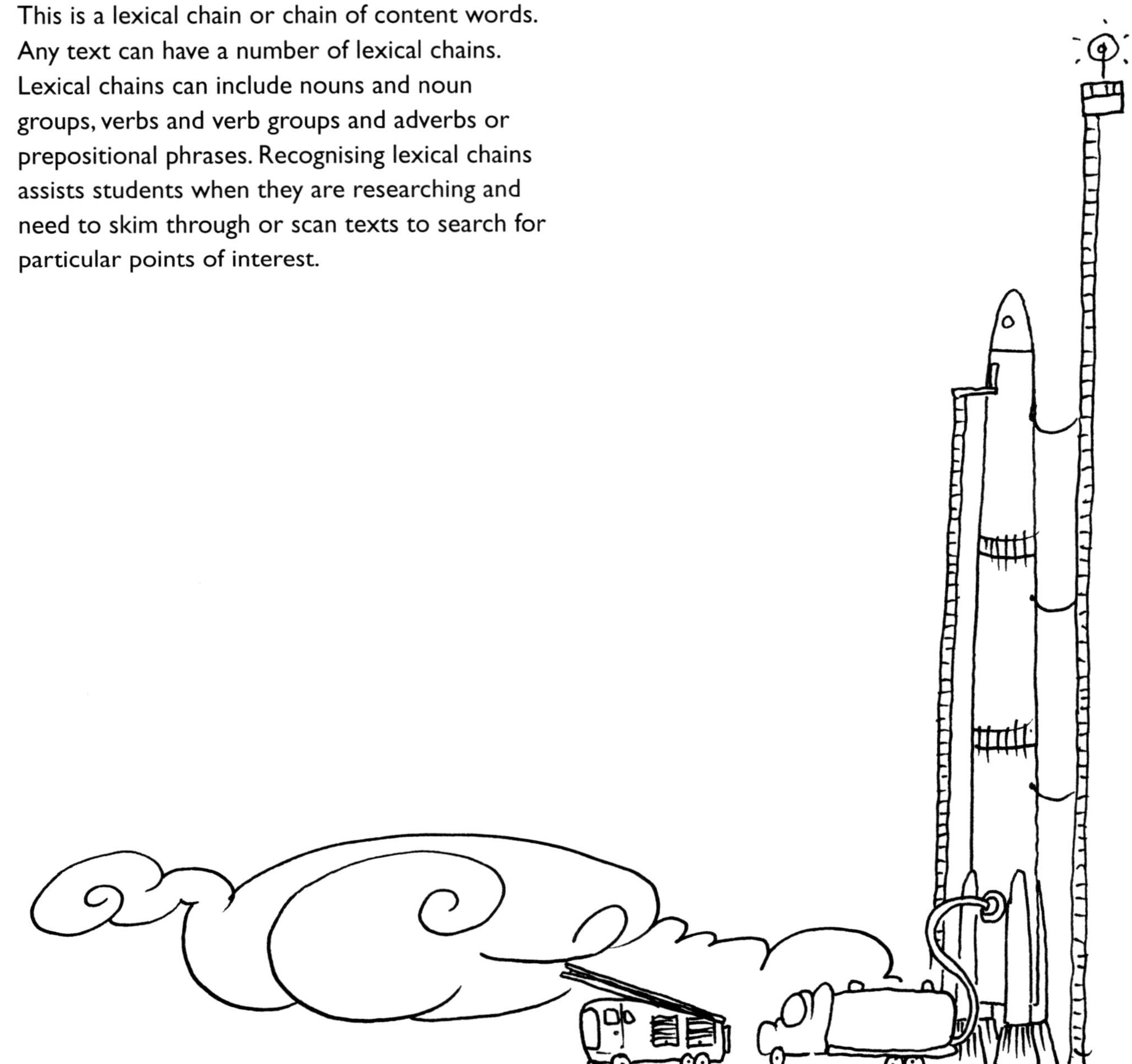

Student Book 6

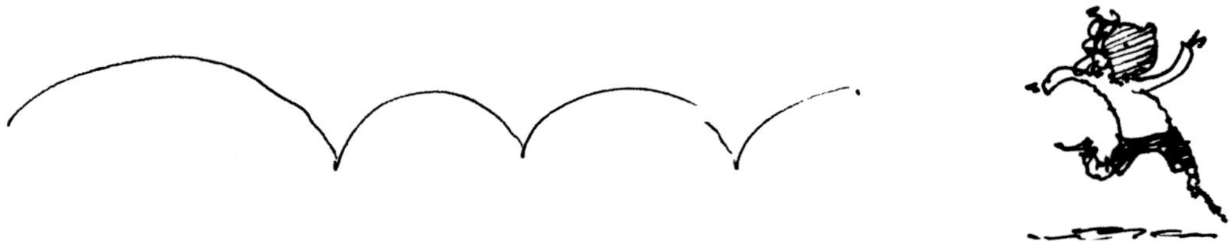

Scope and Sequence

This scope and sequence chart is based on the requirements of the Australian Curriculum.

Unit	Unit name/ Type of text	Clause to whole text level			Word and word group level		
		Sentences and clauses	Cohesion: theme, pronouns, lexical chains, connectives	Mood and modality, language and vocabulary	Nouns and noun groups	Verbs and verb groups	Adverbs and prepositional phrases
1	**Dear Grandma and Grandpa** Recount/Email		conjunctions (connectives)			verb groups; auxiliary verbs; past tense; verbs	adverbs
2	**Green Sea Turtles of the Great Barrier Reef** Description			similes; subjective and objective language	noun groups: descriptive and classifying adjectives		
3	**My Trip to the Zoo** Recount	simple and compound sentences; clauses	conjunctions (connectives)				adverbs that modify adjectives; adverbs that modify verbs
4	**The Monster in the Labyrinth** Narrative/Myth			similes; antonyms	number adjectives; descriptive adjectives; classifying adjectives		prepositional phrases
5	**Sea Lion Encounter** Response		personal pronouns; possessive pronouns: *his, hers, theirs, yours, mine, ours*		possessive adjectives: *his, her, their, your, my, our, its*		
6	REVISION						
7	**The Defender** Narrative/Radio play		ellipses	statements, questions, commands, exclamations	adjectives	doing verbs	
8	**My Journal** Response/Journal entry				noun groups; determiners; possessive adjectives; number adjectives; descriptive adjectives; superlative and comparative adjectives; absolute adjectives		
9	**The 'Most Famous' Famous Landmark** Discussion	quoted (direct) speech; speech marks				verb groups; regular and irregular verbs; past, present and future tense; saying verbs	
10	**Sydney Shows Off** Information report/ Newspaper article	reported (indirect) speech		synonyms; emotive language; sensationalism			
11	**Greetings from the North-West** Recount/Postcard	addressing mail		contractions; abbreviations; apostrophes; colloquial language			
12	REVISION						
13	**Travel Bugs** Procedure/Instructions	clauses	theme; reference chains; pronouns		noun groups	doing verbs	
14	**Curse of the Pharaohs** Narrative	complex sentences; clauses; comma	connectives; relative pronouns: *who, whose, that, which*; ellipses			verbs	
15	**Safe Travelling** Procedure/ Recommendations	main clauses and subordinate clauses: adverbial and adjectival	connectives; relative pronouns			relating verbs; doing verbs	
16	**Come to China!** Advertisement		theme	modality; emotive language; synonyms	descriptive adjectives	modal auxiliaries	adverbs

Unit	Unit name/ Type of text	Clause to whole text level			Word and word group level		
		Sentences and clauses	Cohesion: theme, pronouns, lexical chains, connectives	Mood and modality, language and vocabulary	Nouns and noun groups	Verbs and verb groups	Adverbs and prepositional phrases
17	**Uluru** Response	compound and complex sentences; clauses		relative pronouns; conjunctions (connectives)	adjectival phrases	verb groups	
18	REVISION						
19	**Where Would You Go?** Exposition			fact and opinion	collective nouns; apostrophes for possession; word sets		
20	**Land Sale!** Persuasive/Parody			collocation; parody; synonyms	compound nouns		
21	**A Future** Poem		lexical chains: reference chains, antonyms, subclasses, part/whole relationships		definite and indefinite articles (determiners); proper nouns		
22	**Mummification** Explanation		connectives		subject of verb	active and passive voice	
23	**Time Travel** Narrative		personal pronouns		noun groups with adjectival phrases		adverbs; adverbial phrases
24	REVISION						
25	**Correspondence** Response/ Correspondence			vocatives; questions; question tags; informal and formal correspondence			
26	**The Taste of Travel** Description/Menu		lexical chains	metaphor; synonyms	noun groups; proper nouns; descriptive adjectives	verbs	
27	**The Rights of the Child** Exposition/Radio interview			proverbs; fact and opinion; emotive words; acronyms		subject-verb agreement	
28	**Top Wonder** Discussion		connectives	evaluative language		relating, thinking and feeling, and doing verbs; complex verb groups	
29	**Why Mount Everest is Still Growing** Explanation				subject of verb	active and passive voice; auxiliary verbs; relating verbs	
30	REVISION						
31	**Chichén Itzá** Interview transcript		internal (anaphoric) and external (exophoric) reference; personal pronouns; demonstrative pronouns		determiners		
32	**African Lion Safari, Kenya** Advertisement			personification; homophones; synonyms; antonyms; metaphor; prefixes	nominalisation	verbs	
33	**Indigenous Languages** Information report				abstract and concrete nouns; nominalisation; collective nouns; adjectives	verb groups	
34	**Multicultural Australia** Information report	brackets	lexical chains	etymology; prefixes; suffixes	noun groups; compound nouns		
35	REVISION						

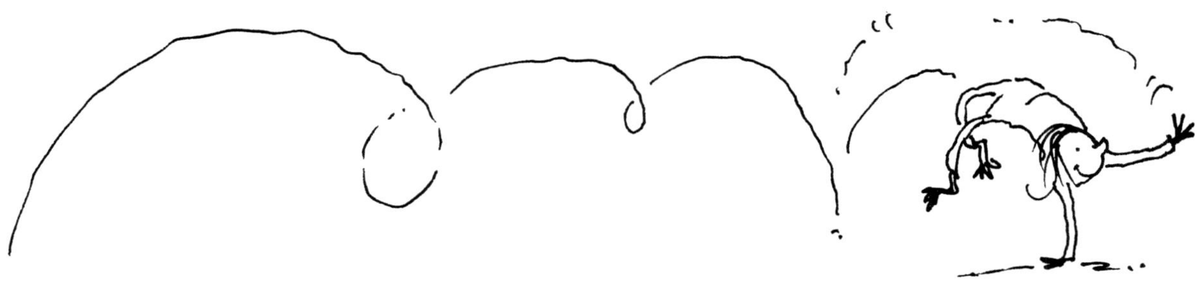

Grammar Focus: Past tense verbs, adverbs, conjunctions
Type of Text: Informative – Recount/Email

Student Book 6
Unit 1

The focus of this unit is words and word groups that function to represent the time frame for events in the text. Time is represented in the past tense verbs *(arrived, went, had travelled)*, adverbs *(yesterday, today)* and time conjunctions *(when, then)*.

Time adverbs such as *yesterday* and *today* can give information about when events occur or occurred, as well as details about where, how, with what or about whom they occurred. Recounts often make use of time words.

Divide the class into groups. Have groups work on a storyboard for a video clip of Kenan's holiday. Imagine he was being filmed. What images and scenes would be presented in the footage? Students will need to firstly list the events recounted in the email. Then they will need to note the setting for each event. Then they should decide on a type of shot (long, mid, close-up). Instructions for storyboards are included on page 19. Tell students to caption or label their storyboards.

Display and discuss the representations of the events in the recount in each storyboard.

Revise the four types of verbs with students: action, thinking and feeling, saying and relating (being or having). Make a class chart or poster for each kind to display in the room. Brainstorm examples of each kind with students and discuss their functions in a text. Include examples of verb groups on the posters as well as single verbs. Make sure students recognise auxiliary verbs (helping verbs) as part of the verb group. Have volunteers illustrate the posters.

Grammar Focus: Noun groups, similes
Type of Text: Informative – Description

Student Book 6
Unit 2

Descriptions can be found in narratives, information reports, poems and other texts. Descriptions make use of noun groups to build detailed images of the person, place, animal or thing. Read the description *Green Sea Turtles of the Great Barrier Reef* with students. The description is not from a scientific report or information report. Ask students to identify the words and phrases that would be out of place or inappropriate in a scientific description *(love to eat, tasty seaweed, gentle, the shell is a cross between circular and heart-shaped, might grow, like a canoe, like little aliens, tropical paradise)*. If possible, find scientific descriptions of green turtles or any other creature and discuss the way descriptions are represented factually and without emotive language *(love, paradise)*.

Discuss where this description could be found: travel brochures, guides for tourists to the Great Barrier Reef, conservation brochures requesting donations to protect the green turtle, for example. These uses for the description allow for more emotive use of language and more literary descriptions of the turtle and its environment.

Simile is common to literary descriptions, narratives and poems. Similes function to describe an aspect of a noun. Ask students to search for examples of simile in class novels and poetry anthologies. In each case, ask students to identify the particular description represented by the simile.

It is possible to find hundreds of examples of simile on the internet to share with students. Students can create posters, illustrations or a class book of similes to display in the classroom.

The unit deals with classifying and descriptive adjectives in the noun group and how they function to build meaning. Other possible components of the noun group will be dealt with in later units (possessive adjectives, articles, number adjectives, phrases and clauses).

Grammar Focus: Sentences, adverbs
Type of Text: Informative – Recount

Student Book 6 **Unit 3**

This recount uses time connectives and past tense verbs to retell events in a time sequence. It starts with an orientation, describes events in chronological order, and concludes with a summing up or judgement statement.

A clause is a group of words that expresses an idea and contains a verb. A simple sentence is a single, independent clause. Independent clauses make sense on their own. Some clauses depend on other clauses in sentences to make sense. Clauses that cannot stand alone, or make sense on their own, are called dependent clauses.

Use jigsaw cloze activities to help students recognise simple sentences and independent clauses. Have students work in pairs or groups of three. Have each group write five independent clauses on strips of cardboard. Tell students to cut their sentences into individual words and place each sentence in an envelope. Distribute the envelopes to different groups of students and have them reassemble the sentences.

The first group to complete the task is rewarded in some way that is appropriate in your school.

Unit 3 deals with compound sentences. Compound sentences are formed when two or more independent clauses join together in one sentence. They usually join together with a conjunction such as *and, but, or, until, so, whereas.*

Students need to understand the concept of a sentence and the punctuation marks involved. They also need to know that the clause is the basis for meaning in texts. How clauses are linked across different types of texts helps the text to make sense and be cohesive, logical, chronological and organised in order to achieve a social purpose.

Grammar Focus: Prepositional phrases, adjectives
Type of Text: Imaginative – Narrative/Myth

Student Book 6 **Unit 4**

Remind students of the structure of narrative texts and the function of orientation, complication, series of events and resolution. The sample text *The Monster in the Labyrinth* is a portion of the Greek myth 'Theseus and the Minotaur'. Myths are ancient stories that developed to try to explain a natural phenomenon such as thunder. Myths often involve supernatural beings, monsters and superhero characters. Display other examples of myth in the classroom.

Extend students' knowledge about noun groups. Discuss number adjectives and the information they provide about precise or vague quantities, and cardinal numbers *(one, two, twenty)* or ordinal numbers *(first, second, last)*. Ask students to identify the noun groups in the text sample and discuss how the descriptions build an image of the Minotaur and the labyrinth.

Prepositional phrases function in narratives to set the scene for events. They can tell where, when, how, or with whom. Make sure students can readily recognise prepositions and then find the prepositional phrases to explore how they function in the text. Make a class poster that lists prepositions.

Have students work in pairs to draw complex scenes or settings for narratives on art paper. They can draw any combination of roads, paths, gardens, bridges, waterfalls, rivers, trees, cliffs and so on. Photocopy the scenes. Then have them add characters to one copy of the scene. Have them devise sets of questions such as *Where is the cat?* Specify that answers to the questions need to be prepositional phrases such as *on the branch, in the tree.*

Have them write instructions for the other copy of their scene: *Draw a cat in a tree.* Give the prepositional phrases games to classmates, younger classes or ESL teachers within the school for students to consolidate their understanding of prepositional phrases, especially prepositional phrases that tell where.

Grammar Focus: Pronouns
Type of Text: Persuasive – Response

Student Book 6
Unit 5

Talk to students about the use of pronouns in texts. Pronouns are words that replace nouns, or refer to nouns that have already been mentioned in a text, or are understood in the context.

Written text: *The sea lions . . . they*

Spoken text: *Pass it to me*. (The pronoun *it* refers to is understood in the context but not mentioned in the wording of the text.)

Recounts, responses, diaries and narratives make use of the pronoun *I*. Using *I* can help a writer to tell what the character is thinking and feeling and so develop readers' empathy for the character. *Sea Lion Encounter* is a persuasive response. The speaker or writer is speaking from a personal perspective and relating events that impacted on him or her. Display examples of response texts in the classroom.

Words in the noun group function to point out *(that sea lion)*, or show ownership *(her pup)*.

Point out to students the difference between possessive pronouns that show ownership (such as *mine, yours, hers*) and possessive adjectives, which also show ownership. Possessive adjectives are part of the noun group. They function to give information about the noun. They are called possessive adjectives because they add to the description of the noun.

That hat is mine. (possessive pronoun)

That is my hat. (possessive adjective)

Determiners in the noun group will be covered more comprehensively in Unit 8 of the student book.

Grammar Focus: Types of sentences, verbs
Type of Text: Imaginative – Narrative/Radio play

Student Book 6
Unit 7

Explain the concept of a radio play to students. Radio plays are written to be performed on radio or recorded and played on radio. Historically, radio plays were performed live to air, in the radio studio, in front of a live audience. At some venues in Australia, particularly in regional centres, radio plays are still performed. Radio plays have different requirements to stage plays because over the radio there are no visual effects, gestures or body language. Sound effects, music and voices are used to create the desired atmosphere and impact. Narrators fulfil the role of describing visual information for listeners. Point out the list of characters, their dialogue, the use of colons before each character's speech, and the directions for the actors' voices, as well as the background noises.

Record students performing *The Defender*. Have students organise the sound effects for tigers, the roaring crowd, cages being flung open and so on.

Talk to students about the pace of the text *The Defender* achieved by the number of very short sentences. Point out that the short sentences work to speed the reading and help make Ishmael sound very frightened. The variety of sentence types used in the play also help to add atmosphere to the narrative.

Have four pairs of students create posters to define statements, questions, commands and exclamations. Have them include examples on their posters. Make sure they realise that all sentences commence with a capital letter and that sentences must end in a full stop, question mark or exclamation mark.

Have students work in groups to write, perform and record their own radio plays.

Grammar Focus: Determiners, adjectives
Type of Text: Persuasive – Response/Journal entry

Student Book 6
Unit 8

My Journal provides the writer's personal response to the issue of immigration. It begins with an opening statement, presents opinions and reasons, and then concludes with a final opinion or evaluation.

Select a few students who enjoy the challenge of researching for information, and have them investigate the difference between an 'asylum seeker' and a 'refugee'. Have students present their findings to the rest of the class as their own response to the information they found, or as an information report.

Ask students to identify words in *My Journal* that represent the writer's opinions and evaluation *(strange, new, lucky, scared)*. Discuss the concept of a journal as a person's private thoughts and feelings. Your school library may have narratives that use journal entries to propel the story. Ask your librarian to find some examples of private writing to share with the class.

This unit deals with determiners in a noun group that point out (including the articles *a, an, the*) and possessive adjectives that show ownership. Discuss these with students. Make posters for display in the classroom.

Revise other types of words that are used in noun groups: descriptive adjectives, classifying adjectives and number adjectives. Help students learn to build interesting and accurate noun groups to represent people, places, animals and things, including abstract nouns for things such as *friendship*.

Ask for volunteers to create a poster defining comparative and superlative adjectives for display in the classroom.

Have students write response texts to current affairs issues that you have discussed in class or that students have seen on the news.

Grammar Focus: Verb tense, quoted (direct) speech
Type of Text: Persuasive – Discussion

Student Book 6
Unit 9

The 'Most Famous' Famous Landmark is a discussion text. Discussions offer differing viewpoints on a topic. Discuss the structure of the text with students. Point out the introductory statement; the first viewpoint, introduced by the words *many people suggest*; the second viewpoint, introduced by the words *other people believe*; and the writer's opinion in the final paragraph presented as a summing up and a judgement.

Revise auxiliary verbs with students. *Auxiliary*, as a word, means to 'support or provide back-up'. Auxiliary verbs support main verbs by:

- representing tense: *I did walk the dog. I have walked the dog. I am walking the dog. I will walk the dog.*
- matching verbs to the number of subjects (ie singular or plural nouns): *The cat is eating dinner. The cats are eating dinner.*

Modal auxiliaries indicate degrees of certainty *(will, would, might)* or obligation *(should, could)*. Modal auxiliaries are useful in presenting viewpoints. Help students understand the function of parts of the verb group.

Verbs have a base form that is regular or irregular. Regular verbs form their past tense by adding *–ed* or *–d (shopped, danced)*. Irregular verbs form their past tense in a variety of other ways including adding *–t* or *–en (kept, have chosen)* or changing the middle vowel *(sank, has sunk, knew)*. Student need to learn the various rules and exceptions for spelling past tense verb forms (see the notes for *Student Book 4*, Unit 31, on page 72).

Demonstrate for students how to write a discussion text. The topic could be the construction of a landmark in your local area. Propose a landmark such as a bronze sculpture of your principal or some other icon relevant to your community. Ask students for viewpoints 'for' and 'against' the landmark.

Grammar Focus: Reported (indirect) speech, emotive language
Type of Text: Informative – Information report/Newspaper article

Student Book 6 **Unit 10**

Newspaper articles use sensational language, and emotive words and phrases to capture and hold readers' attention. Newspaper articles are sometimes presented as recounts with events described in time order. This newspaper article, *Sydney Shows Off*, is an information report. It presents information about the event. The information is not written in chronological order. It is written in 'newsworthy' order. Have examples of newspaper articles available for students to read to determine how the events are written – as information report or as recount. Examine, also, the way people are quoted in newspaper articles. Sometimes people are quoted in direct speech using speech marks. Sometimes there are quotes presented as reported or indirect speech.

Divide students into groups and ask each group to role-play a scene where a newspaper reporter is interviewing people about New Year's Eve. The people interviewed could be any person who has something to say about New Year's Eve. Have students decide on their roles in the scene and rehearse and then perform for the rest of the class.

After the performances, have students work in the same groups to write newspaper articles based on their role-plays. They should use sensational and emotive language to present the information. Tell them to use quoted and reported speech to record what the interviewees said. Make sure students write a sensational headline. They can provide an illustration to show what sort of photos would accompany their articles. Tell each group to add a caption to their photo.

Provide time for students to present their newspaper articles to the rest of the class. Discuss their efforts.

Grammar Focus: Colloquial language, contractions
Type of Text: Informative – Recount/Postcard

Student Book 6 **Unit 11**

Greetings from the North-West is a postcard written by grandparents to a grandchild. The postcard is for a familiar audience so it uses colloquial language and slang. Discuss some of the slang terms used by students in the school or that they have picked up from television or the internet. Start a class list of these terms with their definitions. Tell students that these terms change over time and are generational. Tell them some of the slang terms used when you were their age or have them interview parents and grandparents for slang terms popular when they were younger. Display the list in the classroom and add to the list as the school year progresses.

The postcard also includes contractions. Contractions are shortened words that have an apostrophe where a letter or letters have been left out. Contractions are more commonly used in informal language than in formal language situations.

Verbs can be contracted after a pronoun: *we've (we have), we're (we are).*

Verbs can be contracted after a noun: *Broome's (Broome is), countryside's (countryside is).*

Jointly construct with students a letter that Nonna and Poppy would write to their accountant, informing her that they will be away longer than expected. They can advise their accountant that they are having a good holiday and tell her about some of the things they have seen in the north-west. The writing will be more formal than the postcard to Tatiana and more formal again than the postcard students write for question 3. Demonstrate for students the way language choices are affected by audience. Talk to students about ways to start correspondence, and ways to sign off.

Ask students to identify the three compound words in *Greetings from the North-West: countryside, grandparents, upside.*

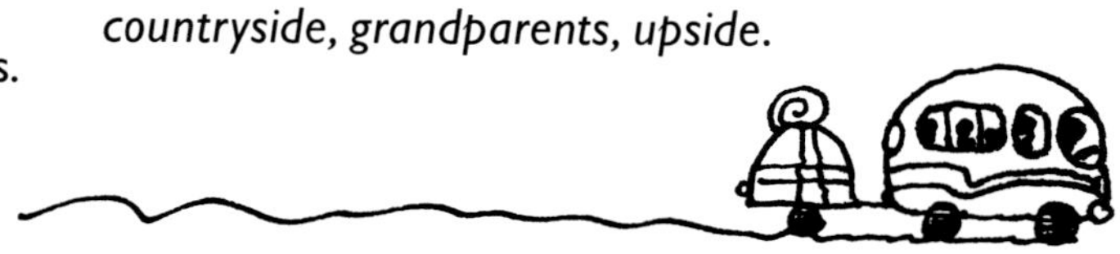

Grammar Focus: Theme, reference chains
Type of Text: Informative – Procedure/Instructions

Student Book 6
Unit 13

In grammar, the term 'theme' refers to the first grammatical component of a clause. It could be a noun group or pronoun, a prepositional phrase or adverb, or a verb or verb group. A conjunction may be included in the theme if it links to previous information in the text.

The cat curled in a ball but he did not sleep.

The cat curled in a ball and (he) went to sleep. ('He' is an ellipsis – it is understood.)

Into her kennel crept the dog. She was ready for sleep.

Yesterday was too hot. Today should be cooler.

Wash your hands. Dinner is ready.

Theme is typically what we can take for granted as the 'given' in the text. Understanding how theme works to hold a text together and assist a reader to access the flow of information in the text is useful for students when constructing their own texts or interpreting the texts of others.

Each type of text has a typical pattern of theme. Instructions based on commands often use a verb in theme position. If all the commands begin with a verb but one command has a different theme, the different theme stands out. This is called a marked theme.

Write the following instructions on the board or chart paper. Ask students to identify the theme in each clause. Ask them to identify the marked theme.

Add the carrots. Add the pumpkin. Stir in the potatoes. Heat through. Carefully pour into a blender. Blend thoroughly.

Grammar Focus: Joining clauses, commas
Type of Text: Imaginative – Narrative

Student Book 6
Unit 14

The text *Curse of the Pharaohs* provides the orientation and complication for a story. The function of the orientation is to introduce the characters and set the scene for events. The complication is where something has to happen to change the lives of the characters in some way. The complication in a narrative is usually a problem or a series of problems that the characters had to solve, overcome or learn to deal with.

Talk to students about narrative texts that they know and the various complications the characters have faced in the texts. Make a class chart under the following headings:

Title and Author

Orientation: list the characters and setting

Complication/s: what problem/s are faced by the characters?

Events: list the series of events

Resolutions: how were the issues resolved? (Point out that sometimes in novels the problems are not solved – the characters just learn to live with them. Also, usually, in narratives the characters learn about themselves and others in the process of overcoming their problems.)

Narratives can have different structures or sequences to deal with orientation, complication, events and resolution. Narratives are not necessarily written in chronological order. They can start at the resolution and then provide the orientation and complication. They can flash back, flash forward, commence with a prologue, cover dual time frames and so on.

Narratives can also take different forms: picture book, novella, novel, play script, storyboard, radio play, cautionary tale, fable, folktale, fantasy, science fiction, historical recount, legend, myth, mystery, realism, social realism, crime, romance, diary, journal, ballad.

Display a variety of narratives in the class for students to explore.

Encourage students to reflect on the structures of the novels they have read and consider how the authors presented orientation, complication and resolution.

Grammar Focus: Subordinate clauses, relating verbs
Type of Text: Informative – Procedure/Recommendations

Student Book 6
Unit 15

Remind students that clauses must contain a verb and that independent clauses make sense on their own while subordinate (dependent) clauses depend on other clauses for their meaning.

Tell students that subordinate clauses can function as adjectives or adverbs, adding extra information to clarify the meaning of main clauses. The underlined subordinate clause below is an adjectival clause – it describes the shirt. It is a clause because it contains a verb.

Wear the shirt,/which ***has*** *red stripes.*

Compare the subordinate adjectival clause above with the following adjectival phrase (which has no verb): *Wear the shirt with the red stripes.* *the shirt with red stripes* is a noun group.

This subordinate clause is an adverbial clause – it adds information to the verb (it tells when).

You can eat / when you ***are*** *hungry.*

Don't let students get confused – the key to a clause is the verb! If they keep the verb in mind they will be able to identify clauses. But, at this stage, it really doesn't matter whether they add phrases or clauses to their texts, as long as their meaning is clear.

If possible, display some comic strips in the classroom for students to examine.

Have each student choose one of the *Safe Travelling* tips in the sample text and draw a three-panel comic strip to show what might happen if you did not follow the tip. Tell students to exaggerate the consequences so that the comic is more humorous. They can use captions. They can use speech balloons. They can also add words to assist with time frames, such as *Meanwhile . . .; Later that day . . . ; the next day . . .* Display and discuss the comic strips.

Grammar Focus: Emotive language, modality
Type of Text: Persuasive – Advertisement

Student Book 6
Unit 16

The social purpose of an advertisement is to persuade people to buy something or to take some form of action. Advertisements use high modality to sound more convincing. Read the advertisement *Come to China!* with students. Allow students opportunities to read the ad aloud to each other in groups and practise using high modality vocal tones.

Discuss aspects of modality with the class. Modality is the way a text communicates certainty, obligation, usualness or inclination. Use of modality varies across types of texts. Information reports, for example, use high modality because they deal with the way things are rather than the way things might be. *Whales are mammals.*

Discussions often use low modality to express possibility or probability. Low modality keeps the discussion open to negotiation: *We could go to the movies.*

Thinking verbs can contribute to the modality of a text.

Low modality: *I think I agree with that.*
I wonder if you've considered this.

High modality: *I know that for a fact.*
I believe I am right.

Modal auxiliaries and adverbs contribute to the modality of a text.

Mum really loves banksia trees. They probably will plant a grevillea.

You absolutely must get your homework finished.
Maybe you shouldn't eat that cake.

Have students work in pairs and write an anti-ad for an advertisement of their choice. An anti-ad is an advertisement based on antonyms. An **antonym** is a word that means the opposite: *tall* → *short, happy* → *sad.* The anti-ad will state the opposite of what is actually written in the real advertisement. Students can illustrate their ad if they wish. Display and discuss high modality, persuasive language and emotive language.

Grammar Focus: Compound and complex sentences
Type of Text: Persuasive – Response

Student Book 6
Unit 17

Uluṟu is a response. Read the text with students. Discuss the aspects of the text that let readers know it is not a scientific explanation or part of an information report. *Uluṟu* is a persuasive response. It uses evaluative words such as *beautiful, amazing* and *fascinating*. It includes a simile that compares Uluṟu to an iceberg. It concludes with a statement that makes a personal judgement.

Uluṟu includes the three types of sentences: simple, complex and compound.

In the examples below, verbs are underlined and clauses are separated with a /.

Simple sentence example: *I recently visited Uluṟu with my family.*

Compound sentence example: *Uluṟu stands 340 metres tall / and it is 9.4 kilometres around its base.*

The complex sentences are the most important kinds to discuss with students at this point. Students should explore the way information is connected across clause to clause.

The relative pronoun *that* is used to link these subordinate (dependent) clauses to their independent clauses.

*It is the most incredible place /**that** I have ever seen.*

It is filled with small native shrubs and flowers / **that** *miraculously survive in the dry red earth.*

The following complex sentence consists of two clauses linked by the adverb *when*.

*It is really amazing /**when** Uluṟu changes colour during the different stages of the day, such as sunset and sunrise.*

Discuss the noun groups constructed to describe different aspects of Uluṟu:

the most incredible place that I have ever seen; The vast, open, flat land around Uluṟu; small native shrubs and flowers that miraculously survive in the dry red earth

Grammar Focus: Fact and opinion, apostrophes
Type of Text: Persuasive – Exposition

Student Book 6
Unit 19

The text *Where Would You Go?* is an exposition text. It presents the speaker's opinion about visiting Antarctica. The viewpoint is supported by reasons. Before attempting the **Try it yourself!** activity make sure students understand that everyone is entitled to have an opinion, but that opinions should be supported by logical and well-presented reasons or arguments. Tell students that it also helps to have factual evidence to back up opinions in an exposition. Tell students that sometimes people make assertions that are untrue in order to persuase someone.

Learning to recognise opinions is important for students to deconstruct other exposition texts, such as advertising, as well as newspaper editorials, magazine editorials that accompany advertisements, political speeches and so on. When trying to determine whether a statement is fact or opinion it helps to look at the context of the statement. Who has made the statement and under what circumstances?

A magazine article promoting a vitamin company placed alongside an advertisement for vitamins made by that company should alert students to 'read between the lines'. Another example of the need to read between the lines would be a television advertisement that claims nine out of ten dentists recommend a certain toothpaste. The viewer of the ad would need to ask which ten dentists made that statement. The statement would be factual if ten dentists were given the specified toothpaste to compare with, for example, a garlic-flavoured toothpaste, created for the survey. The facts, though, may have been distorted to suit the purposes of the advertisers. Ask students if they can think of examples of misleading advertising or exposition texts.

Question 2 has two statements that some people would consider to be factual and others would consider as opinions. Discuss this with students.

Grammar Focus: Parody, collocation
Type of Text: Persuasive – Parody

Student Book 6
Unit 20

Read the ad with students. Have a number of students pretend to be real estate spruikers. They can role-play making a vocal sales pitch to sell the land to the rest of the class. Tell them to use their voice, gestures and body language and add any extra words and phrases that they need to the ad.

To appreciate parody, the reader or listener needs an understanding of the type of text and the subject matter. Have a few students locate information about the Great Victoria Desert on the internet and share their findings with the class. They can find out about the size and geography of the area, as well as any other issues.

Discuss how the advertisement is a parody. Ask students how the ad pokes fun at real estate advertising: what language choices tell us the ad is a parody? *(peaceful and tranquil, pristine wilderness, development opportunity, paradise)*

The name of the Real Estate company 'Burke and Wills' is another clue that the ad is a parody. It refers to Burke and Wills, the explorers who became famous because they were the first white people to cross Australia from south (near Melbourne) to north (Gulf of Carpentaria). They made the trip in 1860 but both died in the desert on the way back south.

Many students for whom English is a second language struggle to learn how certain words collocate. For example, the word *make* collocates to words such as *money, lunch, mistakes* and *friends* but not to *homework, business* or *study* (you don't 'make homework', 'make business' or 'make study'). Students also might have difficulty working out which prepositions are appropriate, for example *having something on your mind and having something in mind; the prisoner is accused of stealing; good will triumph over evil; this is a once-in-a-lifetime opportunity; I give up.*

Grammar Focus: Lexical chains, articles
Type of Text: Imaginative – Recount/Poem

Student Book 6
Unit 21

The cohesion of a text depends on factors such as lexical chains, theme, connectives and reference. 'Cohesion' means how a text holds together. Chains of content words in a text represent the field or subject matter. Chains of content words in a text are called lexical chains. Dictagloss is an activity that focuses students' attention on the content words in a text. See page 14 for an explanation of how to conduct a Dictagloss.

Poetry often condenses, or synthesises, language down to content words. The poem *A Future* is lexically dense. The poem consists of seven chains of content words. If we wrote the first stanza in full sentences we would need to add a lot more words:

Yousif's grandparents migrated to Australia from Greece in 1949. Yousif's grandfather worked as an engineer on the Snowy Mountains Hydro-Electric Scheme. This scheme was considered a miracle of engineering in the Snowy Mountains.

Reconstruct the other stanzas of the poem as sentences to show students how poetry often does away with words that are not content words and are excess to meaning.

Talk to students about the inverted commas around *'home'* in stanza three. They signify that home in Australia is a different home from the home they had in Bosnia.

The poem illustrates the contribution to Australia made by asylum seekers, refugees, boat people and immigrants. Discuss the definition of each term with students. Verbal-linguistically gifted students, or students interested in further research on this topic, could visit the government immigration websites for information to share with the class.

Discuss the cultural backgrounds of students in the class. Display their stanzas written for question 4. Have students perform recitations of their stanzas on assembly.

Grammar Focus: Active and passive voice
Type of Text: Informative – Explanation

Student Book 6
Unit 22

'Active voice' and 'passive voice' are ways of describing whether the 'doer' (agent) of the action is the subject of the verb or whether the 'done to' (affected or goal) is the subject of the verb.

In active voice, the subject of the verb is the 'doer' of the action. The 'doer' of the action is in theme position in the clause.

The Egyptians	*built*	*pyramids.*
subject	verb	object
doer	verb	**done to**

Who <u>*built?*</u> The Egyptians – they were the 'doers' of the action. The goal of the action was the pyramids. Active voice is the most common pattern in texts.

In passive voice, the subject of the verb has the action done to it. The goal or the affected is in theme position, not the 'doer' of the action.

Pyramids	*were built*	*by Egyptians.*
subject	verb	object
done to	verb	**doer**

What <u>*was built?*</u> The pyramids – they were the 'done to' of the action.

Passive voice can be used to make texts appear more objective. The 'doer' becomes less prominent than what is actually being done. The focus shifts from 'doer' to 'done to'.

Their cat was run over by a car. (passive)

A car ran over their cat. (active)

Some passive voice clauses leave the 'doer' out altogether. This is called 'agentless passive'.

The cat	*was run over.*	
subject	verb	(no object/ agentless passive)
done to	verb	no 'doer'

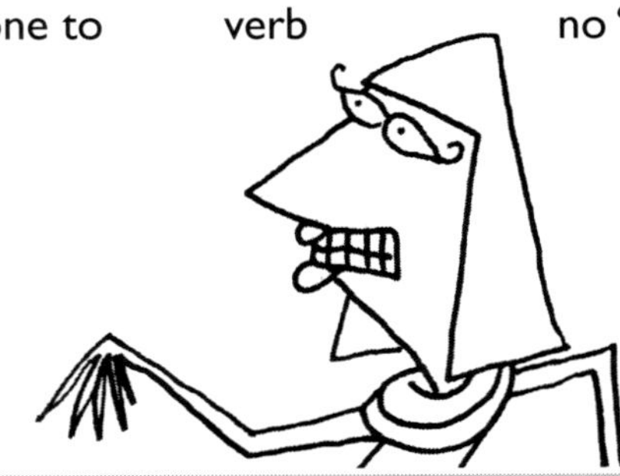

Grammar Focus: Adverbial phrases, personal pronouns
Type of Text: Imaginative – Narrative

Student Book 6
Unit 23

Talk to students about the character of Vince and what they know about him from *Time Travel*. Talk to students about the way the point of view of characters is revealed in narratives. This occurs through the voice of the narrator and dialogue. Sometimes stories are narrated in the 1st person; 1st person pronouns *I* and *we* are used to tell readers what the character is thinking and feeling. Sometimes a story is narrated in the 3rd person but from the perspective of one particular character. Sometimes there is a voice of the narrator, which is usually the author's voice. Dialogue can be used to reveal what characters are thinking and feeling. Thinking and feeling verbs also help readers to understand a character's feelings and motives and enable readers to empathise with characters.

Ask students to write how they would feel if they were in Vince's position. Tell them to write a paragraph to describe Vince's feelings as he realises what has happened to him. Share and discuss their writing.

Help students to empathise with the characters in novels they are reading. Point out the thinking and feeling verbs, adjectives and voice of the narrator that contribute to our understanding of the character. Have students write diary entries for a character or letters to the characters telling the characters that they understand what they are going through. They can deal with main characters and also peripheral characters.

Some students can find it difficult to maintain 3rd person in their own narratives. They start writing in 3rd person but by the end of their stories they have switched to the 1st person. Increasing students' awareness of the narrator of a story will assist them in their own writing.

Grammar Focus: Vocatives, questions
Type of Text: Informative – Response/Correspondence

Student Book 6 **Unit 25**

In any context of language use, the relationships between the writers and readers, and between the speakers and listeners, determine the language choices made. The purpose, the subject and also the audience affect language choices.

Whether something is a question or a statement can also depend on the relationship between the people involved. A parent saying *Will you tidy your room, please* is not actually asking a question but making a command. The tone of voice used in the command will affect the way the command is received. Alternatively, the parent could use a question tag on a statement: *You will tidy your room, won't you?* This implies that a tidy room is expected and the question tag asks for confirmation. Questions can be formed by adding a question tag to the end of a statement, command or even a question.

When asking a spoken question the voice usually rises at the end. This is called a rising inflection. A rising inflection can indicate a question when grammatically there is no question. *You're coming* → *You're coming?*

Have students work in groups. Ask half the class the write an email from Tony to Andreas. Ask the rest of the class to write a letter from Mr Wilson back to Andreas. Discuss students' writing for different audiences.

If appropriate in your school, discuss students' understanding of the conventions of text messaging or emailing and computer correspondence. Discuss the evolution of short-hand terms such as LOL, :-) and ;-) and spelling such as c u l8er (see you later), which are used in emails and in text messages. Discuss how technology has created the need for new conventions.

Grammar Focus: Metaphor, lexical chains
Type of Text: Persuasive – Description/Menu

Student Book 6 **Unit 26**

Have students read the menu items in *The Taste of Travel* out loud so that they notice the alliteration in the menu. Alliteration is when a number of words start with the same consonant sound, for example *beef burritos; spices with the sweet flavours of sultanas*. Ask students to find all the words starting with the alliteration pattern s in *A Taste of Travel*. Add other s food words to this lexical chain.

Discuss the menu items in *The Taste of Travel* with students. Have they tasted these items before? Discuss the structure of the menu and the ways the noun groups provide detailed descriptions of the foods. Talk to students about the purpose of such detailed descriptions in a menu: to whet the appetite, to help patrons make the right choices from the menu, to tempt people to try things they might not have eaten before. Display recipe books containing foods from various countries, especially recipe books that show photographs of the foods.

Point out the term *waitstaff* used in *The Taste of Travel*. *Waitstaff* is a gender inclusive term for people who wait on tables at a restaurant. Discuss with students the way some words indicate gender.

Masculine examples include: *he, his, uncle, son, prince, drake, bull.*

Feminine examples include: *she, her, aunt, daughter, princess, duck, cow.*

Gender inclusive language should be used whenever appropriate (for example, *actor* for male and female actors rather than *actress, flight attendant* rather than *air hostess*). Words that are gender inclusive do not indicate a particular gender but apply equally to both genders.

Brainstorm a class list of gender inclusive terms for occupations: chef, pianist, pilot, doctor, judge, dentist, accountant, driver.

Point out the spelling of the term *complement* in *The Taste of Travel*. Compare its meaning to the word *compliment*.

Grammar Focus: Subject-verb agreement, proverbs
Type of Text: Persuasive – Exposition/Radio interview

Student Book 6
Unit 27

The Rights of the Child provides factual information as well as opinions to support an argument. It includes proverbs to illustrate the points of view.

Proverbs are short sayings that have a message or moral. Some proverbs come from old stories such as Aesop's fables. These stories were often told as lessons to children and were passed orally from generation to generation. Share some Aesop's fables with students. For example, *The Hare and the Tortoise* and its proverb 'slow and steady wins the race' or *The Lion and the Mouse* and its proverb 'one good turn deserves another'. Have students choose a fable of their own to reconstruct as a play script, comic strip, newspaper article or other form of their choice.

Some students might be allocated the task of researching the history of Aesop or the history of other collections of fables. Other students might research, for example, the work of UNICEF globally, The Universal Declaration of Human Rights, or the work of UNICEF in Australia with Indigenous Child Rights. Students can present their research findings to the rest of the class. They can present their research findings as an information report or as an exposition text that presents the points of view they have formed as a result of their research.

Have students create acronyms for themselves or work in pairs and create positive acronyms for each other. They should illustrate and display the acronyms in the classroom.

Grammar Focus: Verb groups, evaluative language
Type of Text: Persuasive – Discussion

Student Book 6
Unit 28

Point out to students the structure of the discussion text *Top Wonder*. The first paragraph introduces the topic. The second paragraph presents one viewpoint on the topic. The third paragraph presents an alternative viewpoint on the topic. The final paragraph sums up the opinions and then makes a judgement.

Remind students about the structure of the verb group. Verb groups can be defined as single verbs or a group of words with at least one main verb as well as one or more auxiliary verbs.

Auxiliaries help set the time frame. *Inez has played her trumpet.*

Modal auxiliaries help establish certainty or possibility. *Inez must have played her trumpet.* The modal auxiliary comes first in a verb group. Students can refer to them as helping verbs because that is their function. Explore how they affect modality. Teach students how to contract auxiliary verbs: *might* → *might've*.

When a verb group has two main verbs it is sometimes called a complex verb: *considered leaving, loved eating, hated losing, tried working.*

People evaluate or make value judgements in every context of language use, consciously or subconsciously. How you judge things depends on the sum of everything you have experienced and all the things in your life that have contributed to making you 'you' (ethnicity, gender, education, experiences, socio-economic background, religion, family background, employment, social group and so on). These things determine the 'who' you bring to any social interaction or context for using language. Your evaluation of the message will be biased based on 'who' you are. Discuss topics relevant to the class and endeavour to have students recognise differing points of view and the reasons for these. Help them to recognise that people should not be judged as inferior if their points of view differ from ours.

Grammar Focus: Active and passive voice, verbs
Type of Text: Informative – Explanation

Student Book 6
Unit 29

Read *Why Mount Everest is Still Growing* with the class and then have students construct flow diagrams to illustrate the sequence of events in the explanation.

Review active and passive voice with students. In active voice the subject of the verb does the action. The object has the action done to it. In passive voice the verbs are verb groups containing a main verb and an auxiliary verb. The subject of the verb has the action done to it. Clauses do not always need an object.

	Subject	Verb	Object
Active	*Jack*	*caught*	*the ball on the full.*
Passive	*The ball*	*was caught on the full.*	

(See the notes referring to Unit 22 on page 103 for more detail.)

Discuss *Why Mount Everest is Still Growing* with students. Talk about the structure of the explanation text, the use of technical or subject-specific terminology, and the words used to help sequence events. Discuss the component of theme position in each clause and then decide whether active or passive voice has been used. Passive voice is sometimes used in explanations when the agent is not as important as the effect. Placing the 'affected' or the 'goal' in theme position gives it more prominence.

Discuss the differences in the following pairs of sentences:

Your book was left out in the rain / I left your book in the rain.

We mixed yellow and blue paint to make green. / Yellow and blue paint were mixed to make green.

The charity group donated $1000 to the flood victims. / $1000 was donated to the flood victims.

Grammar Focus: Reference, demonstrative pronouns
Type of Text: Informative – Interview transcript

Student Book 6
Unit 31

Have two students read the interview *Chichén Itzá* as a play script. Allow practice time before they perform for the class.

Cohesion is a term used to describe how texts 'hang together'. A number of grammatical devices help with cohesion. These are: reference, lexical chains, ellipsis, connectives and theme.

Reference works in spoken language to link items within a text as well as items not expressed in words. Gestures also assist reference. Words in a text refer to other items in a text (or outside the text in the context of a spoken text). These reference words form the reference chains. Reference chains consist of nouns, personal pronouns and demonstrative words.

Demonstrative words include demonstrative pronouns: *this, that, these, those* (*<u>This</u> is my bus*). Remind students that pronouns replace a noun.

Demonstrative words can include words that point out, in the noun group *(This bus; that fish)*.

In spoken language reference is often accompanied by gesture and this can assist comprehension. Reference can also be made to things outside the immediate context and this form of reference in spoken texts can be difficult for students to follow, especially as the texts they deal with become more complex in school. Students for whom English is a second language can also find it difficult to follow the chain of reference in a spoken or written text.

Grammar Focus: Personification, nominalisation
Type of Text: Persuasive – Exposition/Advertisement

Student Book 6
Unit 32

Read the travel advertisement with students. Ask students to comment on any words or phrases that they find interesting or that they would like to discuss.

Discuss the lexical chains of antonyms and synonyms, as well as the use of words that appeal to the senses or are based on the senses for evoking the sights, sounds, smells and textures of Africa. Ask students:

Why would you listen as night descends rather than watch it descend? Why would you breathe in the immensity of the plains rather than look at their size? Why does the poet say that you sense the pride of the lions? What does stalking of the lion as it stalks its prey mean? How does night convey safety and danger?

The advertisement evokes the beginning of a trip, the journey and then the end of the trip as well as the passage of one day in time from dawn to night.

Have students create a series of visual art panels to represent the lines of the advertisement. Allocate one line to each pair or group of three students. Provide paint and cardboard for the series of large panels. Display the panels in sequence along with their line of the ad.

African Lion Safari, Kenya uses the poetic devices of personification and metaphor. Discuss these with students. You may also wish to discuss allegory, symbolism, assonance and alliteration. Discuss the difference between speaking figuratively and literally. Discuss the use of onomatopoeia in texts to represent the way things sound.

Have students write a response to the advertisement. Would they want to take an African lion safari, based on reading the advertisement? Why or why not? Have them justify their opinions with reasons.

Grammar Focus: Noun groups, abstract nouns
Type of Text: Informative – Information report

Student Book 6
Unit 33

Indigenous Languages is an information report. Its tenor is formal. It is lexically dense. It makes use of technical terminology. Read the report with, or to, students. Tell students that 'Indigenous' is a term used to refer to people or animals and plants that are native to a particular geographical area. Indigenous people live in all areas of the earth from the Arctic to the Amazon regions and throughout Australia. Indigenous cultures are distinctly different from each other but many share an affinity for the earth.

The various Indigenous 'nations' of Aboriginal peoples in Australia speak their own languages. Discuss the concepts presented in *Indigenous Languages* and the information provided about the number of Indigenous languages under threat of extinction. Discuss how a language can become extinct and ways to prevent this from happening. Discuss, for example, the importance of protecting culture and heritage, protecting sacred and significant sites and objects, passing on knowledge to others, and making sure younger generations are bilingual – maintaining their home languages as well as developing proficiency in English. Tell students that just as some conservationists work to save animals and plants, other types of conservationists are currently working to save Indigenous languages, worldwide.

If you have any picture books or word dictionaries available in Standard Australian English, Aboriginal English and Indigenous languages, display these in the room and provide time for students to explore the different language versions of the same words or stories. Consider viewing *Rabbit Proof Fence (2002)* with students.

Invite an elder from a local Indigenous community to talk to students about aspects of culture and language. If this is not possible in your area then consider organising penpals with students from a school in an Indigenous community. Exchange photos, letters, emails and stories.

Grammar Focus: Word origins, lexical chains
Type of Text: Informative – Information report

Student Book 6
Unit 34

Use *Multicultural Australia* to raise awareness of cultural diversity and languages. Talk to students about their cultural backgrounds. Have students create family trees or create posters of words in home languages to teach other students. Invite family members to share information about their cultures. Invite members of local community groups to share information about their cultures or show students photos or objects that have cultural interest or significance.

Tell students the definition of an 'Australian' is any citizen of Australia, regardless of their ethnic or cultural background, religion or country of birth.

Ethnocentrism is a belief that your own cultural group is superior to all other cultural groups. When society, organisations or institutions are ethnocentric it means that racial stereotypes are perpetuated.

Stereotyping is a concept that could be dealt with at this point in the program. Stereotyping means defining and labelling someone according to a simplistic view of a particular group or a characteristic, such as a physical feature, an occupation, their age, gender, cultural background or intellect. Stereotyping is usually discriminatory and misleading.

The term 'inclusive language' is used to describe language that does not exclude or discriminate against any particular group of people based on gender, disability, race, culture, religion or ethnicity.

Teach students how to use language that does not stereotype or show bias or prejudice. Endeavour to raise their awareness of the ways language contributes to stereotyping. For example, examine images of people used in advertising. Make sure that your school displays positive and appropriate images of Australians from all cultural groups as well as males and females, the elderly and people with disabilities.

Using inclusive language means that when discussing people with disabilities, you need to refer to the person first and the disability second and only if it is relevant. For example, use *people who are visually impaired* rather than *the blind*, or *blind people*. Also, do not label a person according to a disability: *He's a paraplegic*. Refer to the person in the following way: *He is a person with paraplegia*. It is also inappropriate to refer to people with disabilities as 'victims' or 'powerless': *wheelchair bound; polio victim*. Say instead that the person *uses a wheelchair* rather than is *confined to a wheelchair* and *had polio*.

Gender inclusive language should be used when you don't want to exclude one gender. Avoid stereotyping inanimate objects such as boats, ships and cars as *she*. Use *it*. Consider the gender inclusive alternatives for the following: manmade (manufactured), mankind (humanity/the human race/people/humankind) waitress (waitperson, waiter), weatherman/weathergirl (weather presenter), actress (actor), cameraman (cameraperson), fireman (firefighter), policeman (police officer), sportsman (athlete), chairman (chairperson), salesman (sales representative).

Avoid using gender suffixes such as *–ess (actress)* and *–trix (aviatrix)*. They are unnecessary in modern Australian English.

When addressing letters to an unknown recipient, write Dear *Sir/Madam*, or *Dear Madam/Sir*. When addressing correspondence to a female, always address the letter to *Ms* unless you know for a fact that she prefers to be addressed as either *Mrs* or *Miss*.

GRAMMAR PROGRAM CHECKLIST (*GRAMMAR RULES!* STUDENT BOOKS 3 AND 4)

	Concept	Date	Comment Evaluation/Follow-up
Clause to whole text level	**Paragraphs**		
	Sentences Statement Question Command Exclamation		
	Clauses		
	Modality		
	Quoted speech **Reported speech**		
	Personal pronouns		
	Reference chains		
	Theme		
	Lexical chains		
	Connectives		
Word and word group level	**Nouns** Proper Common Collective Plural and singular **Possession** **Adjectives**		
	Verbs Doing Saying Thinking and feeling Relating (being or having) **Tense** **Regular and irregular verbs**		
	Adverbs **Prepositional phrases** When Where		

 GRAMMAR PROGRAM CHECKLIST (*GRAMMAR RULES!* STUDENT BOOKS 5 AND 6)

	Concept	Date	Comment Evaluation/Follow-up
Clause to whole text level	**Paragraphs**		
	Sentences Simple, compound, complex Statement, question, command, exclamation		
	Clauses Independent and subordinate (dependent)		
	Modality		
	Quoted (direct) speech **Reported (indirect) speech**		
	Pronouns Personal, relative, demonstrative		
	Reference chains		
	Theme		
	Lexical chains		
	Connectives		
	Ellipsis		
Word and word group level	**Nouns** Proper and common Collective, abstract, concrete, compound **Determiners** Definite and indefinite articles **Apostrophes for possession** **Nominalisation** **Adjectives** Descriptive, classifying, number Superlative, comparative, absolute **Adjectival phrases**		
	Verbs Doing, saying, thinking and feeling, relating **Tense** Past, present, future **Regular and irregular verbs** **Auxiliary verbs** **Active and passive voice** **Subject/verb agreement**		
	Adverbs **Adverbial phrases** **Prepositional phrases** When, where, with what/with whom		

Student Book 3 Answers

Unit 1

1 people: mum, kids
places: museum, area, home
food: sandwiches, milkshakes, lunch
2 National Museum of Australia, Canberra, Lake Burley Griffin, Museum Café
3 options include: car, tree, film, bees, table, people, museum
4 dog, cat, bird, swan, wombat
5 ate, drove, worked, built, played
6 drove, took, saw, ate, closed
7 visited, swam, slept, worked

Unit 2

1 sandwich, games, day, game, hours, slices, bread, meat, players, meat, bread, hand, cards, friends, bread, meat, invention, sandwich
2 John Montagu, Montagu, Montagu, Earl of Sandwich
3 John Montagu lived in England.
The Earl of Sandwich was very rich.
Uncle Jack lives on Woodland Road.
Today is Friday.
My friends are Jin and Waiyin.
4 Answers will vary. For example:
apples, bananas, sandwiches; cards, toys, friends; pencils, crayons, chalk; parents, animals, friends
5 loved, hated
6 liked, hoped, loved, enjoyed
7 Answers will vary.

Unit 3

1 I, I, you, we, I, you, us, me, I, you, I, you, you, I, YOU
2 Answers will vary.
3 The finish it hungry dog: Not a sentence
The dog ate my homework: Sentence – needs a full stop or exclamation mark
Nan and Pop: Not a sentence
Dad told me which: Not a sentence
Can Mum cook pancakes: Sentence – needs a question mark
4 Answers will vary.
5 think, had thought, miss, love
6 like, hope, love, think

Unit 4

1 he, he, them, he, They. Note: Some students may circle *himself*.
This is a **reflexive pronoun** not a **personal pronoun**.
he: the inventor they, them: the robots
2 He, them, They, She
3 It, He, them, It, It, They
4 Options include: peaceful, clever, fast, finished, robot, huge
5 inventor, island, explosion, boat
6 happy → smile angry → frown
scary → ghost ferocious → pirate
whiny → voice
7 Answers will vary. For example: fluffy cat, cute piglet, strong gorilla, smart scientist, old boat, noisy baby

Unit 5

1 complained, said
2 stated, asked, told, announced, cheered
3 Answers will vary.
4 I enjoyed it.
5 happy face
6 opinion, opinion, fact, opinion, opinion
7 Answers will vary.
8 Answers will vary.

Unit 6

1 Aunty Flo lives in Darwin.
Today is Wednesday.
School holidays start in April.
2 Answers will vary. For example: book, biro, pencils, chairs, desks, students, teacher, walls
3 jumped, invented, cooked
4 The cow jumped over the fence. The cat licked its paw.
5 loved, hated, believed, hoped, wished, heeded
6 them, They, We, us
7 I think potato chips are tasty.
I love to eat pancakes for breakfast.
Are you going to watch the movie? or You are going to watch the movie.
Go away!
8 cute → kitten sore → knee
bossy → king old → dog
beautiful → island
9 fact, opinion, opinion, fact
10 Answers will vary. For example: shouted, spoke, talked, cheered

Unit 7

1 at, of, under, through, into, beneath
2 over, under, through, on, behind
3 over, beside, from, around, above, along
4 near, towards, under, around, beyond
5 Answers will vary. For example:
at the swimming pool; under the water; through the jungle; into the building
6 Answers will vary. For example:
The lorikeets chattered in the tree.
The dog squeezed through the gate.
The tiger prowled along the riverbank.
The worms wriggled under the ground.
7 special, scraggy, prickly, dark, still, quiet, secret, discovered, hidden
8 Answers will vary.
9 Answers will vary.

Unit 8

1 has, was, was, was, had, is
2 was, is, are, belong, had
3 Donkey Kong game/Nintendo company
4 They, He, it, them, she
5 They/~~Them~~ ~~Him~~/He It/~~She~~ ~~they~~/them She/~~Her~~
6 child-friendly, video game, inventors, storyline, electronics, Pac-Man, international company
7 monitor, mouse, program, delete, screen saver
8 Donkey Kong, Nintendo, Beauty, Beast, Pac-Man, Japanese

Unit 9

1 Alexander Fleming was studying bacteria growth in 1928.
Bacteria are germs that can cause infections in people.
Penicillin was discovered by Dr Howard Florey and his colleagues.
Howard Florey was from Australia.
Penicillin works by killing bacteria.
2 Where is the treasure?
What time do you go to bed?
3 In 1928, Ten years later, Since then
4 Answers may vary. For example: soon, now, afterwards, tomorrow
5 5: Today is Saturday and I have a soccer game.
2: The next day my ankle was really sore.
3: By Thursday it felt a lot better.
4: Yesterday I could walk and run again.
1: On Tuesday I had soccer practice and hurt my ankle.

Unit 10

1 and, so, but, and
2 unless, so that, because, therefore
3 I have missed Nick since he moved to Bathurst.
I'm pleased you're here because now we can test our device.
It has buttons as well as lots of dials.
Everyone can come except Benny.
4 dogs, boys, girls, balls, beaches, mouths, toes, lids, caskets
5 person, foot, man, woman, leaf, lolly
6 ~~run~~/runs ~~swims~~/swim eat/~~eats~~

Unit 11

1 Crack!, Snap!, It was her hidden valley!
2 Answers will vary.
3 Answers will vary. For example: Ouch!, Ahhh!
4 carelessly, angrily, unsuccessfully, heavily, suddenly
5 crazily/wildly, fiercely/wildly, carefully, wildly/fiercely
6 Answers will vary.
7 Crack, snap
8 Answers may vary. For example: woof, meow, hiss, sizzle

Unit 12

1 in, beside, under, over
2 between, up, down/along, near/in/on
3 Answers will vary. For example:
I like to swim in the pool.
I wear a hat at the beach.
The mice jumped into the tunnel.
I keep my tools on the back of the truck.
4 Answers will vary. For example: cheeky, little; squishy, old; useful, new
5 have, are, is, am
6 ~~they~~/them She/~~Her~~ ~~It~~/He it/~~them~~ him/~~he~~
7 Answers will vary.
8 Answers will vary.
9 tonight, Tomorrow, today, soon
10 I love playing netball because I am a good goal shooter.
The dog can come inside except when it has muddy feet.
11 hats, tables, children
12 foot, toe, wish
13 Answers may vary. For example: lazily, happily, quickly, slowly

Unit 13

1 Dad's speech: "I'd say that jumping on a trampoline is good exercise, as much fun as jumping on the bed but probably safer than jumping on the bed,"; "What do you think?"; "You certainly are not allowed to jump on the bed. Jumping on the bed is dangerous with all the furniture nearby, so it's just as well the trampoline was invented,"
Henry's speech: "Dad,"; "Do you think the trampoline was a good invention?"; "I really like jumping on the bed but I'm not allowed,"
2 Answers will vary.
3 Answers will vary. For example: "Who invented the trampoline?" asked Henry.
4 Answers will vary. For example: "I don't know but we could find out," said Dad.
5 "I want a turn!" shouted Billy.
"That's so funny," giggled Marie.
Dad whispered, "Santa Claus might bring a trampoline."
"Can I have a turn?" begged Susan.
6 suggested, lectured; asked, reminded
7 whispered, yelled, whined, laughed, asked
8 good exercise, fun, safer than jumping on the bed
dangerous with all the furniture nearby
9 I'd, I'm, it's
10 isn't, can't, would've, should've, I'll, you'll

Unit 14

1 Deni's speech: "Don't be a chicken. We might discover treasure, and it will be fun,"; "What if? What if? What if? Look, the fact is, there is absolutely no such thing as a ghost,"; "So stay here or come with me but I'm going in." "Well?"
Amy's speech: "No Deni, I really don't want to go in there,"; "You've heard the stories about that house! What if they're true? Also it's trespassing,"
3 Amy folds her arms in front of her.
She is defending herself from Deni's name-calling. She feels threatened and scared.
4 She raises her eyebrows.
She is challenging Amy not to be afraid and to follow her into the house.
5 Amy: doesn't want to go into the house; there might be ghosts; It's trespassing; She's frightened;
Deni: She wants to go inside; There might be treasure; It will be fun; There are no ghosts
6 I really love pizzas, I want to go, It's definitely haunted, It is not yours
7 Answers will vary. For example: Deni because she has a forceful determined personality and she is daring Amy and will go in anyway without Amy. Or Amy will refuse to trespass and Deni will follow her home calling her names like 'chicken' all the way (but will not have been brave enough to go in on her own).

Unit 15

1 Start, Step, Step, Turn, Slither, Dig, reach
2 begin/commence, walk/pace, slide/wriggle, burrow
3 Not a command, not a command, command, not a command, command
4 2: Walk out the door of your bedroom.
1: Start at your bed.
5: Go in and brush your teeth.
3: Turn left and walk down the hall.
4: Walk through the first doorway on the right side of the hall.
5 Answers will vary.
6 at the big oak tree, in the backyard, to your left, towards the dog's kennel, towards the fence, towards the water tank, towards the tank, beneath your waist
7 on your stomach
8 sideways, backwards, down

Unit 16

1 Answers will vary. For example: needed a spare hand, run out of time, enough time to eat, the answer, don't miss out
2 Answers will vary.
3 rush, hasten, act now, run
4 It chops, cooks, cleans and also feeds you your food – it will do everything in the kitchen.
5 I will have a lunch order today, You must hug your teddy, They will be late
6 To convince you that you need the kitchen hand. The questions are designed to make you say "yes".
7 you
8 it
9 we

Unit 17

1 a, a, an, The, the
2 the strangest and most peculiar thing I had ever seen; the way; its hind legs; the way; its huge tail; its beady little eyes; its tail and hindquarters too big for its body; its head too small; the creature; a very tiny brain; that quite frightening-looking tail; a weapon; some damage; the creature; the safety of the ship
3 strangest, peculiar, huge, beady, little, big, small, tiny, frightening-looking
4 taller, tallest; darker, darkest; smaller, smallest; greater, greatest
5 more, most, most, more
6 strangest, most peculiar

Unit 18

1 "Take me with you!" screamed Louie.
"I would like to go, too," suggested Rhami.
"I think that's a good idea," replied Pop.
Marty sniggered, "Good."
2 Answers will vary. For example: "Oh dear! The fish is dead," said Dad.
"What a good reader you are," announced Mum.
3 I'm, can't, I've, could've, don't, isn't
4 I am very pleased, I will go, I lost my ball, Dad will be home soon.
5 explode, read, jump, run
6 2: Turn on your computer.
4: Open your file.
1: Sit at your desk.
3: Log in your name.
7 Answers will vary. For example: Run to the shop, Jump on the trampoline, Reach for the stars
8 Jetto, because the children look happy and friendly and the can has stars fizzing out of it and looks exciting
9 louder, loudest; smarter, smartest; kinder, kindest
10 funnier, funniest, tidier, tidiest
11 Answers will vary.

Unit 19

1 Davy Jones's locker
2 If they find Davy Jones's locker it means their ship has sunk to the bottom of the sea and they are dead.
3 fit as a fiddle → very healthy shake a leg → hurry up
nothing to sneeze at → something worthwhile
crook as Rookwood → very sick
kick the bucket → die high and dry → stranded
4 wind's, waves', ship's, Jones's
5 Molly's map, Oliver's compass, The sun's rays
6 the twins' chest, the sailors' yachts, the birds' nests
7 slept like → a log as blind as → a bat
the ship tossed like → a cork stubborn as → a mule
dry as → a bone

Unit 20

1 because, Firstly, Secondly, Finally, and so, So, and
2 5: So, choose sandwiches for lunch today.
2: To begin with, sandwiches are healthy.
4: Finally, sandwiches can easily be packed for school lunches.
1: I think sandwiches are good for lunch.
3: In addition, sandwiches are economical.

3 Firstly, and, Secondly, while, In addition, Finally
4 Fact: a black horse, the wattle tree in Nan's yard, a bottlenose dolphin, Pop's poodle
Opinion: a beautiful horse, the doddery old man, the lazy dog, annoying children
5 So, get active now and collect and recycle those cans!

Unit 21

1 "I'm going to invent a cure for stinky feet – or in scientific terms, 'curus maximus stinkolata footitis'," announced Professor Snodgrass.
"Oops!" proclaimed Professor Snodgrass.
"Back to the drawing board," sighed Professor Snodgrass.
2 Answers will vary.
3 Answers will vary.
4 The term could mean a cure for very stinky feet.
5 Real-life scientist: works in a laboratory or in the field, dresses professionally, intelligent, works safely, male or female, may or may not wear glasses or contact lenses
Stereotype comic-strip scientist: works in a laboratory only; wears daggy, nerdy clothes; male only; nutty and mad; wears crooked, broken glasses; does crazy experiments and always causes explosions

Unit 22

1 A real live dinosaur was found at the school.
2 Dinosaur Bone Found at Local School
3 Answers will vary – all acceptable as long as students justify their reasons.
4 Principal Chan said that the school community is very excited to have uncovered these incredible pieces of history.
5 Principal Chan said that she would like to thank UQ for its help.
Angeline Frolie, a parent, said that her children were too excited to sleep.
Teacher José Ramon said that at first they didn't realise what they had found.
6 Answers will vary.
7 Answers could include: Students and teachers at Sunny Side Public School; The principal, Julie Chan; the vegetable garden; The University of Queensland; the bones.

Unit 23

1 Every year, One night, until morning, The next morning, eventually
2 noticed, decided, climbed, reached, discovered
3 Present, Past, Future, Present, Past
4 I am eating. I will eat; I skipped. I will skip; I am playing. I will play; I am writing. I will write; I helped. I am helping.
5 Answers may vary. For example: climbed, raced, asked, fetched
6 Answers will vary.
7 correct order: during breakfast, before lunch, after dinner, at bedtime

Unit 24

1 Dad's keys, cat's paw, children's skateboards, teachers' cars
2 5: Therefore, I recommend soccer to everyone.
2: Firstly, it gives you a lot of exercise.
4: My third point is that it teaches you how to be part of a team.
1: I think soccer is a great sport.
3: Secondly, it teaches you lots of skills.
3 Answers will vary.
4 Nana said, "Your dad was fast as lightning when he was your age."
Dad said, "Nan's memory is a shot duck."
"What's a shot duck?" I asked.
"Something that is kaput," replied Dad.
"Well, what's kaput?" I asked.
"Guess," said Dad.
5 Answers will vary – make sure students sensationalise the topic.
6 The principal said that she was so happy to give the children a wonderful holiday.
Katy Chung from Year 6 said that she's always wanted to go to Fiji.
Teacher Nadia Vonstag said that at first they didn't believe him.
7 Present, Past, Future, Present, Past, Future
8 ~~go~~/went ~~buyed~~/will buy played/~~plays~~ ~~rid~~/rode
9 4: After school, we had gymnastics.
2: Before lunch, we marked our homework.
3: After lunch, we had art.
1: Before school, I went to the library.

Unit 25

1 A number of amazing inventions, Many people, Other people, Every child
2 Paragraph 1 → Introduce the topic.
Paragraph 2 → Present an opinion and give reasons.
Paragraph 3 → Present a different opinion and give reasons.
Paragraph 4 → Make a final recommendation or judgement.
3 because, because, however, because, and
4 because, since, so, unless, otherwise
5 I think
6 The Arguer: You are absolutely wrong, That is a stupid suggestion, Your opinion is ridiculous, You can't be serious.
The Discusser: I see what you mean but I'm not sure I agree, I understand what you're saying, That's a good point but I can't agree, Maybe you have a point.

Unit 26

1 The toaster is a hero.
2 Toaster: Kitchen hero; Working every day; Making hot, crispy breakfasts; champion
Cereal: Wholegrain flakes; Breakfast of champions; Crunchy, nutty, fruity, delicious breakfast
3 Answers will vary.
4 toast: hot, crispy
cereal: crunchy, nutty, fruity, delicious
5 fluffy → possum blue → iceblock prickly → cactus
square → box hideous → monster
6 Colour: white, red, green Shape: circular, round, square
Size: enormous, gigantic, tiny Quality: hungry, slow, filthy
7 Answers will vary. For example: delicious, superb, scrumptious, great, fantastic

Unit 27

1 1, 100, 1, 10, 2, all, four: precise
2 a pinch, enough, 1 cup, 1 L, 2 tablespoons
3 third, few, second, three, Many, hundred
4 Mix, Apply, Bandage, Avoid
5 Briskly, Gently, Carefully, Totally
6 mix, fry, stir, bake

Unit 28

1 1. Alarm rings and starts off five-minute timer.
2. Sleeper has five minutes to get out of bed.
3. If sleeper is not out of bed after five minutes, a latch is released, which causes the bed base to catapult forward.
4. Sleeper is ejected from the bed.
2 when, Once, when, then
3 because, if, in turn
4 rings, starts, finishes, is released, catapult, ejected
5 Catapult: a device for launching objects through the air.
Ejected: forced out of a position.
Pressure: the exertion of force onto something.
6 bed base, mattress with springs, alarm clock, timer, a latch
7 Answers will vary.

Unit 29

2 plastic-lined suction hose, dog's lead, environmentally safe chemicals, dog treats, drinking bowls, dog trolley
3 oak tree, Siamese cat, goldfish, rain cloud, money box, chocolate cake, football boot, fruit juice, handbag, marsupial mouse
4 Answers will vary.
5 Answers will vary. For example: kept on the footpath, any dog pulls too hard, it's pushed into grass, it is environmentally safe.

Unit 30

1 Since, in case, Otherwise, Unless, so
2 Colour: grey, black Shape: rectangular, narrow
Size: minuscule, gigantic Quality: cool, smooth
3 Answers will vary. For example: terrific, cute, lovely, great
4 Answers will vary. For example: Bells work when a small round bead bangs from side to side inside the bell making it clang.
Dog leashes work because they allow owners to hold on to their dogs and stop them running away.
5 Answers may vary: 2, some, many, 2, 1
6 first, few, Most, some, Thousands
7 Answers may vary: Clearly, Slowly, Carefully, Gently
8 exciting football game, ferocious male tiger, cute boxer puppy, fresh orange juice, healthy breakfast cereal

Unit 31

1 an Aboriginal or Torres Strait Islander person
2 problems, polluted, took, hunted, killed, no place, vanished
3 Answers will vary.
4 We, us, He, it, You
5 A tribe is a distinct group of people.
7 You, it, I, you, me, you, us
6 flock → seagulls   library → books
pod → whales   pack → wolves
herd → horses   bunch → flowers
7 a litter of kittens, a clutch of eggs, a team of players, a herd of cows, a flock of ducks, a school of fish

Unit 32

1 Billy: "Why can't we work on our project a bit longer?"
Mum: "Pack up all your equipment, now,"; "We need to set the table for dinner. Your experiment will have to wait until tomorrow,"; "No! There's no time. I think it's a great project but it can wait. Finish it tomorrow,"
Aggie: "But Mum, we just got everything organised. Can we just have another half an hour?"
2 requested, whined, insisted, added, declared
3 No!
4 Answers will vary. For example: Finish it tomorrow
5 Why can't we work on our project a bit longer? Can we just have another half an hour?
6 Answers will vary. For example: There's no time.
7 Answers will vary.
8 "Wow!" yelled Lucy.
"Where is my hat?" questioned Karl.
"I love lasagne," stated Fema.
"Stop!" shouted the coach.
9 Answers will vary. For example: whinged, complained, protested
10 Answers will vary. For example: ordered, stated, decided
11 Answers will vary. For example: stated, declared, yelled, announced, decided, ordered, bossed, sang, whispered, recited, giggled, shouted, laughed, nagged, sniffed, shrieked, kidded

Unit 33

1 My brother, the little scallywag, ruined everything, my meddling pest of a relative, the one whose name is Ben, broken the trap, set the mice free, Monster brother, laughing his head off, That five-year-old
2 Mice, my favourite pets, furry little rodents, likeable, Their cute little whiskery faces, their little paws
3 carrots, pumpkin, potatoes, apples, bananas, milk, bread
4 She is angry with him for ruining her invention and getting her into trouble with her mum. She thinks he is a pest.
5 Mum is angry that mice have escaped into the garden. She is angry with Katy for capturing the mice in the first place.
6 Ben thinks it's all a great joke. He thinks it's funny.
7 Answers will vary. For example: "I'm sorry I ruined your invention," apologised Ben.
8 "You shouldn't have kept all the mice in the invention. It's your fault," announced Ben.
9 Answers will vary. For example: To Katy: "Stop being angry with Ben and catch those mice," said Mum.
To Ben: "Help your sister catch the mice again and apologise for breaking her invention," declared Mum.
10 Answers will vary. For example: mouse, tiny, grey, scurrying creature, running around the garden, scaring Mum, nuisance
11 lime, green; predict, forecast; soaked, wet; enjoyed, liked; laugh, chuckle

Unit 34

1 the first money, coins, a mixture of gold and silver, the invention of money, the first true paper money, invented in China
2 They, the Greeks
3 the first money, people, a farmer, a cow, two pigs, rice, tobacco, animal furs, whale teeth, gold, people, pieces of paper, true paper money
4 Greeks, China
5 Answers will vary. For example: traded – exchanged goods; invention – a new original thing that no one has thought of before
6 Answers will vary. For example: Betty, Barbara, Rachel and Hannah
Joe, Tim, Stevie and Israel
Tiny, Squeaky, Jumpy and Cactus
Comics, books, marbles and pens
7 too
8 sail, weather, Their, By, flour

Unit 35

1 Answers will vary. For example: team, audience, herd, flock, pod
2 Answers will vary. For example: What time is it?
3 Answers will vary. For example: Hurrah!
4 Answers will vary. For example: Turn off the TV.
5 I, they, She, him
6 Answers will vary. For example: jump, skip, hop
think, believe, hope
is, am, are
yelled, shouted, whispered
7 Answers will vary. For example: huge, gigantic, enormous
8 greedy, funny, heavy, cool
9 We will need a hammer, some nails, a piece of paper, a pen and our thinking caps!
10 "Oh!" gasped Ralph.
"Does anyone have the football?" asked Jordan.
"Come here!" commanded the teacher.
"We need to finish our group project today," reminded Sunita.
11 Answers will vary. For example: playing, reading, writing, drawing, calculating, working, listening, watching, laughing, sharing, sitting
12

p	u	n	c	t	u	a	t	i	o	n	x
r	a	v	e	r	b	n	t	e	n	s	e
e	d	a	x	c	x	t	m	b	b	x	e
p	j	d	w	e	r	o	o	i	o	c	v
o	e	v	u	y	t	n	f	v	n	o	i
s	c	e	i	i	p	y	r	e	z	m	t
i	t	r	f	o	p	m	t	e	i	m	c
t	i	b	g	h	j	n	r	t	u	a	e
i	v	d	c	n	e	s	a	r	h	p	n
o	e	x	u	s	p	r	o	n	o	u	n
n	e	o	c	l	a	u	s	e	o	p	o
s	n	o	i	t	c	n	u	j	n	o	c

Student Book 4 Answers

Unit 1

1 the people: grandparents, grandma, grandpa
a place to stand: jetty
a place to live: home
the food they ate: fish, chips
2 Grandma lived in a caravan.
Dad cooked noodles.
I stood on the footpath.
The children rode bikes to school.
We saw dolphins in the waves.
3 mum, beach, sand, bird, ice
4 jumped, cooked, fixed, swam, walked
5 fished, caught, threw, kissed, bought
6 rode, ate, bought, bounced
7 ate, made, sailed, ran, chased

Unit 2

1 people: family, sister, Mum
places: Sandy Bay beach, home
things: sunscreen, waves, sandcastle, sand, car, ice-creams
2 Did Jasmine and Daniel have a holiday in Darwin?
I hope Maria can come to my party on Wednesday.
My birthday is in March and Nellie's birthday is in May.
3 Answers will vary. For example:
at the beach: sand, towels, seagulls
in your car: seats, steering wheel, windows
at an ice-cream shop: ice-cream, cones, scoops
in your kitchen: plates, toaster, sink
4 said, yelled, called, stated
5 and 6 Answers will vary.

Unit 3

1 thought, think, cares, wonders
2 loved, worried, hoped, felt
3 I like carrots but I don't like pumpkin.
It rained all day so we had to play inside.
I won the spelling contest because I studied hard.
I invited Ludmilla to my party because she is my friend.
4 Answers will vary.

Unit 4

1 relay: a twenty-five metre medley relay
race: a twenty-five metre backstroke race
carnival: its annual swimming carnival
Ms Ng: our school principal, Ms Ng
2 Answers will vary. For example:
her crazy little kitten
my school friend
the most difficult game
3 I, I, I, We, I, I, I, me, I('m), I, I, I, I
4 Answers will vary.
5 I, me, me

Unit 5

1 ocean: the deep, dark ocean; fish: tiny, jittery fish; appetite: a very big appetite; problem: a major problem
2 eat, swim, think, see
3 Answers will vary.
4 you, you
5 He, He, him
6 My friends and I are going to the bowling alley after school. We enjoy ten-pin bowling. The owner of the alley lets us have the same lane each week.
7 Bill: he; the boat: it; Diane: she; Helen and Kirstin: they; the house: it

Unit 6

1 The children went fishing off the wharf.
Nan and Pop cooked porridge for breakfast.
Bethany rides a bike to school.
I like tadpoles.
2 stepped, grated, mowed, cooked, picked
3 hopped, ate, bought, walked
4 Answers will vary. For example: said, mumbled, shrieked, demanded, announced
5 My aunty likes the music of the band, The Beetles.
I told Andre to come after school on Friday.
My birthday is in September and Emily's birthday is in October.
6 believe, think, worried
7 worried, thought, believed
8 I walked to the shop but I caught the bus home.
It was a beautiful sunny day so we went on a picnic.
I was allowed to watch television because I had finished all my homework.
9 Answers will vary.
10 My family and I like playing tennis together. We play each Saturday afternoon during the summer. The exercise keeps us fit.

Unit 7

1 insects: vigorous, pulsing, strident; flowers: vibrant, desperate; landscape: rocky, parched; air: steamy, heated
2 colourful grasshoppers
hungry dangerous crocodiles
timid little quolls
large grey cranes
3 Answers will vary.
4 Answers will vary.
5 Answers will vary. For example:
The funny old gentleman stepped out of his shiny new car.
The fussy young lady ate her enormous evening meal.
The lazy brown dog waited for her loving owner.
6 Answers will vary.

Unit 8

1 deep, wide: dam/hole; noisy: backhoe/cows/ducks; heavy, soaking: rain; hard-working: parents/mum; favourite, fresh: vegetables; generous, helpful: neighbour
2 we, I
3 precise: last; second; eight;
vague: few
4 halves, kangaroos, radiuses/radii (both acceptable), children, women, babies
5 herd, flock
6 a pod of whales; a pride of lions; a team of footballers; a fleet of ships; a string of pearls; a bouquet of flowers
7 Answers will vary.

Unit 9

1 his, theirs, hers, yours, mine, ours (Answers may vary.)
2 mine
3 Her, their, their, their, our
4 His, her, Their, its/her
5 Those are the twins' shoes.
Where is Amiri's dog?
The children's presents are here!
That is the teacher's desk.
Those are the sailors' yachts.

Unit 10

1 is, has, was, belongs
2 equals, was, is, are, belongs, had
3 conducts, are, had, crashed, thought, was
4 It is 2520 kilometres long.
It travels through New South Wales and South Australia.
Australia's longest river is the Murray.
5 I eat sea slugs.
Freya and Wilma said no.
Water flows.
6 Answers will vary.

Unit 11

1 How much fresh water is frozen in Antarctica?
Seventy per cent of the world's fresh water is frozen in Antarctica.
Which continent is the driest on earth?
Antarctica is the driest continent on earth.
Which continent is the windiest on earth?
Antarctica is the windiest continent on earth.
Where was the coldest temperature ever recorded?
The coldest temperature ever recorded, -89°C, also belongs to Antarctica. (Answers may vary.)
2 When will we eat dinner? question
Where are my keys? question
We'll eat dinner at 6 pm. statement
Did you phone Uncle Van? question
I'll set the dinner table for six people. statement
3 Answers will vary.
4 Antarctica is called a frozen desert because it is so dry.
Antarctica is windy and Antarctica is cold./Antarctica is windy and cold.
The old television doesn't work so we need to buy a new one.

Unit 12

1 Answers will vary. For example: five cranky crabs, some beautiful dolphins, etc.
2 its, my, his, Our
3 The shoppers' groceries; Mum's tea; Aunty Laura's dog; The teachers' cars; The library's books
4 is, are, was, belongs
5 Not sentences: I like to go to the; Too many sharks; By the way
6 Many children walk to school each day.
Cover your mouth when you sneeze.
We will visit our grandfather during the school holidays.
7 yours, mine, hers, his, theirs, ours
8 I'll clean my room **so** you can sleep over.
I would like sprinkles **and** topping on my ice-cream.
I can play **because** I have finished my homework.
The dog is hungry **because** he hasn't been fed yet.
The cat has been fed **but** she's still hungry.

Unit 13

1 in, inside, beside, from, near
2 on, beside, on, near, with, above
3 during the night; under the door; over the moon
4 their, their, there, They're, their
5 Answers will vary.

Unit 14

1 of a prince's hair, off the back, of the troll, under the bridge, of ogre's swamp, from a mermaid's tail, from the bottom, of the ocean, to the frog
2 Mix, Make, swallow, Close, (students may include chant but technically this is a saying verb)
3 Answers will vary.
4 stir, bake, cook, blend, fry
5 Answers will vary and should use four of the verbs: type, spit, throw, argue, yell, tell
6 1 Mix together the flour, butter and sugar.
 2 Add the sultanas and coconut.
 3 Make little balls of dough.
 4 Place balls of dough on an oven tray.
 5 Bake the biscuits for 35 minutes.

Unit 15

1 Get, Attach, Dangle, Sit, Pull, Bring, Keep, Release
2 Answers will vary. For example: Let me go!
3 quietly, patiently, swiftly
4 quickly, carefully, slowly, sweetly, bravely (Answers may vary.)
5 Answers will vary. For example: Carefully, Patiently, gently
6 Cross briskly.
 The children played happily.
 The dolphin jumped easily over the boat.

Unit 16

1 a dark-coloured sun shirt with long sleeves
 some SPF 30+ sunscreen
 a wide-brimmed, legionnaire or bucket-style sunhat
 some Cancer Council Australia recommended sunglasses
 some shade, the sun
2 house, photo, Rowan.
 Answers will vary. For example: She lives in the old run-down house across the street. etc.
3 Answers will vary.
4 She ate salad for lunch. Tibby jumped on the bed. Gran drove to work. Dad listened to music. My dog slipped on tiles.
5 slipped, slopped, went, slapped, slid
 When I went to the beach I slipped on a shirt, slopped on some sunscreen and slapped on a hat. I also slid on some sunglasses.

Unit 17

1 get, Turn, Walk, Cross, Turn, walk, come, Cross, turn, Walk, Cross, arrived (will have arrived is also acceptable as a verb group)
2 Walk, Fly, Catch, Swim, Crawl
3 Olsen Avenue, Olsen Avenue, Olsen Avenue, Smith Street, Smith Street, Charles Road, Charles Road
4 Aunty Freda, Dingle Street, Tiggles, Dimitri, Watson's
5 The letter is addressed to Robyn Nguyen at 29 Alfred Street, Pentiville.
 Uncle Hien lives in Ascot, which is a suburb of Brisbane.
 Cradle Mountain is a beautiful area in Tasmania.
 Frozen World Ice Rink is on Boona Street in Forestville.
6 Answers will vary.

Unit 18

1 Jacob threw three coins in the fountain.
 I dropped a shell on the floor.
 My neighbour stood at the window.
 The street was flooded after the storm.
 A bridge swung over the river.
2 Answers will vary.
3 hurried, ran, chased, was, enjoyed
4 mistakenly, greedily, noisily, frantically
5 Answers will vary. For example: stir, bake, fry, chop, mix
6 Answers will vary. For example: Keep your desk tidy.
7 Cross the road carefully. The children played noisily. The horse jumped clumsily over the fence. Mum sang loudly.
8 Answers will vary.
9 Santa Claus lives at the North Pole.
 My teacher's name is Ms Hickman.
 Debbie and Lucy went together to Frankie's house on Shark Island.
 The dog's collar stated its address as 101 Hill Street, Fairlight.
 King Neptune Child Care Centre is on Trident Street.

Unit 19

1 "I love you," said Dad.
 "Where are you?" called Louella.
 "Go away!" shouted Bindi.
 "How many apples will I get?" asked Teresa.
 "Eddie, please sit quietly at your desk," said the teacher.
2 "Help! Help!" called the little fish.
 "Does someone need my help?" asked Super Crab.
 "Super Crab to the rescue!" yelled Super Crab.
 "You're my hero!" said the little fish.
 "I can see lunch!" roared the big fish/shark. (Saying verbs may vary.)
3 Dad said that he loved me. Louella called out to ask where we were. Bindi shouted at them to go away. Teresa asked how many apples she would get. The teacher told Eddie to sit quietly at his desk. (Answers may vary.)
4 Answers will vary. For example: Hurray it's raining!; He's going to get soaked. I wish I had an umbrella.
5 Answers will vary.

Unit 20

1 The first Australian to ride a surfboard, Isabel, Isabel, Isabel, Isabel, she
2 Australia, The surf life saving movement, Surf Life Saving Australia, Swimmers
3 Answers will vary.
4 On Tuesdays, Eating fruit and vegetables, Occasionally
5 Practise, Apply, Swim
6 Rips are strong currents. They are stronger when the surf is bigger. They run out to sea. A tired swimmer can easily get caught in a rip. The worst thing you can do is panic.

Unit 21

1 is, developed, is called, evaporates, condenses, move, release, forms, flow, begins, has been recycled
2 The water has been recycled.
 It was developed a long time ago.
 It is called the water cycle.
 Water has been carried in clouds.
 The clouds have moved to the mountains.
3 had (past); have (present); were (past); was (past); is (present); are (present)
4 will, will, will
5 walked, hopped, ran, ate, borrowed

Unit 22

1 Install, Collect, Beat, Help, Reduce, Call, arrange
2 Answers will vary. For example: Harvest, Buy, Combat, Ring, Decrease, Save
3 Eat, Cross, Sit, Jump, Look
4 I will collect my own rainwater.
 I will beat water restrictions.
 I will help the environment.
 I will reduce my water bills.
 I will call now on 1309 999 99.
5 Answers will vary.
6 I, We, us, you, me

Unit 23

2 Lake Eyre is in South Australia. Lake Eyre is a salt lake.
 The Lake Eyre dragon is a lizard. The Lake Eyre dragon does not like to have hot toes.
 The Lake Eyre dragon is a reptile. The Lake Eyre dragon eats ants and tiny insects.
3 when, however, so
4 Lake Eyre dragons have sharp claws so the females can dig holes to lay eggs.
 Lake Eyre dragons have sharp claws; however, they cannot hurt people.
 Lake Eyre dragons and Pebble dragons live on Lake Eyre.
5 largest, deepest
6 bigger, biggest; smaller, smallest; slower, slowest; funnier, funniest
7 more, most, most

Unit 24

1 "Put it in the oven now," said Dad.
 "Where are you going?" asked Tahlee.
 "Stop!" shouted Roberto.
 "How is your new goldfish?" asked Zac.
 The pirate announced, "Be careful on the gangplank."
2 Liesl Jones is an Australian swimming champion.
 Andrew 'Boy' Charlton won an Olympic Gold Medal for the 1500 m freestyle in 1924.
 The first Australian Olympic swimmer was Freddy Land in Paris, 1900.
 The 2000 Olympic Games were held in Sydney.
 Ian Thorpe is one of Australian's all time greatest swimmers.
3 was held, has been competing, is recognised, was born, have proven
4 ran, hopped, said, read, chopped
5 past, future, present, present, past, future
6 I, us, it, you
7 slower, funniest, funnier, slowest, bigger, biggest
8 more, most, most, more

Unit 25

1 sewerage system, Sewage, all the used water and waste, Sewage, sewerage system, It is, sewage, no sewerage system, the waste
2 plugholes, toilet, kitchen sink, washing machine, dishwasher, bathroom sinks, showers, bathtubs
3 Answers will vary. For example: kitchen sink, toilet, garden hose, fish tank
4 Answers will vary. For example: swim, drink, splash, wash, squirt, cook
5 sewage: waste matter that is carried away by underground pipes
 sewerage: the removal of waste matter
6 Answers will vary.
7 Answers will vary. For example: On our holiday we went surfing, swimming, snorkelling, waterskiing and scuba diving.
8 Wash, Thoroughly wash, Germs, Flush

Unit 26

1 are made, begins to coat, keeps adding, keeps adding
2 past, present, future, past, present, present, present
3 when, then, until, so, therefore, and
4 because, however, when, After
5 Answers will vary.

Unit 27

1 Cane toads, They, Cane toads, Cane toads, they, the cane toad, Cane toads
2 Australian indigenous animals, such as snakes, lizards and water birds, are poisoned and killed when they attempt to eat the cane toad.
3 to change the focus to indigenous animals and the fact that they have no defence against the cane toad
4 Australia, Hawaii, Queensland, Australia
5 cane toads, Queensland sugar cane farms, sugar cane crops, Australian indigenous animals
6 long tennis | big humpback | webbed hind
 Australian | South Pacific
7 library → books | polar → bear
 snake → venom | shark → teeth

Unit 28

1 It's fierce, intelligent and an incredible predator, don't you think?
 To give his own opinion and because he expects Ali to agree.
2 You're coming aren't you? I can have it, can't I? You will give me one, won't you?
3 love, love, like, think, agree, sure
4 Answers will vary.
5 I love whales but I don't like eels. (to compare)
 Whales breed in warmer water, so they migrate from Antarctica up the coast of Australia. (to show one thing causes another)
 I like sharks; however, I prefer whales. (to compare)
 I love whales because they are gentle giants. (to show one thing causes another)
6 Ben: but, because; Ali: however, so

Unit 29

1 Places: the Daintree area in North Queensland; a great travel destination; the Daintree Rainforest; the Great Barrier Reef; the Daintree; the Daintree Rainforest; the ocean; the 135-million-year-old rainforest; a school holiday destination
 Animals: a cassowary; Cassowaries; flightless birds
 Things: the ocean; half-day and whole-day guided walks; the number of plant, tree and bird species; four stars
2 North, great, travel, Daintree, half-day, whole-day, guided, 135-million-year-old, flightless, endangered, rare, school holiday
3 Answers will vary.
4 The dog eats sausages. The baby cries for hours. The author visits all schools in the district.
5 will amaze, love, am sure, will love
6 Answers will vary.

Unit 30

1 our new soccer uniforms, Our boots, shorts, clean jeans, shoes, our jerseys
2 The cat, It, it
3 After a long time, The blue whale, The largest whale, The lake
4 Answers will vary.
5 boat, baby, hind, computer
6 You'll be late. statement
 You'll be late, won't you? question
 Don't be late. command
 Will you be late? question
 I hope you're not late. statement
7 so, until, and, but, because
8 Answers will vary. For example: carefully, swiftly, slowly, quietly, silently
9 The children ran past the teacher.
 The babies cry for an hour.
 The dogs eat a bone.
 The authors visit the school.
10 My friend Gemma is travelling to North Queensland for the school holidays in December.
 The Great Barrier Reef Marine Park is beautiful.
 Cassowaries live at Cape Tribulation.

Unit 31

1 Relating verb groups: is, was
 Doing verb groups: are mainly caused, erupted, caused, can also occur, reached, move, to be hit, erupts
2 mainly, quickly. Sentences will vary.
3 playing, played; walking, walked; receiving, received; laughing, laughed
4 flying, flew; taking, took; fighting, fought; drinking, drank; teaching, taught

Unit 32

1 forced, abandon
2 Answers will vary. For example: slaughtered, were forced, ripped off
3 reported speech: Local resident, Ted Egan, said he had advised Wickham Council last year that the council's drainage system would not cope with the amount of run-off that would result from a tropical cyclone combining with a high tide.
 quoted speech: "No school today!"
4 Terri said that her teacher would miss her.
 Mary Egan said that Ted had warned the council to look out for the next cyclone season.
5 Wickham Council member Deanne Cole said, "We will investigate the matter further."
 "Gee, I wish I could go to school," Terri Egan complained.
 Terri's brother told me he thought the flood was good fun.
 Mary Egan said, "I managed to rescue my cat, budgie, photo albums and handbag before climbing up to the roof."
6 The drains might not cope with the run-off.
 The council might/could do something.
 Homes might/could be ruined.
 People might/could be angry.
 People might not give up hope.

Unit 33

1 1. Anyone who wants to swim will swim outside of school so swimming in school is a waste of time.
 2. Swimming increases the risk of developing skin cancer.
 3. School time should be spent on indoor activities like spelling and grammar.
2 Firstly, A second reason, In addition
3 do not think, believe, wants, like, be expecting, feel
4 high modality, low modality, high modality, high modality
5 should, will, should not, would
6 Answers will vary.

Unit 34

1 at the bottom; of the swamp; on a quest; under a huge willow tree; inside a waterfall; towards it; through the cascading water; into a cave; on the other side; under it
2 Answers will vary.
3 Answers will vary.
4 Answers will vary.
5 Answers will vary. For example: Wearily, Stealthily, Hopelessly, Luckily, Happily

Unit 35

1 saw: irregular; bought: irregular; jumped: regular; tickled: regular; thought: irregular
2 "I love swimming at school!" exclaimed David.
"Why can't we swim every day?" asked Poppy.
"It wastes too much time," replied Tom.
"That's the whole idea," said Rachael.
3 The drains will not cope with the run-off.
The council must be able to do something.
Homes will be ruined.
People will be upset.
4 First of all, Secondly, Finally
5 Answers will vary. For example: are excited, chugged, is, sped, believe, are
6 Answers will vary.
7 Answers will vary.
8 Answers will vary. For example: Noisily, Carefully, Slowly, Quickly

Student Book 5 Answers

Unit 1

1 seven
2 simple, compound, simple, compound
3 correct conjunctions: so, because, but
4 Laika was harnessed into the spacecraft so she didn't move around too much.
Some scientists believe Laika showed no ill effects of her space flights until the oxygen ran out and she died.
Laika was a stray dog so no-one protested Laika's journey into space.
Laika died in space and she became famous.
5 she, she, she, she
6 she, he, it, it, her, him
7 Laika was a stray dog so the media named her 'Muttnik'.

Unit 2

1 Answers will vary. Students may use adjectives from the narrative, or think of some others.
Ferling: kind, gentle, nomadic
Moonberries: sweet, juicy
space: deep, wild, lonely
Grimly: not-so-friendly, fierce, huge
Planet: rocky, distant
Jupiternuts: tasty, little
2 Answers will vary. For example: busy, noisy classroom; happy, tidy school; annoying, boring homework; quiet, crowded library
3 the deep wilderness of space; a peaceful community of Ferlings; kind, gentle, nomadic creatures; the not-so-friendly Grimlies; sweet, juicy Moonberries; tasty little Jupiternuts; a gang of huge, fierce Grimlies; a nearby rocky outcrop
4 Australians, Earthlings, Iraqis, Germans, Japanese, Martians, Somalians, English
5 was flying, were giggling, is jumping, was shouting, has exploded
6 community, group, gang
7 is, were, was, are, is, is, is

Unit 3

1 An estimated 700 million people around the world watched in awe/ as the lunar module *Eagle* landed in the dusty Sea of Tranquillity,/and its Commander, Neil Armstrong, and Lunar Module Pilot, Edwin 'Buzz' Aldrin, stepped onto the surface of the Moon,/while the Command Module Pilot, Michael Collins, orbited above them.
2 An estimated 700 million people around the world watched in awe. The lunar module *Eagle* landed in the dusty Sea of Tranquillity. Commander Neil Armstrong, and Lunar Module Pilot Edwin 'Buzz' Aldrin, stepped onto the surface of the Moon. The Command Module Pilot, Michael Collins, orbited above them.
3 Over half a billion people watched televisions around the world/as Armstrong climbed down the ladder of the lunar module/and took his first footstep on the Moon's surface.
Aldrin joined Armstrong on the lunar surface/and described the moonscape as 'magnificent desolation'.
The astronauts were trained to control all equipment/ and land the module themselves/ if the computers broke down.
4 The *Daily News* sold out on the 20th July so the paper had to be reprinted because everyone wanted souvenir copies of the paper.
Armstrong and Aldrin walked on the Moon and Collins orbited above the Moon as the team on Earth watched excitedly.
5 watched, landed, stepped, orbited
6 The astronauts collected materials. Clause
rocks, soil and dust – not clause
They reprinted the paper. Clause
souvenir copies of the paper – not clause
the Kennedy Space Centre – not clause
7 During their walk, Armstrong and Aldrin collected rocks, soil and dust from the surface.
Because of their Moon mission, Neil Armstrong, Buzz Aldrin and Michael Collins are very famous.
During his time in orbit, Collins checked his instruments and equipment.
He was not injured, luckily.
Neil Armstrong, Commander of the mission, was the first person to walk on the Moon.

Unit 4

1 gentle, quiet, terrible, devastated, frightened, weird, mystical
2 Answers will vary. For example: Descriptive adjective – distant, special, happy
Classifying adjective – space, glitter, moon
3 later, Last night, tomorrow, Before, soon
4 Answers will vary. For example: quickly, swiftly, carefully, badly, hungrily
5 Answers may vary: below, above, inside, here, there
6 Answers will vary. For example: The man who was supposed to sprinkle glitter on the moon was on holiday.
Here is the blueberry pie that the restaurant is famous for.
The koala, which had a sore toe, climbed to the top of the tree.
The man who came to dinner was Dad's friend from work.

Unit 5

1 suggested, told, cheered
2 Answers will vary. For example: yelled, cried, whispered, shouted, announced
3 loved, remembered feeling, remembers thinking, will definitely enjoy, believe
4 Answers will vary. For example: hope, wish, love, believed, think
5 will, should
6 definitely, extremely
7 I really must go to the toilet!
8 You must stop – because it sounds more determined and forceful. It is higher modality.
9 high modality, lower modality, lower modality, high modality
10 Answers will vary. For example: extremely, absolutely, definitely, positively

Unit 6

1 It is cold in space so I need to wear a jacket.
I need to wear a coat because I don't want to get cold.
I could put my jacket on or I could just go in my T-shirt.
I'll wear a jacket and I'll wear gloves.
I could take my coat but I don't want to carry it around.
2 she, he, it, her
3 were, were, were, is, is, is
4 Ben bought a jumper, shorts, socks and a pair of jeans.
During the television commercial, Dad made a snack of cookies, milk, cheese and crackers.
Even though it was raining, the soccer team practised corners, penalty kicks and shoot-outs.
5 Answers will vary. For example: Descriptive adjective – shiny, tasty, dirty
Classifying adjective – space, meat, football
6 Answers will vary. For example: soon, Last night, tomorrow, Before, later
7 Answers will vary.
8 The person who normally answers the phone is sick.
Here is the pizza that has ham and pineapple topping.

Possums lived in the tree that burned down in the fire.
The astronaut wore the spacesuit, which has a hole.
9 Answers will vary. For example: I really really want a new bike.
Or: I absolutely must have a softball mitt.

Unit 7

1 out her window, from the neighbourhood park, out of the closet, out the back door, onto the street, down the road, to the park, from a small shoe-sized box, next to it, in the centre, before her eyes
2 out, at, from, out, of , out, without, onto, on, down, to, from, next, inside, in, without, before, into, inside.
The prepositions set the scene. They provide places where events happen.
3 Answers will vary.
4 Adverbs: recklessly, cautiously, inquisitively, clearly, carefully, loudly
Verbs: pushed, peered, looked, could see, decided to approach, buzzed
5 Students to underline word *her* in text.
6 my, their, your, her, his, our

Unit 8

1 was, was, had to leave, could help support, continued, learned, set up, worked, led, had sent, was keen to send, spent, landed
relating verbs and doing verbs
2 Answers may vary. For example: spent, returned, survived, arrived, experienced, landed
3 is, being, deserves, contributed, symbolises
4 are destroyed, was discovered, can reach, have totally evaporated
5 the first woman in space, She, Valentina, she, she, she, she, she, Her parachuting expertise, The Soviet union, it, Valentina, she
6 The Soviet Union is in the theme position to draw attention to it.
7 Magpies, They, Adult magpies, They, Magpies, magpie families
Nouns, noun groups and pronouns for magpies.
Mercury, It, Mercury, It, Temperatures on Mercury
Nouns, noun groups and pronouns

Unit 9

1 See, Fly, Book
2 Answers will vary. For example: Remain seated for entire flight. Fasten your seatbelts firmly. Press your buzzer for assistance. Switch off mobile phones for the duration of the flight.
3 Verb group: is, will train, are, must not fly
Galactic Airways is safe. /Galactic Airways is not safe.
Galactic Airways will train you for zero gravity. /Galactic Airways will not train you for zero gravity.
Seats are limited. /Seats are not limited.
You must fly Galactic Airways./You must not fly Galactic Airways.
4 High modality – definitely positive: I have finished; You must stop; Dinner is ready; The postie has been.
Low modality – maybe positive: I might be hungry; I might be able to hear; I might be finished; You might stop; The postie might have been.
Low modality – maybe negative: I might not be hungry; I might not hear; I might not be finished; You might not stop; Dinner might not be ready.
High modality – definitely negative: I'm not hungry; I definitely can't hear; Dinner is not ready; The postie has not been.
5 Answers will vary. For example: I recommend the Galactic Airways flight to all potential passengers. It was comfortable, safe and exciting. The training at zero gravity was easy. I had a terrific trip and I know you will enjoy the flight too.

Unit 10

1 Yuri's
2 the cosmonaut's spaceship, the pilots' training, the children's space-boots
3 hers, ours, theirs, his, yours, mine
4 that – refers to the spacecraft
who – Christopher Columbus
5 Yuri Gagarin, whose spaceship was called *Vostok 1*, was the first person to orbit the Earth.
Yuri Gagarin, who was a famous Soviet cosmonaut, died on a training flight.
The spaceship, which was call *Vostok 1*, circled the earth at 27 400 kilometres per hour.
The spaceship that circled the Earth at 27 400 kilometres per hour was flown by Yuri Gagarin.
6 It was hot so we went for a swim in the pool that the neighbours had just built.
My mum bought me a bike and a helmet, which I had always wanted.
My friend who lives across the road has a dog that bites.

Unit 11

1 Regular verbs, past tense: stopped, visited, looked
Irregular verbs, past tense: drove, saw, was, didn't have, had to get
Verbs not past tense: is, has, can look, using, visit, that's (that is)
They tell about actions that might happen if you visit the Observatory again.
2 can, didn't, had
3 looked, looked; visited, visited; stolen, stole; eaten, ate; grown, grew; drunk, drank; seen, saw
4 Prepositional phrases that tell <u>when</u>: During the last school holidays, for a night, during the day
Other prepositional phrases: to Dubbo Zoo, in country New South Wales, on the way, outside on a viewing platform, through the telescope, at the surface, of the Sun, to the Zoo.
5 Answers will vary.
6 Answers will vary.

Unit 12

1 Answers will vary. For example: in a faraway galaxy, on the beach, Above the Earth, through the jungle, beside the spaceship
2 Answers will vary. For example: before breakfast, During the school holidays, after dinner, during the school holidays, before I go to bed
3 adverbs: loudly, brightly, wildly, patiently, annoyingly
verbs: honked, smiled, giggled, sighed, chimed
4 his, hers, theirs, ours
5 An alien spaceship, An alien, Its head, It, It, It
6 Mum's car, the teacher's flowers, the magpies' warbling
7 The house that was owned by Jack's great, great grandpa was built in 1901.
My sister has a cat named Bozo, which she loves.
My aunt, who writes books, is very famous.
The man whose car was towed away is very angry.
8 I took the bike that Mum bought me back to the shop because it has a crack in the shaft.
My dad is putting in a basketball hoop so I can practise for the finals, which are coming up in July.
9 High modality – definitely positive: I will moved to Venus; Mercury is warm; I have refulled the rocket.
Low modality – maybe positive: I might be able to sing in tune; Mercury might be warm; I might have refuelled the rocket.
Low modality – maybe negative: I might not move to Venus; I might not sing in tune; Mercury might not be warm.
High modality – definitely negative: I won't move to Venus; I can't sing in tune; I have not refuelled the rocket.
10 broken, broke; kept, kept; asked, asked; written, wrote; blown, blew

Unit 13

1 must agree, absolutely agree, really must accept, definitely look
2 Answers will vary. For example:
We really must save the planet.
We can definitely do something.
We must take action.
Australia is definitely not doing enough to save the planet.
All countries must do more about controlling pollution.
We definitely have a better record on the environment than most other countries.
3 4: It will definitely rain tomorrow.
1: It could possibly rain tomorrow.
3: It will rain tomorrow.
2: It's likely to rain tomorrow.

3: I'm not going.
4: I'm definitely never going.
2: I probably won't go.
1: I don't think I'll go.
4 Answers will vary. For example:
I definitely must get a haircut.
I probably should get a haircut.
I might get a haircut.
I will definitely not get a haircut.
I probably won't get a haircut.
I might not get a haircut.
5 think, believe, agree
6 Answers will vary.
7 Answers will vary.

UNIT 14

1 The first Earth Day; U Thant, The United Nations Secretary-General; peaceful and cheerful Earth Days; our beautiful Spaceship Earth; frigid space; its warm and fragile cargo of animate life;
the Burmese language; a title; every year; a day; the promotion of global environmental issues and environmental awareness; an official Earth Day flag; an image of the Earth taken from space by NASA
2 first
3 Answers will vary.
4 Answers will vary. For example: Goldilocks and the Three Bears, Three Billy Goats Gruff, Snow White and the Seven Dwarfs, The Three Little Pigs
5 "May there be peaceful and cheerful Earth Days to come for our beautiful Spaceship Earth as it continues to spin and circle in frigid space with its warm and fragile cargo of animate life."
6 "I read a poem on assembly," said Tara.
"We gave my little cousin a book for his birthday," said Victoria.
"My teacher read us a quote by U Thant about Earth Day," said Bing.
"Did you know that U in Burmese means Mister?" asked Lauren.
"Imagine travelling on a space flight to Mars," said Phoebe.
7 Nouns: attendance, requirement, behaviour, attraction
Sentences will vary.

UNIT 15

1 the very existence, an attack, the process
2 Nouns: the control, the growth, the threat, the need, the destruction, the mutiny
Sentences: Answers will vary. For example:
The inhabitants were under the control of the invaders.
The growth of the black hole was terrifying.
The black hole posed a threat to all planets.
The need for a plan became apparent.
The destruction of the planet was caused by the Xematars.
The mutiny was defeated by the Xematars.
3 who had lost their family during an attack on their planet by the feared Xematars; who were intent on controlling all other life forms
4 Answers will vary, for example:
Jackie has a horse that she loves but it's getting too old to ride on anymore.
Helen is a clever girl who does well in maths but maths is not her favourite subject.
Martin was surprised that his dog wasn't under the house.
5 The brothers will think of a plan – the story is to be continued.
6 Answers will vary. For example: puddle/mud; like to dance?; the magpie dive-bombed Evie
7 Answers will vary.

UNIT 16

1 connectives that compare: however, if
connective that shows cause: so
connective that show addition: in addition
2 Answers will vary.
3 Life might exist on other planets or life might not exist on other planets.
Because scientists are always curious they will keep searching and wondering.
Life might exist; however, it might not be like ours.
Life developed on Earth. Similarly, life could have developed elsewhere.
There has never been any evidence that life exists elsewhere in the universe. On the other hand, it would be arrogant to think we had the only planet able to support life.
4 Unidentified Flying Object, Queensland and Northern Territory Aerial Services, National Aeronautics and Space Administration, radio detecting and ranging, Australian and New Zealand Army Corps, Personal Identification Number
5 Answers will vary.

UNIT 17

1 supports, has, need, to survive, need, need, was, consisted, were, use, called, take, make, is, became, began to evolve, is, burn, involves, uses, use, are, regenerate, will die
relating and doing verbs are used
saying and thinking and feeling verbs are not used
2 Paragraph 1: Planet Earth has air, which allows plants and animals to survive.
Paragraph 2: Plants create oxygen for animals in a process called photosynthesis.
Paragraph 3: Humans are using up all the oxygen and if there are no plants to create oxygen, people might not be able to survive on Earth.
3 Options may vary. For example:
Paragraph 1: Plants are very important for the survival of humans on Earth.
Paragraph 2: Plants are very specialised in the way they make oxygen.
Paragraph 3: People need to be more careful about burning oxygen and destroying forests around the planet.
4 Answers will vary. For example:
How is oxygen created?
What is the relationship between plants and animals?
How does human activity affect oxygen supplies on Earth?
Have animals always lived on Earth?
5 Answers will vary.
6 will you? aren't you? won't you? can't you? isn't he? won't we?
7 am, is, is, are, are, be, are, am, will

UNIT 18

1 Answers will vary. For example: We should have spaghetti for dinner/We need to have spaghetti for dinner.
Scrub the decks./You must scrub the decks.
Have a quicker shower./You must have a quicker shower.
2 Answers will vary. For example:
4: You will prepare for take-off.
2/1: Would you mind preparing for take-off?
3: You should prepare for take-off.
2/1: Would it be possible for you to prepare for take-off?
3 believe, hope, wonder, love
4 Answers will vary.
5 "Mum gave me a chemistry set for my birthday," said Lennie.
"Do you know the poem Jabberwocky?" asked Ryan.
"I would love to travel on a spaceship," commented Lara.
6 Nouns: the arrest, the growth, the death, the leap
Sentences will vary.
7 Answers will vary. For example: dirty water/bath water/bubbles; that show/the TV/my show
8 Answers will vary.
9 will you?; will you?; will we?; can't they?
10 Random Access Memory, light amplification (by) stimulated emission (of) radiation

UNIT 19

1 cream, add, beat, fold, refrigerate, place, bake
2 Chop, Mash, Whip, Stir, Mix
3 Answers will vary.
4 Ingredients, 70 cookies, 250g butter, 370g caster sugar, 2 teaspoons vanilla essence, 1 egg, 250g plain flour, 250g self-raising flour, 120g desiccated coconut, butter, sugar, vanilla, egg, all flour, desiccated coconut, 2–4 hours, dessert-spoon-sized flat mounds of mixture, a greased oven tray, 15 minutes, 180 degrees
5 I creamed the butter, sugar and vanilla until they were fluffy, then I added the egg and I beat the mixture well. Then I folded in all the flour and desiccated coconut. I refrigerated the mix for 2–4 hours and then I placed dessert-spoon-sized flat mounds of the mixture on a greased oven tray. Finally I baked the cookies for 15 minutes at 180 degrees.
6 laughed, laughed; burnt/burned, burnt/burned; wept, wept; drove, driven; brought, brought; forgot, forgotten, baked, baked
7 4: Mash potatoes
6: Serve hot
5: Add milk and butter to mashed potatoes and stir until smooth.
1: Place potatoes in a saucepan of water.
2: Boil potatoes until tender.
3: Drain water from potatoes.

UNIT 20

1 Fact, Evaluation, Evaluation, Evaluation, Evaluation, Evaluation, Fact
2 usually, don't, was, really, actually, quite, definitely, highly, has, totally
3 Answers will vary. For example: The plot was extremely boring.
The acting was atrocious.
The characters were not believable.
Everyone will hate this movie.
It's the worst science fiction movie of all time.
4 longingly, lovingly, typically, hopelessly
5 favourite, lucky, exciting, scary, special, clever, outer, believable, superior, microscopic, good, family
6 Answers will vary. For example: boring, stupid, dull, annoying, ridiculous
7 I loved it!
8 Answers will vary.

Unit 21

1 lunar module, jigsaw puzzles, Saturn V rockets, commemorative coins, space memorabilia, commemorative sterling silver spoon, Apollo II Zero Gravity Space Pen, Kennedy Space Centre
2 Thank you for your courage in travelling into space and inspiring so many people like my grandad.
3 you have been his hero
4 Answers will vary. For example: wonderful, brave, courageous, intelligent, special
5 Answers will vary.
6 Answers will vary.
7 Rd → Road / km → kilometre
NW → north-west / Dr → doctor
Ave → Avenue / Qld → Queensland
NSW → New South Wales / L → litre
8 Gopal bought flour, eggs, butter, jam and cream for scones.
The horse was spectacularly, amazingly fast.
After it rained, the grass was very green.
9 My grandpa collects space memorabilia too. He collects coins, pendants, photos and posters. He said that the astronauts were brave, heroic and intelligent. He said that he would have been too incredibly, sickeningly terrified to do what they did. He can't help but admire them very much.

Unit 22

1 The new child at the school is an alien.
2 Answers will vary. For example: crazy chimpanzees, a fairy princess, a pirate battlefield, a giant sentinel
3 It is used to introduce three different definitions for the word 'Alien'.
4 Scene 1: Inside the spaceship
Commander: We are counting down to blast off.
2nd office: All systems check.
The rules on this rocket are:
5 The first stanza uses 'or' as a contrasting connective to imply one or the other meaning. You can be strange without being foreign and you can be foreign without being strange. The third stanza uses 'and' to imply a new child at school feels both strange and foreign.
6 Answers will vary. For example: distinct, different, weird, unusual, odd, unknown, unfamiliar, peculiar, freakish, eccentric, bizarre
7 'Here' means any place where a person is new, such as the new school, new country, new town. 'Here' in the poem specifically means 'new school'.
8 Answers will vary.
9 Answers will vary.

Unit 23

1 This impact, the waste, consumption, pollution
2 the measurement, the creation, the calculation, the prediction
Sentences will vary.
3 resources: supplies of things
pollution: waste products that make the environment foul
ecological: refers to the relationship between living things and the environment
eliminated: got rid of something
conservation: saving resources or minimising use of resources
consumption: the using up or destruction of something
4 Every human being uses resources such as food and energy,/and creates waste such as pollution./ This impact on the environment, which each person makes,/can be called an 'ecological footprint'./Each person's footprint can be measured,/and each community, organisation, workplace and country can also have its ecological footprint measured./Ecological footprints are measured by calculating goods and services used,/and the energy and resources required to create them,/ as well as the waste products left over/and the ways the waste is dealt with, stored or eliminated./Conservation groups have predicted/that to continue with current global consumption and pollution levels/we'll need the resources of 12 planet Earths.
5 which
6 My mother, who is an accountant, works for the government.
The house, which is 100 years old, is owned by the Historical Trust.
Sarah, whose dog ate her homework, needs to do it again.
My sister, who is on the football team, has trained hard.
7 The car had a flat tyre so Joan was late for school.
Both Bill and Jenny have new pencil cases.
Either Chen or Hamish will help you calculate your ecological footprint.
Neither Jana nor Jim have new pencil cases.
Because we don't have 12 planet Earths we need to make sure that whatever resources we use, we can renew or reuse, and whatever waste products we create, we can dispose of safely.

Unit 24

1 Answers will vary. For example: Tidy the cupboard.
2 I went to visit my sick uncle in hospital.
3 dance, I danced, I have danced
keep, I kept, I have kept
jump, I jumped, I have jumped
run, I ran, I have run
bit, I bit, I have bitten
4 fact, opinion, opinion, opinion, fact
5 My dog won't win. / My new bicycle was well made.
I hate summer the most. / My dad is a dreadful dancer.
6 Answers will vary. For example:
The clumsy gymnast tumbled badly.
A huge man fell heavily.
The tiny baby cried pitifully.
The hungry child grumbled constantly.
7 Fred Tims
2181 Fisher Rd
Dee Why
NSW 2099
8 St → Street / SW → south-west
it's → it is / Ave → Avenue
SA → South Australia / km → kilometre
WA → Western Australia / mL → millilitre
9 We saw: raccoons, squirrels, prairie dogs and meerkats.
Commander: We are setting course for Alpha Beta Gamma Nebula.
Mission Control: Roger that, Commander. Setting course.
The class rules are:
10 Answers will vary.
11 Answers will vary.

Unit 25

1 Answers will vary. For example:
sudden – quick / attack – contact
abandoned – left / ominously – quietly
terrified – concerned
2 Frank Neal is the voice of authority on the issue so including comments he has reportedly made add to the authority of the article.
3 Answers will vary.
4 Answers will vary. For example: One Melbourne worker commented that the UFO is terrifying. Police Commissioner Frank Neal stated that police have been unable to communicate with the spaceship.
One reporter suggested that the spaceship was a solitary vessel.
A police officer warned the public to stay clear of the area.
5 People/Humankind can no longer afford to be complacent about the environment.
Every student is required to bring his or her own lunch on the excursion/ All students are required to bring their own lunch on the excursion.
When any president visits the city, he or she stays at the conference venue.
Cave people developed simple tools to assist them in their daily lives.
Phone all the schools and ask all the principals if they can attend our meeting.
6 chairperson, police officer, firefighter, flight attendant, cleaner, astronaut

Unit 26

1 Answers will vary. For example: a snow-capped mountain; regular dust storms; extreme temperatures, shiny, mirrored surface; distant spinning planet
2 heroic, colourful, troublesome, disastrous
Sentences will vary.
3 are, belong, is, has been, will become
4 Answers will vary. For example:
crunch – crater cookies
slobber – solar system stew
swallow – succulent Martian strawberries
chew – chunky crater chips
gnaw – gigantic green grubs
5 The dog with the loud bark lives next door.
The player in spiked shoes is disqualified.
The plant with the dead leaves gets too much sun.
Any child without a hat must stay indoors.
The bike with the big motor is Grandma's.

6 Comparative: dustier, emptier, more remote, more unusual
Superlative: dustiest, emptiest, most remote, most unusual

Unit 27

1 magnet: a body that has the ability to attract certain substances
magnetic field: a force that attracts magnetic objects in its vicinity
iron: a metal element that can conduct electricity
molten iron: melted iron/iron liquefied by heat
electric current: a flow of electricity
rotates: turns around like a wheel
2 of the Earth, of iron, Around the solid core, of molten iron, As the Earth rotates, in this molten iron layer, in turn, of a magnet, of kilometres, into space, through the air
3 Planet Earth could be said to have a magnet at its centre.
Around the solid core is liquid iron.
Magnetic fields are caused by electric currents.
As the Earth rotates, the electrons move and cause magnetism.
It would be unpleasant to be hit on the head with an iron.
An iron pan flying through the air would cause damage.
4 Answers will vary.
5 Planet Earth has a lot of iron at its centre.
The magnetic field extends for thousands of kilometres.
Electric currents are generated as the Earth rotates.
6 The centre of the Earth was solid and mostly made of iron.
Around the solid core was a liquid layer of molten iron.
The electric currents generated a magnetic field.
Earth had the properties of a magnet.
No, the past tense does not make sense because the processes occurring are ongoing. They continue to happen and need to be written in the present tense.

Unit 28

1 Firstly, Secondly, Lastly
2 absolutely must ditch, would definitely be much less interesting, obviously doesn't realise, could well have remained living in caves
3 Answers will vary. For example:
School children definitely need more exercise so we will have sport and games more often.
School children must have excursions to chocolate factories.
4 Answers will vary. For example:
Brussels sprouts might be a little bit good for us.
Schools might like to consider the possibility of stargazing sleepouts in their playgrounds once in a while.
5 Answers will vary.
6 madam, ladies and gentlemen, dear reader, Colleagues, honey
7 Editor, Readers, N. Baines
8 The writer does not know N Baines. The relationship is distant.
9 Answers will vary.

Unit 29

1 cruel, immoral, absolutely unnecessary, murdered by scientists, intelligent audience, what possible benefit to human space flight can result from sending tortoises and guinea pigs into space
2 Answers will vary. For example: Conducting experiments on animals is not humane.
Five countries conduct animal experiments to assist research for space travel.
Some animals were given autopsies after their space flights to gain information for use in human space travel.
3 It is supposed to make the reader feel sorry for the animals and angry about their use in experiments.
4 Using the monkey's name personalises the monkey like a pet and makes it seem even more horrific that he drowned as a result of human experiments on animals.
5 Ladies and gentlemen – the relationship is formal. The speaker does not personally know the audience members.
6 adult to children – may or may not know each other
audience is known to speaker; friendly
audience is not know by name
speaker and audience are very familiar – a close relationship
polite, formal – speaker does not know audience by name
polite, formal – audience is known by name but not as a friend
7 Answers may vary. Discuss with students to determine the situations they envisaged for each vocative.
For example: 1, 5, 3, 1, 4

Unit 30

1 We're going to invite firefighters to talk to the students.
People/Humans are responsible for the environmental issues.
I'll find a doctor and have her or him call you.
2 I think I quite like your new puppy.
We might possibly paint the wall green.
The doctor said I should keep off my feet for a week.
3 prepositional phrases that tell how: by the wind, As the Earth
prepositional phrases that tell where: at the cinema, around the tree
4 Answers will vary.
5 is, have, were, are, becomes
6 windy, scenic, dangerous
Sentences will vary.
7 The beach towel with the yellow stripes is Kara's.
The dancer in the leather jacket is my favourite.
The painting of the actor is for sale.
The speech by the principal was very moving.
Children with hats can go outside.
8 Comparative: dirtier, more spacious, busier, hungrier
Superlative: dirtiest, most spacious, busiest, hungriest
9 Answers will vary. For example:
The vandals' rampage cost thousands.
Maitland was devastated by floods.
10 Answers may vary: 2, 4, 3, 5
11 Firstly, In addition, Finally

Unit 31

1 wanted, think, think
2 metaphor: parents are jail keepers; simile: like a prison. Remaining answers will vary.
3 Adjectives could include: restrictive, prohibitive, excessive, unreasonable, interesting
Sentences will vary.
4 my restrictive, prohibitive, excessive, unreasonable parents
5 My smart, witty, talented friend, Tasha's family, my bedroom window, many constellations, Many stars, the city lights.
6 Answers will vary.
7 Short sentences increase the pace of the reading and make it more exciting and action-packed. The long sentences reinforce the message they are trying to get across.
8 cool: good, terrific
jail-keepers: strict parents who limit your freedom
9 Answers will vary.
10 could have, would have, should have, might have

Unit 32

1 Instructions to hide under the bed or bang pots and pans; the instructions to throw water bombs or bite the aliens; the instruction to roll in the dirt so you won't taste any good if the aliens bite you.
2 Answers will vary. For example: or: used to show alternatives (hide in a bed or a tree)
and: used to add things (run and don't look back)
3 Synonyms may vary. For example: stay/remain, don't go/avoid, hide/conceal yourself, take/carry, scare/frighten, keep/stay, drop/fall, roll/wriggle, report/attend
4 Try hiding in a cupboard.
Keep quiet while you hide.
Make water balloons to scare them off.
Scream at the aliens when they approach you.
Taste an alien./Bite an alien.
5 am hiding, am keeping, am taking, am banging, am screaming, am running, am not looking, am biting, are tasting, am dropping, am rolling, am reporting

Unit 33

1 first, third, fourth
2 During, While, When, At first, finally, Because, since, After, before
3 then, before, and
4 Answers will vary.
5 Andy Thomas, He, Andy, Andy, Andy, him, Andy, this amazing astronaut, our Adelaide boy, Andy Tomas
6 The Space Shuttle *Discovery*, It, it, This amazing spacecraft, *Discovery*
7 fact, opinion, opinion, fact, fact, fact, opinion
8 The writer thinks Andy is an amazing astronaut and is proud that he is Australian. The writer says Andy has had an incredible career. The writer fondly refers to Andy as our Adelaide boy.
9 citizen, scientist, footballer, commander, pianist, adviser, journalist, inhabitant

Unit 34

1 A space program, enormously costly, The cost of the US space shuttle program, $175 billion dollars, the space program, critically important, will benefit all humankind, advances in technology, the space program, benefits do not justify its costs, a space program, money isn't squandered, tangible advances in science
2 Many scientists believe the space program will lead to benefits for all humans.
Some people think that Australia should become more involved in the space program.
On the other hand, critics of the space program think that the space program costs too much and is a waste of money.
The average person thinks schools, roads and medical research are better things to spend money on than the space program.
Conclusion: Nevertheless, most people are happy to support the space program as long as money isn't wasted.
3 Answers will vary: students could justify that the writer supports or opposes the space program. For example: I think the author is opposed to the space program because the words "enormously costly" and "squandered" are used to describe the program.
4 Balanced viewpoint because different sides of the issue are presented evenly and fairly. The author does not present a personal opinion but leaves readers to make up their own minds – the author does not make a recommendation.
5 As an astronaut I would support the space program totally and hope that governments continued with space research.
6 I would think that spending money on space travel is a terrible waste when millions of people around the world don't have food or water or medical supplies or vaccinations.
7 Answers will vary.
8 or, on the other hand, or, as long as
9 Answers will vary.

Unit 35

1 Answers will vary.
2 Answers will vary.
3 Answers will vary.
4 Answers will vary.
5 could have, might have, should have, would have
6 Can you/Will you go to bed?
Can you/Will you put that away now?
Will you finish your dinner and then get ready for bed?
Could you/Will you put it on the shelf?
7 opinion, fact, fact, opinion
8 The comet flies across the sky.
I am launching the rocket.
I can see Mars through the telescope.
Patrick is writing a list of instructions.
9 Answers will vary.
10 teacher, actor, photographer, lawyer, baker, dictator, librarian, tiler
11 Answers will vary.
12 The Martian, its purplish skin, six arms, sharp teeth.
13 the ape Albert, Albert, one of many animals, this ape, a hero

Student Book 6 Answers

Unit 1

1 verb groups: arrived, went, had travelled, spotted, headed, got, stopped, drifted, observed, were breaching, breached, leapt, flopped, noticed, meandered, poked, spied, hung, were, loved, love
human doing verbs: had travelled, spotted, headed, drifted, observed
whales doing verbs: were breaching, meandered, spied, hung, flopped, leapt
2 Answers will vary. For example: leapt, flopped
3 had travelled, were breaching
4 loved
5 advised, waved, shouted, attracted, swam, wanted
6 had, did, have, been, was
7 yesterday, today, when, when, Not long after, today
8 since, now, When, After
9 yesterday, now, First, then, Finally

Unit 2

1 Classifying adjectives: nesting area, the critically endangered green turtle, The adult green turtles, the Pacific Ocean, These gentle plant eaters, quite distinctive face markings, Green turtles, oar-shaped flippers
Descriptive adjectives: a magnificent habitat; the tasty seaweed and algae; the warm waters; These gentle plant eaters; some brown, reddish-brown or black markings; quite distinctive face markings; a creamy colour; little aliens; their watery tropical paradise
2 Answers will vary.
3 Answers will vary. For example: fierce Pacific ocean, freezing Atlantic ocean, etc.
4 gentle plant eaters, tropical paradise, little aliens
5 turtle flippers are compared to oars of a canoe
turtle heads are compared to the heads of aliens
6 as dry as → a bone
as cold as → ice
fight like → cats and dogs
work like → a dog
sings like → an angel
7 Answers will vary. For example: as hungry as a pig, as sparkly as a star, snores like a rhino, sings like a cockatoo, eats like a horse

Unit 3

1 Last Saturday my cousin, Satoshi, and I **went** to the zoo./ We **visited** the apes first./My favourite ape **is** the orangutan/ <u>because</u> they **are** so clever and human-like./ We **watched** one orangutan/ <u>as</u> he **gathered** a pile of empty potato sacks/ <u>and</u> carefully **stacked** them/ to **form** a seat. He **fussed** with the sacks/ <u>and</u> **tested** his seat/ to **make** it more comfortable./ Then he finally **sat** on the pile./ It **was** really funny to watch./
After the apes, we **visited** the bears/ <u>and</u> we **visited** the elephants/ <u>but</u> we **decided** /that our favourite animals for the day **were** the mountain goats./ They **were** totally amazing./They **climbed** up their rock mountain so nimbly, even the babies./
Overall, I **enjoyed** the day very much/ <u>and</u> I **hope to go** back soon./
2 The meerkats were cute but the otters were cuter.
We liked the lemurs and we liked the sun bears.
It wasn't very crowded yet we couldn't find a seat.
You can watch tennis at 7 pm or you can watch cricket at 7 pm.
3 Answers will vary. For example: We had lasagne for dinner and we had ice-cream for dessert.
The beach was crowded but we found a place for our towels.
I can travel to New Zealand or I can travel to Fiji.
Either Terry will go to India or he will go to Thailand.
4 The lions **roared** <u>loudly</u>.
The koalas **dozed** <u>peacefully</u>.
The bears **looked** at us <u>occasionally</u>.
Long, blue giraffe tongues **poked** out <u>stickily</u>.
5 The bears looked <u>very</u> **relaxed** in their rock pool.
The whole thing was <u>totally</u> **terrifying**.
Zoos are <u>extremely</u> **interesting** places.
The goats were <u>really</u> **clever**.
6 carefully, finally, nimbly
really, totally, very
7 Answers will vary.

Unit 4

1 In, beneath, of, on, of, of, of, on, into, of, At, of, to, into. Note: *as* can also be a preposition.
2 5. Their function is to set the scene and tell where events occurred.
3 At the beginning
4 Answers will vary. For example: in the dark writhing jungle, on an island shrouded in mist, near the equator
5 Its horns were sharp as swords: it provides an image of the Minotaur to help readers visualise what it looked like.
6 Answers will vary. For example: The maze was as frightening as your worst nightmare.
The Minotaur's head was as big as a bull's.
The Minotaur's bellow was like a ferocious dinosaur.
7 seven
8 last, thirty, Many, every, dozen, Each, Some
9 Gigantic, sharp, dark, cavernous, dreadful, blood-curdling
Answers will vary.
10 underground, young
11 Answers will vary.

Unit 5

1 I, We, She, they, us, we, us, I, I
she: the park's interpretive officer
us and we: the writer and his/her family or travel companions
they: the sea lions
2 they, it, I, it, us, you
3 them, they, They, they, they
4 their (their pups)
5 yours, ours, his, hers, theirs
6 I, me, Bernie and I, them and me

Unit 6

1 ate, swam, drank, brought, enjoyed
2 have, did, will, do, was
3 before, since, now, finally, tomorrow, now
4 'It' is Woofy's chew toy.
5 My dear old Aunt Amy loved pickles. She even ate pickles for breakfast.
6 Answers will vary.
7 Answers will vary. For example:
As tedious as a school concert
As stubborn as a mule
Laughs like a hyena
Tickles like a feather
8 The neighbour's cat is vicious but our cat is more vicious.
We stayed up late as the movie was really long.
We can't go to the zoo unless we tidy our bedrooms.
It was great fun so we stayed all day.
9 Answers will vary. For example: noisily, swiftly, extremely, totally
10 Answers will vary. For example: underneath the abandoned house, in the crowded basement, between the rows of stolen goods
11 them, They, yours, hers.
12 Iris and me, We, Boris and I

Unit 7

1 Short sentences speed up the pace of the reading and so make a story sound more exciting. Short sentences often lead readers to a climax in the story.
2 statement, command, command, statement, exclamation, statement, exclamation, question, exclamation
The pattern of sentences make the text sound varied and interesting. They make the emotions of the characters seem more real.
3 Answers will vary. For example: [You] Do not be afraid, Stay near me [you], [you] see those tigers
4 There's ice-cream on the floor.
The elephant will sneeze on you if you get too close.
Madeline skidded and crashed her bike.
5 stay, protect, look, see, pacing, heard, flung, listen, hear
6 Adjectives tell how the characters are thinking and feeling: trembling, frightened, afraid, panicked
7 Answers will vary. For example:
Adjective: brave, courageous, determined, resigned
Noun: bravery, courage, determination, resignation
8 Answers will vary.
9 Answers will vary.

Unit 8

1 a new home, a new school, a new language, the most important thing, a better life, a different country, those people, the world
their countries
many people
a different country, a new home, a new language, new friends, the most important thing, better life, a new country, new friends
2 A, An, That, These, The
3 Whose, Which, What, How
4 his, my, her, your
5 the most important thing
6 Comparative: more frightening, larger, scarier, more terrific, better
Superlative: most frightening, largest, scariest, most terrific, best
7 prettier, more worried, fastest, most pleased
8 different

Unit 9

1 verbs/verb groups: are, suggest, is, is, was built, has been, believe, is, was, remained, think, is, building, gave, became, climbed, became
saying verb: suggest
2 is: Present; built: Past; is: Present; means: Present; was obscured: Past
3 past tense verbs: was, has been, remained, became obscured
present tense verbs: are, suggest, is, believe, think
The buildings were all built in the past but the discussion presents opinions that represent what people think <u>now</u>.
4 Past tense with-*ed* suffix I asked, I stopped, I visited, I wasted
Past tense with auxiliary: I have asked, I did stop, I have visited, I did want
5 ate or have eaten, wore or have worn, sang or have sung/did sing
6 "The Statue of Liberty is more famous than the Empire State Building," stated Logan.
"Do you really think so?" asked Aleisha.
"No way," interrupted Peri. "The most famous landmark in the world has got to be Sydney Harbour Bridge."
7 would, will, could, might

Unit 10

1 According to Balmain resident Ravi Barba, the only way to get a good view is to get into position by midday, take all your food and drink supplies for the 13 hours, and stay put.
Police said they were kept busy dealing with incidents involving alcohol.
Event organisers said that they were extremely pleased with the evening's celebrations and that the few isolated incidents attended to by police did not impact on the success of the event.
1. Ravi Barba 2. Police 3. Event organisers
2 Ravi said that he loves the New Year's Eve fireworks on Sydney Harbour.
Penny stated that other cities have fabulous celebrations too.
Gopal said that he loves the river of fire in Brisbane.
Louie bragged that Melbourne has fireworks coming from the top of city buildings.
Kala offered that her favourite New Year's Eve is watching the sun set on Cable Beach in Western Australia.
3 Answers will vary. For example: Alcohol Ruins Sydney's New Year Festivities
Police Arrest New Year Revellers
Drunks Arrested for the New Year
4 Answers will vary. For example: heart-stopping, best/unbeatable, triumph
5 Students Learn Respect/ "Respect" School Subject
New Driveway for Elderly Residents
6 Answers will vary. For example: Eucalypt Public School has decided to teach students the art of graffiti. Teachers will help students design their own tags and provide a wall at the school for graffiti practice.
An angry older resident at Pacific Resort for seniors held other residents hostage today as he demanded better food and service for residents.

Unit 11

1 as red as rust, 'upside-down trees', having a fab time, Love and bear hugs, from your 'grey nomad' grandparents
2 Answers will vary.
3 Answers will vary. For example: Dear Friends/Hello all you workers, we are having a terrific holiday. We enjoyed Broome and the beautiful Buccaneer Archipelago. We are now on our way to Kununurra. Yours sincerely, Fred and Lucy
4 Broome's – Broome is; countryside's – countryside is; We've – We have; they've – they have; We're – We are
5 I am, that is, will not, he will
6 hasn't, don't, we're, it's
7 NSW, Vic, NZ, Ave, ACT, SA, NT, Tas, Rd, Hwy, Qld, St
8 Answers will vary.

Unit 12

2 Answers will vary. For example:
those, two, delicious, toffees
whose, two, toffee, apples,
my, delicious, toffee, apples
3 Comparative: more fabulous, newer, older, lazier, more revolting
Superlative: most fabulous, newest, oldest, laziest, most revolting
4 is: Present; built: Past; was built: Past; (It)'s, (that)'s, used: Present; have: Present; am researching: Present
5 "I'd love to hike around Cradle Mountain in Tasmania," said Robert.
"It snows there," said Phoebe.
"Tasmanian devils live there," offered Yanus.
"I don't think you hike there in the winter," suggested Ngutapa. "The snow would be too deep and it might be dangerous."
6 Answers will vary.
7 Brooke said that Freycinet National Park is truly stunning.
Glenn said that he'd been camping at Coles Bay.
Hari said that he would love to go there.

8 Answers will vary. For example: TV/tele, fridge, old bomb/wheels, dosh/dough, cosi/swimmers/togs, PJs/jammies
9 cannot, they are, has not, she will
10 I've, don't, that's, he's

Unit 13

1 A number of diseases, Five of these diseases, They, The more severe symptoms of malaria, The other diseases, Your only protection, To avoid, Stay, Wear, Wear, Use, Avoid
2 Your only protection
The different theme stands out from the others.
3 verb. The actions verbs are used as theme in the commands because the commands tell people what to do.
4 I, Jump, Under the bed, Slowly, Adrienne and Luca.
5 they
6 Phillip Island Nature Park is home to a colony of little penguins./ The little penguins have become Victoria's most popular tourist attraction./ The little penguins waddle up the beach to their burrows at sunset./ They have been out at sea all day./ They bring back fish for their chicks./ Little penguins only grow to 33 centimetres./
7 Saltwater crocodiles live all along the top of Australia. They can grow quite large and they can be dangerous. They drag their prey under water and do a 'death roll' to drown it. Saltwater crocodiles have been known to attack people. Tourists are advised to be wary of them, especially when camping and fishing.
8 Rules for a safe car journey:
wear a seatbelt
keep your eyes on the road
stay a safe distance from the vehicle in front
don't talk on a mobile phone
don't eat while you drive
indicate if you need to turn a corner
travel at the speed limit
pull over before stopping your vehicle.

Unit 14

1 Egypt used to be my favourite place in the world until the day my life was changed forever – the day when the curse struck!/ My parents are journalists/ and my brother and I often travel with them./ I loved it when they went to Egypt./It was so mysterious./ Jack and I used to fool around/and pretend we were being chased by possessed mummies/ or trapped in undiscovered tombs./ Until one day we didn't have to pretend./
It all began/ when my parents had to interview an archaeologist at The Great Pyramid of Giza./Jack and I wandered away through the pyramid/ and it wasn't long before we became lost./ We found ourselves in a room in the pyramid/ that we'd never seen before./ Hieroglyphics decorated the walls/ and the eyes of the god, Horus, looked down on us from the granite ceiling./ We stood transfixed by the eyes/ as the air became chilly/ and a stone wall slammed across our exit./ We were trapped./
2 We were frightened of mummies as well as of curses.
I was worried but I knew my parents would look for us.
Because a stone wall moved by itself to block our exit we became trapped.
3 adds information, shows cause, compares things, shows time sequence
4 *That* refers to a room in the pyramid not seen by the children before.
5 Answers may vary.
For example: My uncle, who lives in Lebanon, is an archaeologist.
The journalist whose job was to interview the archaeologist was on holiday.
The museum that houses artefacts from the pyramids was closed.
I rode a camel, which had a red blanket on its back, around the pyramid.
6 My parents interviewed an archaeologist who specialised in hieroglyphics.
I love Egypt because it is so mysterious.

Unit 15

1 that will not be offensive to local people or their religions and customs; the clause adds information to tell what sort of clothing should be worn.
2 Answers will vary. For example:
Ask for advice from a person who is an expert on travelling safely.
Wear a hat that shades your face and neck.
Wear sunscreen that is waterproof.
Wear walking shoes, which are comfortable.
Avoid drinks that are not in bottles.
Eat fruit that you can peel.
Travel with people who you can trust.
Travel with a person whose advice you can trust.
3 have
4 had, become, equal, are, belongs
5 Answers will vary.
6 unless, or
7 Answers will vary.
8 check, avoid, wear, wear, wear, drink, avoid, eat, eat

Unit 16

1 Have you ever yearned to visit China?, Now is the best time, very short time only, outstanding, value-for-money, first 100 callers only, small exclusive, amazing, once-in-a-lifetime opportunity, not to be missed
2 best, short, outstanding, small, exclusive, amazing
The reader is meant to feel a desire to travel to China as soon as possible because this trip is an exclusive opportunity.
3 It is used twice to reinforce the idea that only 100 can go on the trip and it's only being offered for a short time.
4 Answers will vary.
5 Now might be a good time; You might travel in a small group; You could possibly see amazing sites; This tour might include some transport; This could be a good opportunity; It probably should not be missed; Maybe book you tour soon.
The reader would be less likely to be persuaded. The reader would not be convinced that the tour was a great opportunity.
6 I will come to your house; I don't like car travel very much;
It definitely won't rain today; It's certainly too late to buy a ticket;
You must come with me; They definitely won't come to China with us; I might like to go to China.
7 "Book" – using one verb as theme makes the verb stand out and therefore makes the command more important. The ad only has one command, Book your tour today

Unit 17

1 visited, is, have ever seen, stands, is, extends, is, is, changes, is, appears to change, is, is filled, survive, is, can understand
3 1) It is the most incredible place that I have ever seen.
2) It is filled with small native shrubs and flowers that miraculously survive in the dry red earth.
4 It is adverbial because it tells when something happened, ie when the colours change.
5 I recently visited Uluṟu with my family./It is the most incredible place/that I have ever seen./Uluṟu stand 340 metres tall/and is 9.4 kilometres around its base./The rock probably extends five or six kilometres under the ground – /so only a small percentage of it is above the ground, like an iceberg./
It is really amazing/when Uluṟu changes colour during the different stages of the day, such as sunset and sunrise./The play of light on the red rock is a fascinating sight./The rock appears to change colour from red to bright orange to a dark, deep burnt orange, to shades of purple and mauve./The vast, open, flat land around Uluṟu is also very beautiful./It is filled with small native shrubs and flowers/that miraculously survive in the dry red earth./Uluṟu–Kata Tjuṯa National Park is world heritage listed./I can understand why./
6 The Aboriginal people prefer that tourists do not climb Uluṟu. Uluṟu is a spiritually significant site for Aboriginal people.
A large number of tourists are choosing not to climb Uluṟu. They are doing this out of respect for the culture of the traditional owners.
The traditional owners of Uluṟu–Kata Tjuṯa National Park are pleased about this.
7 People are advised not to bring plants or seeds into the National Park or camp in the National Park and they should take their rubbish with them when they leave.
8 Answers will vary.
9 for sore eyes, beside the road, in red thongs, on the rock, around Uluṟu, with the small yellow flowers

Unit 18

1 A gremlin, Fly, Through the gate, Quietly, Ali and Katy
2 The Ningaloo Reef, Ningaloo Reef, It, The whale sharks, The reef
3 Perth: Perth, It, Perth
Quokkas: quokkas, these, they
4 Answers will vary.
5 Answers will vary. For example:
In the sun, wear a hat that covers your face, ears and neck.
On holiday, wear shoes that are comfortable to walk in.
For breakfast, eat some fruit, which is healthy.

In class, sit with a person who is quiet.
6 You might visit now.
You might have a good time.
You could possibly be late.
It might be finished.
I might not allow it.
7 become, had, are, belong, equal
8 Answers will vary. For example:
I like train travel but I prefer air travel.
You can catch a bus or you can catch a train.
You should concentrate in class or you won't learn anything.
I'll get an ice-cream and I'll get a chocolate.
9 Answers will vary. For example: bad, mean, a sad event, gaoled/jailed
10 Answers will vary. For example: I was surprised at the dramatic colour changes as I watched the sun set on Uluru and was pleased that all the tourists were quiet and respectful of the site.
Feral animals such as cats and foxes, which prey on small native species of mammals in the National Park, have caused a number of native species to disappear.
11 around Uluru, at Ningaloo Reef, without a hat, under the table
12 Answers will vary. For example: with the crooked fin, in the spotted dress, with the pink stripes, with the googly eyes

Unit 19

1 Reason: to see the animals in their natural habitat; to see the ice, colour and shapes
Supporting facts: Antarctica has seven different penguin species and other large sea birds. It has five species of seals. It has many different types of whales; Antarctica has natural ice sculptures, glaciers and icebergs. The ice looks spectacular.
2 Answers may vary. For example: opinion, fact, fact, opinion. Note: Some people may consider the first and last statements to be fact.
3 A group of whales – pod, a group of seals – herd, a group of birds – flock, a group of ships – fleet, a group of dolphins – pod, a group of people – audience/crowd. (Answers may vary.)
4 albatross's, the penguins' rookeries, the whale's tail, the sheep's wool, Granny and Pa's TV
5 Answers will vary.
6 Answers may vary. For example:
emperor penguin → penguin/sea bird/ bird/vertebrate, animal
droplet of water → puddle/pond/lake

Unit 20

1 Own a piece of the largest, shops, schools and restaurants, Potential plus, Redevelop, once-in-a-lifetime opportunity, invest, Get in now, miss out forever, your last chance to buy
2 desert, guaranteed never to flood, helicopter flight to shops, schools and restaurants, redevelop as a mine, pristine wilderness
3 Answers will vary. For example: barren/empty, loneliness, tepid/hot/humid, cold/freezing, desert, lose money/spend/buy
4 Answers will vary. For example: hot, freezing, loneliness, spend, barren, desert
They make the real estate sound terrible. No one would choose to purchase the real estate described by these synonyms.
5 accused of, make fun of, had an accident, black and white, throw a party, give up/hard
6 Answers will vary. For example: relax in tropical paradise, cheap flights, great deals, 3 nights for the price of 2, buffet breakfast included, paradise awaits you, trip of a lifetime, luxury holiday, a trip to remember
7 Answers will vary.
8 Answers will vary. For example:
Hyphenated: cross-country, roller-coaster, ice-cream
Solid: Sunday, footpath, hairbrush
Written with a space: birthday card, light switch, power point

Unit 21

1 *A Future* means that there is more than one future possible because *a* is an indefinite article.
The Future would mean that the future is fixed and there are no choices that can make any difference to how *the future* turns out.
2 a, The, an, the, the, a
3 family groups: Yousif's grandparents, Tan Le's family, Dijana's parents, Mohamed
countries: Greece, Vietnam, Bosnia, Iraq, Australia
ways to come to Australia: migrants, boat people, refugees, asylum seeker
years: 1949, 1977, 1999, 2007
verbs: engineered, worked, created, made
final phrases: in the snowy mountains, for a new life, far from 'home', in Australia
4 Answers will vary but need to consist of lines as follows: Name, cultural background, how they came to live in Australia, verb for contribution to Australian way of life, final phrase.
5 My name is Gabriella. I have a yellow bedroom inside a red brick house. My suburb is Five Dock in the city of Sydney. My state is New South Wales in the country of Australia. I live on the planet called Earth in a universe that goes on forever.
6 Answers will vary.
7 Night/Morning
descended softly/pounced with a clang
Sneaking up/Crashing down
stealthily enveloping/harshly illuminating
senses/thoughts

Unit 22

1 First, Then, Next, After that, then, then, Finally, then, before
2 Labels on the comic strip should read:
The brain was removed, the empty skull was rinsed, the internal organs were removed, the body was dried for 40 days, the body was stuffed, artificial eyes were stuck on, the body was coasted with resin, the body was wrapped in bandage strips, charms and decorations were attached, the mummy was paced in a coffin
3 verb: chased, travelled, was chased, is, enjoys cooking, placed
subject: The dog, Tamara, The ball, India, Dad, The Egyptians
4 active, passive, passive, passive, passive
5 The car was driven to Taree by Jimmy.
The walls of the temple were climbed by monkeys.
6 The Egyptians removed the brain.
Priests placed the internal organs in jars.

Unit 23

1 adverbs: quickly, narrowly
verbs: spotted, avoiding
2 from the garage, across the hallway, down the stairs, from the shelf, onto his back, onto the floor, to an 'on' position, behind the eye, to his head, in the garage, in front of the Tower of London, to the side
3 after a minute, in January, in time
4 from a postcard, by a horsedrawn carriage
5 The phrases provide information about the verbs – they tell more about the events that happened, such as where, when and how the events occurred.
6 Answers will vary.
7 Answers will vary.
8 a small cube-shaped object with one large button
9 Vince, silver shoes, Vince, the Tower of London, a small, cube-shaped object with one large button
10 Vince's mother
11 Vince
12 Jess is going to Canberra during the next school holidays to visit her Aunty Evelyn and her cousin Gillian.
13 When travelling, people need to be aware of local customs regarding clothing. For example, when entering a Christian Church in Fiji people should cover their knees and their shoulders.

Unit 24

1 Answers will vary. For example:
Copenhagen is a beautiful city.
The statue of the Little Mermaid in Copenhagen looks really cute.
Danish is a difficult language to learn.
2 For example: whales, eggs, players, insects, fish, horses/elephants, people, soldiers
3 echidna/monotreme/Australian mammal/mammal/vertebrate/animal
4 rhinoceros's horns, magpies' nest, dolphin's tail, children's bags, Mum and Dad's car
5 talking to, best wishes, by accident, lost my job
6 Tourists viewed The Little Mermaid at the water's edge.
The family visited Auckland.
The guests ate the whole pavlova.
Feral cats hunt native animals.
7 spend, dance, eat, make
8 Answers will vary. For example:
Hyphenated: dressing-gown, roller-coaster, great-grandmother, passer-by
Solid: backpack, knapsack, rollerskate, seatbelt
Written with a space: full stop, decimal point, mud cake, hot dog

9 a, The, the, an
10 Deciduous trees, their leaves, winter deciduous tree, the Deciduous Beech, gnarled, twisted branches, leaves
11 Answers will vary. For example: into the castle, onto the roadway, above the clouds, onto the rocks
12 Answers will vary. For example: after the goal, During the afternoon, before dinner, in the morning
13 Answers will vary.

Unit 25

1 Mr Wilson, Tony
2 friendly, polite, respectful
3 friendly/close/informal/familiar
4 Opinion presented to Mr Wilson: The beanie will be useful in the snow. It is colourful and warm.
Opinion presented to Tony: The beanie is awful and will not be worn by Andreas but used instead for teapots and orphaned wombats.
5 student speaker at a school → Good afternoon, fellow students
letter to loved ones → Dear Mum and Dad
text message to friend → :) hi how R U? I'll C U L8R.
addressing conference delegates → Welcome, colleages
business letter → Dear Sir or Madam
letter to a government department → To whom it may concern
6 What do you think of the beanie Mr Wilson gave you?
How do you feel about your new school?
What do you think of the snow?
7 . . . won't you?
8 will you?, won't we?, is she?, have they?, didn't he?

Unit 26

1 You can taste the food of various countries because items on the menu include food from destinations all over the world.
2 Answers will vary. For example: a beating drum, fingernails on the window pane, are feeding time at the zoo, a boa constrictor waiting in ambush, a computer
3 Pacific Crepes, A delicious blend of fresh Pacific Ocean seafood, herbed cream sauce, soft French crepes, Mexican beef Burritos, Tasty strips of beef, garlic, Mexican chilli beans, tortillas, sour cream, Moroccan Lamb, Tangy North African spices, the sweet flavours of sultanas and brown sugar, sautéed lamb, a bed of couscous, Scrumptious Greek souvlaki, chilled and refreshing, beetroot and sour cream, Russian borscht, succulent, Japanese tempura prawns, mouth-watering Thai-style coconut rice
4 delicious, tasty, scrumptious, succulent, mouth-watering
(Other answers will vary.)
5 wrapped, baked, rolled, topped, complement, served, ask
(Other answers will vary.)
6 Pacific Ocean, France, Mexico, Morocco, North Africa, Greece, Russia, Japan, Thailand
7 Food answers will vary. For example:
Italian: pasta/lasagne/pizza
Spanish: paella
German: strudel/sauerkraut
Indian: rice/curry
Indonesian: satay
Chinese: chow mein/chop suey
Filipino/Filipina: adobo/sinigang
8 Answers will vary.
9 Answers will vary. For example: strands of seaweed, black plastic beads, a dark cavern, river of life, groping tentacles, brick columns
10 Answers will vary. For example: comfortable, cosy, quiet, happy, busy, popular, colourful, spacious, clean, tidy
11 crowded, noisy, bright, dark, uncomfortable, busy, empty, dirty, greasy, smoky

Unit 27

1 Way back in 1948 the General Assembly of the United Nations proclaimed *The Universal Declaration of Human Rights* to advocate for the rights of all people of all ages, races, religions, genders and economic status. These rights included the rights of children.
2 DEEdee is seeking publicity for the rights of children. He hopes to gain support for the work of the United Nations and other organisations that are working to help children and promote the rights of children everywhere.
3 fame and notoriety; unfortunate circumstances; we all share a global responsibility
4 Queensland and Northern Territory Aerial Services, Technical and Further Education, Languages Other Than English, Asia-Pacific Economic Cooperation, Sudden Infant Death Syndrome, World Health Organisation
5 "Where there's a will there's a way" means that when you set your mind to to do something you can do it.
"Don't sit on the fence" means that you need to make a decision or take action rather than just think about doing something.
6 Don't just talk about what needs to be done, get in and do the job. Do the job straight way and don't wait or put it off.
7 DEEdee has shown that he has a brain and is capable of deep thought and showing a conscientious attitude to helping others. DEEdee is not a superficial person.
8 incorrect verbs: makes, is, are, are, is
9 is, is, are, was

Unit 28

1 Paragraph 1: Introduces the topic – comparing the Grand Canyon with the Great Barrier Reef.
Paragraph 2: Presents arguments that the Great Barrier Reef is the best natural wonder in the world.
Paragraph 3: Presents arguments that the Grand Canyon is the best natural wonder in the world.
Paragraph 4: Presents a conclusion that the Great Barrier Reef is the best.
2 Many people, Other people, Both
3 are, are, are, is, is, is, deserves, is, (that)'s, is
4 believe, think
5 Answers will vary. For example: consider, feel, decide, hope, want, wish
6 have built
7 carved
8 continue to evolve
9 is, are, crashes, can be seen
10 incredible, so vast they can be seen from outer space, spectacular, a miracle of nature, deserves the title, truly beautiful, precious
11 Answers will vary.

Unit 29

1

Subject	Verb	Object
People	visit	Nepal
The Nepalese	do restrict	access
India	crashed into	Asia
The crash	caused	the seabed
The plates	are still moving against	each other
This movement	is pushing	the Himalayas

2 Answers will vary. For example: a fish, pineapple, the dog, money, the garden, a rainforest
3 Nepal is visited by people wishing to see Mount Everest.
The mountain is climbed by some people.
Access to climbers is restricted by the Nepalese.
Asia was crashed into by India.
4 The mountain climber flew a flag.
The Sherpas arranged the climb.
The tourists also visited India.
5 (what)'s, is, is, is, existed
6 auxiliary verb, relating verb, relating verb, auxiliary verb

Unit 30

1 don't you?, is she?, hasn't she?, isn't it?, do they?
2 Answers will vary.
3 Answers will vary. For example: busy/deserted/crowded/tidy/messy/dirty/clean/well-loved/abandoned/old/modern
4 Answers will vary. For example: experiment, monitor, mechanical, digital, analysis, results, invention
5 Answers will vary.
6 is, are, is, were, are
7 relating, relating, relating, relating, auxiliary
8 Look before you leap. → Think about what you are doing before you do it.
Too many cooks spoil the broth. → People get in each other's way if they try to do the same thing at the same time.
Every cloud has a silver lining. → Try to look on the bright side of every situation.
Never put off till tomorrow what you can do today. → Don't delay action or you'll miss out.

Don't count your chickens until they hatch. → Don't count on things that haven't happened yet.

9 Answers will vary. For example:
Subject: The horse, Phillipe, The stars
Verb: munched, danced, lit up
Object: the carrots, a jig, the sky

10 Tourists saw polar bears in Churchill.
The black bears ate the berries.
The racoon smashed the vase.
The hikers ate porridge for breakfast before the hike.

11 verb groups: have made, to conquer, called, became, to survive, must have been, to go, made, broke, going, would have suffered, wasn't, is, healed, have succeeded, died, would want to even try, is
modal auxiliaries: must, would, would

12 stupid/must have been nuts/would have suffered badly/foolhardy individuals/why anyone would want to even try it is beyond me

Unit 31

1 Chichén Itza: the ruins of Chichén Itza, these ruins, Chichén Itza, the Chichén Itza site, Chichén Itza, a great courtyard at Chichén Itza
the Mayans: The Mayans, They, they, They, they, The Mayans
the Gods: a great many gods, those gods, the gods
the ball game: a ball game called pok-ta-pok, this game, the game

2 *We* refers to the compere and the viewing audience. *They* refers to the Mayans.

3 these ruins, this evening, this, those gods, this game

5 Answers will vary. For example: I have a story to tell you about my grandma; I will make a responsible school captain because . . . ; I'm sorry I broke the vase and hid the pieces.

6 I'll tell you this: they were great astronomers, writers and architects but they were also very religious.

7 She, this/that, she, that/this, her, they

Unit 32

1 a family of lions relaxes in the sun; observe the king as he observes his kingdom

2 raged angrily → the wind
smiled kindly → sunshine
screamed in terror → the sails of a yacht in a storm
waited malevolently → the cat
played across my bedroom floor → the shadows
squatted knowingly → the television (Answers may vary.)

3 Answers will vary. For example: guarded its baby; waited patiently for rain; wrapped the daylight in its cloak; stretches her legs after her nap; splashes playfully in its bath

4 the knowledge/the fervent call/ the stalking

5 Answers will vary. For example: He was the hope of his family; The feeling of doom stalked us; We held the belief that the rains would arrive; The performance was spectacular

6 prophecy – The prophecy came true.
practice – Piano practice has been cancelled. (Sentences will vary.)

7 sight, sound, smell

8 wild/untamed; pride/family
begin/end; wake/sleep; fervent/lulling; safety/danger
the lion is king

9 descends/ascends; experience/inexperience

Unit 33

1 colonisation, languages, pronunciation, dialects

2 The text deals with ideas and concepts rather than particular objects so it needs to refer to these things using abstract nouns.

3 Answers will vary.

4 were/spoken/have disappeared/are/is made up of/speak/use/can be/ are written/indicates/need/means/are spoken/curled/can be/to make/ are working to ensure/remain/do not become

5 spoken – the speech; speak – the speech; written – the writing; working – the work; disappeared – the disappearance; use – the use; make – the making of; curled – the curling
Sentences will vary.

6 colonisation: to start a settlement in an area where people may or may not have already been living
pronunciation: the way words are spoken

7 colonise: The English colonised Australia.
pronounce: You need to pronounce your words clearly.
(Sentences will vary.)

8 The Anangu people – traditional owners of Uluru – Kata Tjuta National Park.

9 European, Indigenous, language, Western, Anangu, retroflex, non-Aboriginal, Aboriginal

10 community

11 different, active, long, short

Unit 34

1 democracy, Diwali, Hindu, Ramadan, Hanukkah, Christmas, Easter, Vesak, Buddhist

2 regardless
Answers will vary. For example: reckless, hopeless, helpless, speechless, thoughtless, penniless, clueless, lifeless

3 vocal: related to the voice
advocate: speak out to support or defend someone else
evoke: to call up feelings or memories
evocative: reminds of some feeling or emotion
vocative: term used to address others that shows the familiarity or formality of the relationship

4 celebrated, celebrations

5 Answers will vary. For example: celebrity, celebrant, celebrating

6 backgrounds, Overseas, everyone

7 Hindu people, Diwali, the Festival of Lights, gifts and sweets, the triumph of good over evil, Chinese New Year, a particularly popular celebration, Australia, Lion dances, dragon dances, firecrackers, evil spirits, Vietnamese people, Tet New Year, dragon dances, street decorations, Homes, fresh flowers, people, special foods, A very important festival for Buddhists, Vesak, Buddha day, This festival, the life, enlightenment and death of buddha, People, candles, flowers and food

8 (the anniversary of the Gallipoli landing), (a Jewish festival), (enters stage right), (Stops centre stage), (follows Wayne and stands to his right)

Unit 35

1 Sophia said she enjoys travelling to amazing places.

2 You need to remember to show respect for local customs when you are travelling.

3 "Tahlia, please take my photo in front of the statue," asked Anthony.

4 These, those, This, the

5 Answers will vary.

6 Answers will vary. For example: A flower is a happy little face looking at the sun.
The sun is a cheerful clown looking down on the world.
The gorilla was acting like a big daddy, bossing all the family.
The spider is a tiny acrobat balancing on its rope.

7 Answers will vary. For example: stated, declared, announced, repeated, mentioned, whispered, yelled

8 Answers will vary. For example: please/annoyed, bored/busy, excited/ indifferent, lonely/friendly, long/short, happy/sad, close/far

9 The love I feel for you is amazing.
The fond memory of his trip to Bali filled Joel with a longing to return.
The reading of his poem on stage was very moving.

10 safety, travel, excitement, transfer, pleasure

11 Answers will vary.

12 Answers will vary. For example: authorship, partnership, friendship, citizenship, dictatorship, leadership, mateship

13 Answers will vary. For example: misguided, misplaced, misnomer, mismatch, mischief, mistake, misjudge, mishap, mislay, mislead

14 (a day honouring fathers), (a day honouring mothers), (kneels in front of Flora), (pulls Kyle to stand)

15 During, While, At first, once, when, until, After, finally